FUGITIVE
WRITINGS

FUGITIVE WRITINGS

Peter Kropotkin

Edited with an Introduction by George Woodcock

Volume 10 of *The Collected Works of Peter Kropotkin*

Montréal/New York
London

BLACK ROSE BOOKS NO. W195

Hardcover — ISBN: 1-895431-43-3 (978-1-895431-43-8)
Paperback — ISBN: 1-895431-42-5 (978-1-895431-42-1)

Library of Congress No. 93-70389

Canadian Cataloguing in Publication Data

Kropotkin, Petr Alekseevich, kniaz, 1984-1921
Fugitive Writings

(The Collected works of Peter Kropotkin, ISSN 1188-5708; 10)
            ISBN: 1-895431-43-3 (bound) —
            ISBN: 1-895431-42-5 (pbk.)

    1. Anarchism.
    I. Title.
    II. Series: Kropotkin, Petr Alekseevich, kniaz, 1984-1921. The Collected works of
Peter Kropotkin; 10.

HX914.K678   320.5'7   C93-090100-2

Ordering Information

USA/INTERNATIONAL	CANADA	UK/EUROPE
University of Chicago Press Chicago Distribution Center 11030 South Langley Avenue Chicago IL 60628	University of Toronto Press 5201 Dufferin Street Toronto, ON M3H 5T8	Central Books Freshwater Road Dagenham RM8 1RX
(800) 621-2736 (USA) (773) 702-7000 (International)	1-800-565-9523	+44 (0) 20 852 8800
orders@press.uchicago.edu	utpbooks@utpress.utoronto.ca	contactus@centralbooks.com

Black Rose Books is the publishing project of Cercle Noir et Rouge.
CP. 35788 Succ. Léo-Pariseau, Montréal, QC, H2X 0A4
www.blackrosebooks.com

Contents

Introduction

FROM his schooldays in the Corps of Pages during the early reign or Czar Alexander II, when he essayed fiction and verse, to the disillusioning after years of the Russian Revolution when he worked fitfully on the manuscript of his never-completed *Ethics*, Peter Kropotkin was constantly writing. Already, during the his pre-anarchist period, as an ex-officer of the Cossacks turned geographer, he gave expression to the theories of East Asian mountain forms which he had developed so accurately as he explored large areas of western Siberia and Manchuria as part of his military duties, and for which he is still well remembered by the fraternity of geographers. The monographs and essays he wrote in this field really belong to the geographers as specialists. Here we are concerned with Kropotkin in a wider sense that sees him primarily as a social scientist and social agitator who at a crucial time in his life, as he described vividly in *Memoirs of a Revolutionist*, renounced the mental luxuries of the scientific life to serve the people more directly as an activist.

After his conversion to the service of revolutionary ideals in the early 1870s, which occurred largely as a result of his association with exiled revolutionaries and reformers in Siberia, Kropotkin became an activist militant in Russia and later in western Europe. It was here, while on a trip to Switzerland in 1872, and where he encountered the watchmaker disciples of Bakunin in the Swiss Jura, that he had in fact acquired the anarchist ideas that distinguished him among Russian revolutionaries of that populist era. It was after returning home from this trip that he wrote his first, long unpublished work, "Must We Occupy Ourselves with an Examination of the Ideal of a Future System"; it was a paper that he read to the discussion circle to which he had become attached and which is known in history as the Chaikovski Circle, since its principal convenor — rather than leader — was Nicholas Chaikovski, the brother of the celebrated composer. The Chaikovski Circle, in fact, consisted mainly of vaguely socialist populists influenced to some extent by the ideas of Saint Simon and Fourier, but willing to accept a constitutional rather than a revolutionary solution

1

to Kropotkin's problems. We shall be discussing "Must We Occupy Ourselves...," like the other works included in this volume, in the Preface that accompanies it. But at this point, it is appropriate to point out that Kropotkin, and some of his comrades, did pursue the plan he suggested of visiting the workmen's artels — or living co-operatives — and it was peasants living in these artels and working in the capital as weavers who betrayed him and led him to his imprisonment in the Peter-and-Paul Fortress in 1874.

It was Kropotkin's flight in 1876 from a prison hospital in St. Petersburg that started the career of writing for a publication which continued the rest of his life. He arrived destitute in England, for he had not been able to bring funds with him from Russia, and income from his estate was frozen by the Tsarist authorities, so that he could not have sustained himself as absentee landlord, even if he had wanted to do so, which is unlikely. The only way he could think of earning a living was by writing about the scientific matters of which he had some knowledge, and with this in mind he established a contact with the editors of publications like *Nature*, and with the officials of the Royal Geographic Society, including its secretary, the great biologist Henry Walter Bates, who became his valued friend. Until his last days in England, in 1917, Kropotkin continued this scientific journalism to provide for the needs of him and his wife Sophia and, eventually, his daughter Alexandra. Most of this work was published anonymously or pseudonymously, and now, a century and more later it is virtually impossible to identify it all. In any case, it was the most ephemeral of his work, since it was concerned with science — and particularly the biological sciences — in one of its most mutable periods.

It is with Kropotkin's less narrowly professional writing, much of it done without payment for the anarchist cause, that we are concerned in this edition of his *Collected Works*. This writing covered many fields — anarchist theory and practice, social history and sociology and literary criticism. Here and there, indeed, in his frankly popularising way, Kropotkin blended his socio-political theories with scientific arguments, notably in *Mutual Aid*, which can be seen as one of the great polemics in the evolutionary controversy as well as a study of animal and human societies, and the balancing of scientific knowledge and social theory is done quite openly in *Modern Science and Anarchism* which, with other essays on science and the natural world, will form the next and final volume of this series.

Many of Kropotkin's books, like *Mutual Aid, Fields Factories and Workshops*, and *The Great French Revolution*, and the incomplete *Ethics*, are works of deep thought and original scholarship, though Kropotkin never affected a professorial style and evaded scholarly apparatuses as far as he could. Others of his books, like *Memoirs of a Revolutionist* and, to a less extent, *In Russian and French Prisons*, were autobiographical, developing the narrative vein Kropotkin had tried in his boyhood to turn to fiction. These books and his contributions to reviews like *The Nineteenth Century*, the *Fortnightly Review*, and the *Atlantic Monthly*, to newspapers like the *Times* and the *Daily Chronicle*, and to major compilations like *The Encyclopedia Britannica* and Elisée Reclus' *Géographie Universelle*, established him among the men of letters who flourished in the late Victorian and Edwardian eras in Britain.

But there are two other books which revealed a different role, that of the anarchist activist and polemicist; these were *The Conquest of Bread* and *Paroles d'un Révolté*, only recently translated into English and first published in this series as *Words of a Rebel*. These consisted of the articles he wrote for the periodicals he founded and edited in Switzerland and France from 1878 until 1883, when he was arrested and imprisoned by the French authorities. They were written for working people; Kropotkin had the advantage that, after Proudhon, he was one of the few leading anarchist militants to express himself eloquently on paper. Bakunin was a fiery orator who carried his listeners on the flow of his enthusiasm, but his written prose was turgid, he could never organize his thought so well on paper as he did facing a sympathetic audience, and he rarely finished his ponderous essays. Kropotkin, who wrote in three languages, Russian, the French that came to him easily as a Russian aristocrat trained by French tutors as a child, and with increasing confidence English, deliberately set out to discuss serious things in a simple prose that would be understood by any moderately educated working man. In doing so he wrote the best anarchist literature since Proudhon died.

The Conquest of Bread, and *Words of a Rebel* served as word mines for Kropotkin's contemporary activists and for later generations, with the result that many of the pamphlets by him, translated into languages as far apart as Korean and the Portuguese of Brazil, which spread over the earth during the 1980s and early twentieth century were in fact chapters taken from one or other of these books and turned into quickly printed publications that could be sold for a few pence or sous.

By printing the source books for these numerous Kropotkin pamphlets we have to an extent simplified our task, but there were other works that appeared after the seminal propagandist books and which justly demand a place in this collection. I have naturally left out everything included in the earlier volumes where it belongs, so that the period of Kropotkin's greatest political activism, from the later 1870s and early 1880s in Switzerland and France is virtually absent from the present volume of shorter works. Two other clearly identifiable periods are in fact represented here; his conspiratorial phase in Russia where he lived a double life as gentleman-scientist and sheepskin-clad agitator among the workers and wrote "Must We Occupy Ourselves..." in 1873; and the 1880s and 1890s after his arrival in England in 1896, to which all the other four items belong.

This was the early part of Kropotkin's time in England when, apart from his scientific journalism, he was still active in trying to create an anarchist movement; he was instrumental in founding *Freedom* in 1886 and the Freedom Press as an anarchist publishing house at the same time; both of them survive more than a century later as a testament to the durability of the anarchist ideal. But Kropotkin appears at this time not merely as an anarchist militant, increasingly less active, but also as a member of late Victorian culture, lecturing at universities and staying with professors, making his house at Bromley open to Sunday gatherings of writers and painters as well as radical thinkers, and slowly retreating from the London haunts of anarchist activity, as his health deteriorated, to refuges like Bromley and finally, Brighton.

During the same period as he wrote "The State" and these other pamphlets, Kropotkin also wrote fairly regularly in *Freedom*, where his occasional articles from 1886 to 1907 were devoted to themes he thought would interest English working people, though, in fact, *Freedom* was read — as it is a hundred years after — mainly by middle-class radicals rather than by authentic proletarians. Apparently he intended to collect these pieces in a book similar to *The Conquest of Bread* or *Words of a Rebel*, but never did so, and it was left for Nicholas Walter and Heiner Becker a century later to carry out this task in a collection which they called *Act for Yourselves*. This volume, published at *Freedom's* centenary in 1986, is still freely available from Freedom Press in London, which is why I have not included any of its contents.

There are two other items falling into the category of lesser works which I have omitted from the present volume. One is a shift rather than an omission, for *Modern Science and Anarchism* (1903) represents the beginning of the post-activist phase when he was drawing together his scientific and social interests. I have accordingly made it one of the features of the final volume of this series; the rest of that volume will consist of a never completed series of essays on the subject of evolution and environment published in *The Nineteenth Century* between 1910 and 1915.

The other omission is the material which Kropotkin wrote, particularly at the time of the 1905 Revolution and afterwards, regarding the situation in Russia. Hidden away in anonymous or pseudonymous pieces in the Russian revolutionary emigré press, notably in the publications of the anarchist *Khleb i Volya* (Bread and Freedom) group, there are pieces by Kropotkin — examinations and exhortations. But they are addressed from outside, and in judging even those that can plausibly be attributed to Kropotkin, we have to bear in mind the warning he himself gave in "Must We Occupy Ourselves..." about the different experiences and hence the different viewpoints of emigré leaders and of conspirators actually working in Russia. This difference shows in his writing from England on the Russian situation; he was there — as he was in so many other contexts — and incessant optimist, and if he perhaps rightly saw the 1905 Revolution emerging spontaneously from the will of the masses, he did not understand how the authoritarian leaders of the revolutionary parties were learning the lessons of this situation, so that while 1905 may have begun as a spontaneous uprising, October 1917 would be from the beginning an organized and successful conspiracy simulating a spontaneous outbreak. There really seems no point in my showing that the great social anarchist and visionary was not always perceptive regarding the Russian politics of the moment. The same, after all, might be said of Marx or Engels and even of the early Lenin, and certainly of Bakunin. So, except for "Must We Occupy Ourselves...," where Kropotkin speaks very much to the current Russian situation as one deeply involved conspiratorially in the then and there of Russian circumstances, nothing is included here about the situation in the country to which he remained devoted but which he did not see between 1876 and 1917.

In assembling this volume of short works I have been indebted to many people working beforehand in the field, including Roger Baldwin, who prepared in 1927, Kropotkin's *Revolutionary Pamphlets,* a somewhat different collection from the present because it contained many of the items appearing in *The Conquest of Bread* and *Words of a Rebel,* and Martin A. Miller, who in 1970, published Kropotkin's *Selected Writings on Anarchism and Revolution.* In his collection, Professor Miller included the first publication of the important formative essay, "Must We Occupy Ourselves with an Examination of the Ideal of a Future System," translated by Victor Ripp, and a new translation, better than anything in the past, of "The State," done by Vernon Richards.

I express my appreciation of the willingness with which Professor Miller has allowed me to use these items from his collection, and also I thank Dr. Ripp and my old friend and comrade, Vernon Richards, for permission to reproduce their respective translations.

George Woodcock
Vancouver, 1993

Must We Occupy Ourselves

with an Examination

of the Ideal of a

Future System?

Preface

THIS is the only known statement made by Kropotkin of his revolutionary beliefs during his period of activism in Russia, though in his *Memoirs of a Revolutionist* he does tell us retrospectively and in his own rather vivid terms of the development of his anarchist ideas and his increased involvement in radical activity that would lead to the writing of "Must We Occupy Ourselves with the Examination of the Ideal of a Future Society" in the later months of 1873.

When the Grand Duke Nicholas visited Kropotkin in the Peter-and-Paul Fortress during 1874, and quizzed him—perhaps on the Tsar's behalf—about the origins of his revolutionary ideas, he was somewhat alarmed that Kropotkin may have already developed these subversive beliefs while he was still a member of the Corps of pages and a close personal attendant of Alexander II. Kropotkin's answer was: "In the Corps I was a boy, and what is indefinite in boyhood grows definite in manhood."

It is true that Kropotkin did react as a child against the authoritarian family pattern imposed by his father, who was a military authoritarian untouched by the liberal ideas that had seeped in during the reign of Alexander I and had inspired the Decembrists in the 1820s. Yet through his mother Kropotkin was related to noblemen who had taken up in the surge of reformism that temporarily influenced the Tsar and his advisers and led to the emancipation of the serfs in 1861. It was in the hope of taking part in the projected reforms of the 1860s that the young Kropotkin—with all the privileges of the Emperor's personal page—chose a commission in the humble Mounted Cossacks of the Amur rather than in one of the prestigious Guards regiments. Indeed, Siberia at first did seem a bridgehead for reform to take hold before it swept over the whole of Russia, and on his arrival Kropotkin became involved in a number of investigative commissions, including one on the Siberian prison system.

In the latter part of Alexander's reign the reactionaries regained control, and Kropotkin gave up his hopes of furthering reform and instead carried on the explorations of the East Asian mountains on which his early repute as a geographer would be based. These journeys supplied him with observations of the behaviour of wild animals and of primitive peoples that he would later develop in books like *Mutual Aid*. His enquiries in this direction only became linked with rejection of authority when he and his brother Alexander resigned their commissions in 1867, largely in protest at the barbarous treatment of certain Polish prisoners who had staged a daring escape in Siberia.

Back in St. Petersburg, Kropotkin obeyed the tradition that young aristocrats who did not join in the armed forces should join the civil service, but he combined his light official duties with attending the University and with preparing for the Russian Geographical Society the monographs stating his conclusions on the formation and direction of Asian mountain chains, on the last great Ice Age and on the desiccation of Central Asia, the works on which his reputation as a geographer still remains secure. He was interested in radical ideas, and an exiled writer in Siberia had already moved him in the direction of anarchism by giving him a volume of Proudhon. But he did not become involved in the discussion groups and conspiratorial societies that were beginning to re-emerge in the early 1870s until after what he regarded as his conversion.

This took place in 1871 when he had gone on a geographical expedition to examine Ice Age phenomena in Finland. In the lengthy solitudes in wild country he began to consider the future course of his life, and a decision was precipitated when a telegram came inviting him to become Secretary to the Russian Geographical Society, a post that would enable him to carry on his geographical work and pay him enough to live modestly. The moment had come for choosing the main direction of his life. He rejected science on the grounds that pursuing it exclusively was a luxury in a world where many people survived in the direst of poverty. He returned to St. Petersburg resolved to involve himself with those who were working for radical change.

But instead of seeking the activist groups there, he decided to travel first to Switzerland, which was the destination of many Russians in the 1870s, not only those with radical ideas but also many women in search of a higher education not available to them in Russia. Both Michael Bakunin and Peter Lavrov, leaders respectively of the revolutionary and the reformist populists were living there. But Kropotkin was not then interested only or even primarily in Russian expatriate politics. He had heard of the First International, the International Workingmen's Association, and he was anxious to find out how European working people went about seeking their liberation from authority—political and economic.

He went first to Zurich, where most of the Russian expatriates were concentrated, and then to Geneva. By this time, the International was already becoming sharply divided between its Marxist and Bakuninist trends. In Geneva, it was mostly in the hands of the Marxists, and while Kropotkin enjoyed his first encounters with real workers at the union halls there, he did not find the atmosphere of political calculation congenial. He went to the Swiss Jura, and there, among people like the printer James Guillaume and the watchmaker Adhémar Schwitz-guegel, friends and disciples of Bakunin, he absorbed the doctrine of free socialism that they projected. (He never met Bakunin, who was then living in Locarno, but that is a passage of anarchist history that has remained irremediably obscure.) He was an anarchist by the time he returned to Russia.

He did not have very long to wait for entry into a group of like-minded young people, for his radical views had been observed and it was known that he had returned from western Europe with a collection of pamphlets and journals which were brought over the border for him by a Jewish smuggling ring based in Cracow and which the Tsarist authorities would certainly have regarded as subversive. A fellow student—and later a famous geographer—Dimitri Klemens (whom Kropotkin, in his *Memoirs,* called Kelnitz) approached him with the suggestion that he might be interested in joining the Chaikovski Circle which included members who were later to become famous revolutionists, such as Sophia Perovskya and Sergei Stepniak. Kropotkin agreed, and Klemans proposed him; after some objection to the fact that he was a prince and had close connections in the Tsarist court, he was accepted. Though some of its members were to become tragically involved in conspiratorial groups like *Narodnaya Volya,* the Circle was propagandist and educational in its main intent, aiming at enlightening in a socialist direction the workers of St. Petersburg, who were mainly young peasants coming to the city because or rural poverty and who lived in artels or dwelling communities. Kropotkin showed a talent for assimilating with these people, and very soon, as the sheepskin-clad Borodin, he was well-known among them.

His activity did not last for many months, since the net of the Third Section, the Tsarist secret police, soon closed on the Circle and on the satellite groups its members had founded in other towns and cities. Eventually more than 2,000 people were imprisoned, including Kropotkin who was picked up on March 12, 1874, but many were released because of their tenuous links with the main group, until eventually in 1879, and long after Kropotkin's own escape from Russia, the residue were arraigned at the Trial of the 193.

It was at this trial that "Must We Occupy Ourselves…" made its first appearance, as a piece of evidence for the prosecution. We have no knowledge what motivated Kropotkin to write such a manifesto in 1873, except perhaps to justify a revolutionary extremity which most of his co-workers did not share. We know from the memoirs of various people associated with the Circle that it was discussed at several meetings, and Kropotkin seems to have tried hard and unrealistically to gain acceptance of what must clearly have been a minority position. The rough draft of the manifesto, with its many corrections and notations, was evidently circulated among the members, for it was found unsigned by the police in the apartment of I.I. Gauenstein shortly before Kropotkin's arrest.

After the trial it remained hidden in the archives of the Tsarist police for more than forty years, until after the October Revolution, and it seems to have been forgotten by Kropotkin himself, who never mentioned it in any of his later works. It was first published in an abbreviated form as part of a memorial issue of the magazine *Byloe* in 1921. It was first published completely in 1964—during one of the Moscow thaws—in a volume entitled *Revolutionnoe narodnichestvo*, edited by Boris S. Itenberg. It is from this version that Dr. Brill made the present translation, omitting the marginal notes and crossed-out passages.

* * *

In "Must We Occupy Ourselves...," we find Kropotkin forming the ideas that would dominate the years of his political maturity; he did so against the unshaped background of mid-nineteenth century Russian populism. Like most of his fellow Chaikovtsi, he was in feeling and in action the heir of the 1860s notion of "going to the people," and his essay can be seen as a study of the best way to reach them. Like *Words of a Rebel*, though with less assurance, it deals with the matter of educating the people, not only in general, but also as activists for the revolution, which he believes can emerge only from the spontaneous will of the people. Already—though he still talks of the revolutionists as a party—he sees them only as the instigators, and stresses the anti-Marxist notion that a revolution made by a conspiratorial party will fail; it will only succeed if the people are convinced to carry it out because they see it as necessary; it can only succeed if the myth of the socialist State is abandoned. In suggesting that revolutionary activists should be agitators and inspirers and not leaders, he was in fact prefiguring his own career. For however much loyalty and reverence he inspired, Kropotkin never sought to capitalize on them to gain power of any kind. He aimed to be a militant propagandist and writer, advocating, explaining, clarifying, and ready to fight in the ranks on the barricades; no more.

In all this, the influence of Bakunin, as transmitted by Guillaume and Schwitzguebel in Jura, is evident, and it would be the libertarian, Bakuninist wing of the International to which Kropotkin would give a lasting loyalty during his West European exile in the late 1870s. The influence of Proudhon was there in his anti-Statism, of course, but it was even more evident in Kropotkin's developing economic ideas.

He believed, it is clear, that the means of production and consumption must be expropriated and collectivised, though he wisely did not attempt to foresee an intricate mechanism for fulfilling this aim; he was already showing his rejection of any ideas of utopian planning. But he had not yet developed his anarchist communist ideas; that would come when he returned to western Europe later in the decade. He still saw a collectivist rather than a communist arrangement, and clung to a neo-Proudhonist idea of the exchange of goods and services against labour cheques and their alternatives. Still, all that he said against the State and in favour of the expropriation of private property must have seemed extremely radical to his fellow Chaikovtsi, who would have been content with a parliamentary constitution, open elections and the legalization of labour unions. They would almost certainly have voted him down if it came to an issue. But Borodin, when the Tsarist agents arrested that formidable agitator, was already the Kropotkin we know in history, though his first work was neither published nor remembered.

G.W.

Must We Occupy Ourselves with an Examination of the Ideal of a Future System?

I believe that we must.

In the first place, in the ideal we can express our hopes, aspirations and goals, regardless of practical limitations, regardless of the degree of realization which we may attain; for this degree of realization is determined purely by external causes.

In the second place, the ideal can make clear how much we are infected with old prejudices and inclinations. If some aspects of everyday life seem to us so sacred that we dare not touch them even in an analysis of the ideal, then how great will our daring be in the actual abolition of these everyday features? In other words, although daring in thought is not at all a guarantee of daring in practice, mental timidity in constructing an ideal is certainly a criterion of mental timidity in practice.

In speaking about the definition of the ideal, we of course have in mind the definition of only four or five prominent features of this ideal. Everything else must inevitably be the realization of these fundamental theories in life. Therefore, these things cannot be a subject for discussion now. The forms of the realization cannot be derived by scientific means. In practice they can be derived only by means of repeated practical discussion shortly before and during the realization on the spot, in the *obshchina*,[1] in the artel, but not now at the beginning of things.

There is not the slightest doubt that among different socialists of the most varied shades there does exist a rather complete agreement in their ideals, if these are taken in the most general form. Those social conditions which they would hope to realize in the more or less near future are generally quite the same: their differences proceed not from fundamental differences in the ideal, but rather from the fact that some concentrate all their attention on that ideal which can, in their opinion be realized in the immediate future; others concentrate on the ideal which in the opinion of the former, is more remote.

In fact, all present-day socialists strive toward the fullest possible equality in the conditions of development of private individuals and societies. They all desire the realization of such a system so that everyone would have the same opportunity to earn his livelihood by his own labour, that is, so that everyone would have the same right to use those instruments of labour and those raw materials without which no labour is possible so that everyone would be compelled to earn his livelihood by his own labour; so that the distribution of useful occupations in society would be such as to make impossible the formation of a class occupied for life (and moreover, because of heredity) exclusively with privileged labour, that is, labour more pleasant, less difficult, and less protracted, but giving the right to the same, or greater prosperity as others; so that everyone would have the same opportunity, on a level with all others, to receive that theoretical education which now constitutes the lot of only a few; so that the relations of a private individual to all others would be such that he might be happy and at the same time bear the least amount of restraint on his personal freedom and personal development. In a word, to state these positions briefly, today's socialists are striving for equality; in rights to work; in labour; in methods of education; in social rights and duties, with the greatest possible room for the development of individual characteristics; in those capabilities which are harmless for society.

Such is the programme of the immense majority, if not all of the socialists of our time. Even those who evidently advocate a completely different ideal, those who, for instance, advocate as the ultimate ideal a State communism or a hierarchical system and so forth in the end desire the same thing. If they concentrate strong power in the hands of either a ruling minority or elected representatives and, but this means, sacrifice individual initiative, this is by no means because they attribute no value to it or consider it detrimental, but only because they do not consider possible the realization of such a system in which all four forms of equality would be realized in equal measure and they sacrifice one form for the attainment of others. Moreover, not one of the active followers of these learned socialists believes that any social form whatever could ossify and resist further development.

We will now examine all the above-mentioned various forms and conditions of equality separately, and we will see how compatible they are with one another and how necessary a common realization of all of them is for the durability of each. We will examine in particular the practical measures which now seem useful for the realization of each of these ideals.

The first condition of equality is self-evident and is least subject to dispute.

If each member of society is to have the possibility of earning his livelihood by his own labour—without, as a result, enslaving himself to anyone else, neither to a private citizen, nor to a company, nor to an artel—he must obviously always have the possibility of acquiring that shovel with which he intends to dig, that cocoon from which he intends to spin a thread or to weave a fabric, that bread, those clothes, that room where he must live, that place where he will work, before he manufactures anything having an exchange value for society. It is apparent that in former times production was so simple that all this did not require a vast accumulation of the initial products of personal labour, that anyone, although working only with the instruments of labour available in his family, on those raw products which he took free of charge from nature, could produce useful exchange values. But now—and the progress of society consists in this—the preliminary accumulation of the products of labour for the creation of the instruments of labour and the storing up of raw material must be so great that it can no longer be the business of a private individual or a private group of individuals. It is clear, therefore, that if it is desirable that a person beginning to work not enslave himself, not yield part of his labour, his strength, his independence, either permanently or temporarily, to private individuals whose arbitrariness always will determine how great that part should be. Thus it is necessary that private persons control neither the instruments of labour (tools, machines, factories), nor the places of cultivation of the raw products (the earth), nor the raw products stored up beforehand, nor the means for storing up and conveying them to a given place (the means of communication, warehouses, and so forth), nor the means of existence during work (the supplies of the means of subsistence and housing).

Thus we arrive at the elimination, in that future system whose realization we desire, of any personal property, of any property of an associated joint stock company, an artel, and so forth.

Those writers of a former time who came to this same conclusion saw no way out other than the transfer of all the capital of society to the State, that is, to a powerful organization representing in itself the interests of society and managing all matters which concern the whole society in total.

It was left to it (the State) to guarantee each member of society the opportunity to obtain the necessary instruments of labour, and so forth; it was also left to it to distribute among the members of society those products made by them. But precisely because of this, the brilliant dreams of the followers of these scholars did not find enough adherents among those who would have to realize these dreams in actuality. In the very ideal of these scholars only one aspect of life is considered, the economic. Those who were accustomed to thinking in a concrete manner understood very well that no matter what combination of conditions was contrived in order that this government might express the views of the majority, that no matter how mobile, fluctuating, and susceptible to change its composition might be, the group of individuals to whom society cedes its rights would always be the power, separate from society, trying to broaden its influence, its interference in the business of each separate individual. And the wider the circle of activity of this government, the greater the danger of enslavement of society, the greater the likelihood that the government would stop being the expression of the interests and desires of the majority.

Thus, both the masses and many individual thinkers long ago realized that the transfer of this most essential element of the life of society into the hands of any elected government whatsoever would be the source of the most essential inconvenience, if not simply the suicide of society.

From this realization the most natural transition was to the idea that all capital, no matter how accumulated by preceding generations, must become the property of all, of the whole society, which must itself be the fully empowered manager of it.

The expression of this ideal in its most immediate, direct form, consists of: 1) the recognition of all available capital, whether or not gained through labour, as the property of all members of that territorial unit (group of districts, nations, countries), where the socialist revolution is occurring; 2) the recognition of all public capital which can be worked (arable land, exploitable ore, factories, railroads operative and under construction, apartment houses, and so forth) as given over for use (for a certain period of time) to those individuals who now exert their labour; 3) the taking of necessary measures so that the unprofitable conditions in which separate working groups find themselves would be equalized within the various small territorial units (the town, the province) by means of the mutual agreement of these groups, without eliminating the possibility of a further redistribution to equalize disproportionate conditions within the more extensive unions of small territorial units.

But still clearer is the second condition of equality, namely, that everyone should be compelled to earn his livelihood through his own labour. This aspiration is common to all socialists and is expressed with perfect clarity by them. Disagreements arise only in regard to what is rightfully to be considered personal labour. But this disagreement is to a significant degree the result of a simple misunderstanding. All economists have long since distinguished productive labour from useful labour, counting as the latter the labour of scholars, writers, artists, administrators, and so forth. But this subdivision is hardly appropriate in the present case, and it hardly distinguishes labour necessary for a given group and that which is *unnecessary*. We believe that only that production should be considered as labour, which all society can make use of, and which the significant majority *wants* to make use of. Thus, we would have to include in our formula: "labour for which there is a demand by the majority of society." Clearly, the classification of the different types of labour involving the mutual relations of members within a given group of society must be the business of only that group—but all relations of this group to other similar groups is the business of those groups with which it enters into union or into an exchange of products. Thus, in the *obshchina*, where not all members of the society can read and write, and not all can acquire more advanced knowledge, the teaching of higher algebra can be designated not as labour but as a leisure activity. On the other hand, if the whole society is so developed in musical matters that hearing music has become a necessity for it, then the performance of these pieces can be designated as labour, liable to payment in other equivalent labours—if this designation was made by the *majority* of the group. It is obvious, however, that other groups less developed in musical matters may not recognize the musical instruments manufactured by the first group as a product of labour necessary for themselves, and may not agree on an exchange of them for an equivalent quantity of labour of the type they acknowledge as useful. The immense difference between such a state of affairs and the present one is obvious, in that now a handful of individuals, controlling the labour of others, have the right to make use of it without supervision for the satisfaction of their own needs, and thus use the labour of all to pay for the production and actions necessary to themselves alone. This evil is being eliminated.

But it has often been stated that such an order of affairs as we have in mind in our ideal has another inherent shortcoming. It has been said that the requirements of the majority are not at all the essence of the requirement for the progress of human society; that progress in society always results because some minority, having accidentally fallen into especially favourable circumstances, developed more than all the rest and discovered and laid down to the world new truths, which were absorbed by those individuals who were relatively prepared. Though we doubt (for reasons developed below) that such was the path of progress in society in the majority of cases, or that it must always have been like this, yet even if we grant that such was the sole possible path of progress in a given direction, albeit only in some rare, even unique instance, we must then of course consider whether the classification of labour which we propose in the ideal might not extinguish *this* gleam of progress.

It is clear, however, that those who reasoned in this way were imagining an *ideal* evaluation of labour in *present* society, and assuming the contemporary situation, with its present suffocating conditions in the workshops, with its debilitatingly heavy work, with that unbearable tedium of machine labour which now is necessary in order to have even shelter and a crust of bread. But it is obvious that the classification of labour of which we speak is possible only in a society which has been subjected to that change mentioned in connection with the first condition of equality. And for such a society a lack of considerable leisure time is unthinkable. If some economists asserted that the equal division of all the present income of society's nonworking sector among all members of society would raise each member's average salary only five sous (eight kopecks), these economists once again assumed an impossible condition, that is, they imagined a sharing impossible in present society, one which was to occur while preserving present conditions and forms of production. Now, of course, it is impossible even to define how much time would be required for each member of society to labour on the production of those objects necessary to provide all members of society with comfort, [a comfort] equal to that of people in the lower part of today's middle class. But it can be stated directly that if each worker now supports on the average (in Germany and France) three people besides himself (in France almost four people) of whom only one is a member of the worker's family, whereas the other two (almost three in France) are parasites on the family—then in a better organized society, where the worker need only support one, or more, usually two people (that is, in sum, two to three people counting himself, instead of four or five), he can work half as much (five and a half hours instead of eleven hours a day), in all thirty-three hours a week, and moreover without in any way diminishing his prosperity. Recalling further all the unproductive expenses of society, caused mainly by social disorder (troops, wars, jails and courts, lawsuits, and so forth), recalling further what immeasurable quantities of labour are spent on the production of objects not leading to an increase in the productive power of the people — we, of course, will understand how much leisure there would be in a correctly organized society, leisure even for the satisfaction of such intellectual pleasures as a middling nobleman does not even dream of at present; we will understand then how much closer to the truth was Owen, who was convinced that for this, as well as for much else, three hours labour by all the members of society would be sufficient.

Here is why we believe that (granting the progressive influence of the minority) separate individuals would have the full opportunity to formulate all those progressive ideas which separate individuals can formulate, to disseminate them, to invent all those mechanical tools which could facilitate man's satisfaction of his needs, and to invent and perfect all those pleasures which promote the further development of the individual. The preparation of the groundwork in a society which would consist of members who have since childhood had the opportunity to receive that training which now is the lot of only the fortunate few; the capability of this society, given the elimination of present obstacles, to comprehend all that is good; the ability to identify the good with the socially useful and the bad with the socially harmful; finally, an extension to the presently inactive masses of the spheres of vocational, scientific and artistic creativity — this is the guarantee of progress in the future society, and it is not only not less than any existing today, but ten, even a hundred times greater.

Therefore, we consider our second condition both a necessary condition of equality and the most immediate; but, in addition, we consider that a great stride towards attaining this part of the ideal is the acknowledgement of *social* exchange value only for such objects as will be acknowledged as useful for society by the *majority* of a given group, or a given union of groups.

All the preceding now leads us as well to a belief in the feasibility and the practical expediency of an organization of useful occupations which lacks those groups of individuals occupied exclusively with privileged labour (intellectual labour, the management of some business of industry, the factory, the *obshchina*, and so forth). There can be no doubt that the existence of such a class of people is a manifestation of inequality, in itself obviously undesirable. There can be doubt and objection only in the sense that: 1) the existence of such a class is necessary for the further development of the very society; 2) from the point of view, held by many, that the division of labour is necessary.

We said above that we find it neither just nor useful that public labour should pay for objects useful or necessary only to a minority. We said also that there would be sufficient leisure to produce these objects after the completion of that work required by society, and that the likely extent of this leisure, together with the increase in basic training and an increase in the number of people having the opportunity to use this leisure for every possible occupation, would promote society's progress. This would be a sufficient guarantee against stagnation in the culture and civilization of the society.

Now we proceed. We say that among those occupations which will be acknowledged as necessary by a given group of people there may be occupations which are, so to speak, privileged. From the first, every *obshchina* will require a schoolteacher, a doctor, a bookkeeper; after some time there will be a need for a professor, a scholar, a technician, perhaps a banker, and so forth. It will be asked, will it be more advantageous for the *obshchina* as a whole that this schoolteacher concern himself solely with the education of children for those seven or eight hours which every member of society must devote to a socially useful occupation, without devoting himself to any other work whatsoever; or should he as well daily or regularly perform other duties of so-called unskilled labour, for example, chop wood for the school (if that is necessary), wash or scrub the floors, fire the stoves, sweep the school-yard, provide school supplies, and so on? Should a professor—in such an *obshchina* where it is required—concern himself solely with delivering lectures during the designated seven or eight hours, or should he concern himself as well with the preparation of the physical layout? Should he concern himself, together with the metalworker and the mechanic, with cleaning up the dirt in the university building, and so forth? We believe that, yes, he must perform the latter. Since the formation of a class of intelligentsia, the formation of an aristocracy of skilled labour alongside the democracy of unskilled labour is completely undesirable, the whole question, consequently, is only how profitable for society is such a division of occupations wherein separate individuals do not specialize as now. It seems absurd to people that [someone like] Darwin should concern himself with cleaning up, only because they are unable to rid themselves of the conceptions which they have accepted whole from contemporary society. They forget that for such an individual as Darwin to appear, [a man] who in his intellectual development outstripped his society by a whole century, a certain selection of especially favourable, exceptional conditions was necessary over the course of many years. They assume (without proof, of course) that if Darwin and Wallace had not put forth the hypothesis of natural selection in 1859, then humanity would have remained ignorant of it for many centuries, and that there is no combination of social conditions such that would have allowed this hypothesis to be stated not merely in 1859 but even considerably earlier. They consider the natural or most advantageous path of progress for humanity to be the revelation by separate individuals of those ideas which outstrip those of the mass of society by a whole century or even a millennium. All these opinions and views are, however, utterly untrue.

In the light of all that has been said, we consider absolutely necessary, in the first place:

The acknowledgement of the superfluity of that class which enjoys a privileged type of occupation; in other words, the acknowledgement of the necessity of manual, muscular labour for all members of the society, along with the acknowledgement of complete freedom for each individual in choosing those occupations—if he can prove his capability in the selected type of occupation.

The realization of these two conditions of equality and the transfer of them into actuality guarantees the realization of the fourth condition, equality in education—not merely the possibility of equality in education, but actually, in fact.

Unconditionally denying that the most advantageous, progressive movement in society is by means of the development of a minority which receives a far greater education than the rest of society, we by no means wish to subsidize such a minority with public funds; thus we do not need universities or academies maintained by the public funds, if they are not to be used by every member of society without exclusion. If private individuals, wishing to use their leisure for the further development of intellectual capacities, should establish institutes of higher learning, study societies, conservatories, and so forth, let them maintain these with the products of their leisure, let them visit them during their leisure hours, during that time which the other members of society will spend on entertainment or pleasure-making; but the society which does not want to disturb those conditions of equality which it achieved through its own efforts must not spare even one unit of public labour for their maintenance.

We do not want the educational process to act in the direction of dividing people, from childhood onward, into those who are led and those who lead, of whom the former are mainly familiar with the unskilled labour necessary for their daily lives—and the latter mainly with the methods of management and the so-called higher manifestations of the human mind. Therefore, we have absolutely no need of universities which produce doctors, when the majority of those working in this field are destined to fulfil the duties of watchmen, nurses, orderlies; or lawyers when the majority will be only clerks; or professors—along with office watchmen, or skilled technologists—along with miners.

Repeating this formulation of Proudhon, we say: if a naval academy is not itself a ship with sailors who enjoy equal rights and receive a theoretical education, then it will produce not sailors but officers to supervise sailors; if a technical academy is not itself a factory, not itself a trade school, then it will produce foremen and managers and not workmen, and so on. We do not need these privileged establishments; we need neither universities nor technical academies nor naval academies created for the few; we need the hospital, the factory, the chemical works, the ship, the productive trade school for workers, which, having become available to all, will with unimaginable speed exceed the standard of present universities and academies. In eliminating all the necessary ballast of useless occupations, in devising accelerated methods of education (which always appear only when a demand for them arises which cannot be put off), the school will train healthy workers equally capable of both further intellectual and physical work.

How many hours the student will have to concern himself with actual *production* at each age level (not play at production as in current technical and secondary schools) and how many hours with theoretical studies—and up to what level the latter will be required—will be decided independently by each *obshchina* and district; and, of course, this decision will not be accidental as it is now, but based on rational principles.

We must say, finally, several words about compulsory education, which has been the subject of so many arguments. We believe that the source of these arguments was that those who argued against this requirement always had in mind the contemporary State, with all its attributes. But, obviously, we speak not of compulsory education in present society with its present government, but of a future society with those institutions which will fulfil those useful functions (or, more accurately, potentially useful) which the government now fulfils. Therefore we of course consider that in a future society, education—which up to a certain limit will be defined by the society itself—will and must be compulsory.

In the light of what has been said, we consider necessary for the realization of this fourth aspect of the ideal of equality the recognition of the necessity to close all universities, academies, and other institutes of higher learning, and to open everywhere trade schools, whose volume of instruction will in a very short time surely increase to the level of present universities and surpass them.

To achieve agreement on the fifth point of political equality was always the most difficult of all for all socialist schools. For several decades the learned representatives of socialism could find no other alternative for realizing their ideals than by means of a strong centralized government, a strong government which would have fixed and regulated all social relations, which would have interfered with all the details of people's private lives. These conceptions were particularly developed among the writers of France and Germany. But this caused a natural aversion to other, correct, principles of communism, both among the masses and among especially sincere socialists.

It is clear, however, that all this is the consequence of a simple misunderstanding. Freed of the always dangerous idea of an all-powerful government, communism quickly began to spread even in western Europe—in an altered and limited form under the name of collectivism.

On the other hand, many excellent thinkers of the present century have tried to define in their writings the combination of conditions in which private individuals could be guaranteed the greatest freedom of activity and development along with the least restraint. It is clear, however, that as long as these thinkers limited themselves to working out only purely political relations, they could not achieve any practical results. But with the transferring of the issue to the area of economic relations, the problem is much more simply resolved. The most ideal form devised by the defenders of the idea of the State is a federated republic with the *obshchina* autonomous and deciding independently as much business as possible, with as much independence as possible from the district and ultimately from the State. We see such a form in the United States of America. In Europe one necessary addition to this form is held to be that certain laws must be brought to a vote of all the people, all citizens, as we see in certain cantons in Switzerland and in the Swiss Union at large for laws concerning the alteration of the Code of the Union. Finally, the putting of *all* laws to a vote by the people, while granting the government only the right to promulgate them, is considered a further improvement of this form.

To enumerate here all the inconveniences of these forms, all the infringement of liberty to which they lead, all the inability of these forms to express the will and desire of the majority—would be inappropriate. This criticism has been made many times, and it is sufficient to say that its conclusions proceed not from a logical analysis of the *possibilities* but from a criticism of the actual, contemporary phenomena. Finally, it is sufficient to say that this whole analysis led to the following positions. Apart from all those qualities and characteristics of any government which result from an economic inequality of rights, all the indicated forms lead to this: 1) that the centralized government of a district, state and union is not the expression of the will of the majority of the population; 2) that growing constantly stronger, it usurps the rights of the state, district, *obshchina*; 3) that separate individuals, possessing great energy, can, even if only for a time, seize great power into their hands and paralyze all the necessary measures which the majority wishes to take; 4) that in creating a highly complex State machine, and requiring long practice to become acquainted with the mechanism, such a system leads to the formation of a class especially concerned with State management, which, using its acquired experience, begins to deceive the rest for its personal advantage; 5) that, finally, the boundary between law and decree cannot be ascertained even with approximate accuracy and that it thus is necessary, given the impossibility of daily convening the entire population for voting, to transfer considerable power to the centralized government of a district or state.

All this criticism led Proudhon to the rejection of any government and to *anarchy*.

One feature, common to every government, is that the members of the *obshchina*, district, and State are deprived of a part of their right to decide their own personal matters, and this right is given to several individuals. Moreover, precisely which matters are to be decided by those individuals who make up the local government is defined in general terms. A feature no less central is that this group of individuals is permitted to decide not only any private matters whatsoever but all those matters which arose or could arise in the management of public matters; and they are limited in deciding those matters only by quantity. Another feature common to every government and just as basic is that this same group of individuals, or even still smaller groups, chosen either by the first [group] or by all of the remaining population of the state, district or *obshchina* in total, is permitted to execute the decisions of either the general meeting or the elected government. For this a whole hierarchy of executive organs is created which is obliged to submit to the directions of the executive power of the *obshchina*, district, or state. For the sake of expediency, the executive power of the *obshchina* subordinates itself to the district [power], and this one—in its turn—to the State [power]. Such, in general features, is the essence of all governments. The differences consist only in this—in one place the *obshchina's* circle of activity is wider, in another, more public matters are handed over to the district or central government; in some places the authorities are wholly or partially elected, in other, they set themselves above the people, and so on.

The inconveniences which arise from such a state of affairs are too well-known for it to be appropriate to pause over them. But more important here is not whether these inconveniences are great or small, but that they lie in the most basic conception of the institution, in its very essence, and so cannot be eliminated by any measures such as limitations, control, and so on as long as the very essence of the institution continues to exist.

And as a matter of fact, we know that any group of people entrusted with deciding a certain set of activities often of an organizational quality always strives to broaden the range of these activities and its own power in these activities. And the more intelligent, energetic, and active these people, the greater will be this striving on their part to usurp those activities not entrusted to them. The more energetic, active, and conscientious these people, the more the remaining society becomes accustomed to not overseeing them, to not checking on them. It becomes easier, consequently, for a dishonest but talented person, who has accidentally gotten into the government, to direct the activities of this group for the attainment of his personal aims.

It is well-known that to apply some general principle to the business at hand is most difficult. The newer this general principle and the less familiar its particular applications, the easier it is, with the application of this general principle, to make concessions which can completely paralyze the principle itself. Moreover, in a system of elected leaders who must decide for a certain group of people, they may find themselves forced to make a decision which corresponds to the general principle in theory, but not to its particularities [in practice]. In short, the most difficult part of the decision, which most of all requires the assistance of various opinions, is left by the group to a separate person. Any central authority of the district, State or country must consist of a small number of persons, and the larger this unit, the fewer the possibilities that the elected persons are known to the majority, the less, consequently, is the election of reliable, worthy people assured.

Finally, any government created in the present form must have in its authority the power to execute its decisions. But it is clear that if the decisions of the government were each time considered useful by the majority of citizens possessing equal rights, then there would be no need of such power at all. If there were found small, isolated deviations by separate persons or small groups from the fulfilment of the will of all, then these persons or groups either should be abandoned or should be forced to that fulfilment by the disadvantages of such a deviation, without any physical power. This physical power, which every government possesses, is only necessary because no government whatsoever can be the expression of the will of the vast majority. The closer it is to this expression, the less is the physical power at the disposal of the government (example: the United States of America with forty thousand troops).

But again, all these arguments lead to the idea of the harmfulness of any central authority and, consequently to anarchy.

But let us imagine a country organized without such central authority, without a government, and we will see in what practices of society the need for such a government can be found.

Let us imagine groups of rural *obshchiny* engaged in agriculture and producing grain, cattle, and so on. Let us imagine, that by the common consent of all the inhabitants of a given country these *obshchiny* are not considered the owners of the lands occupied by them, but only the users of them. Let us suppose, that in a separate *obshchiny* there appears a parasite who shirks his work and wishes to live without working. He does not now [in present society] receive money, and without money he cannot live. Then [in future society] he will not receive money or that certification that every day he finished his portion of required labour, and without this he will also be unable to live.

Let us suppose that he begins to steal and so on. Now they send him to the district police officer. In the future, an autonomous communal court will deal with him—by itself or through elected representatives.

In short, it is clear, and about this there can be no dispute, that in all its own internal affairs the *obshchina*, just as now, is and will be able to be in command without creating a government.

But let us suppose that one *obshchina* seizes the land of another, drives its own cattle onto its meadows or ploughs its field. Now from this arises a whole *case* which is decided in all sorts of government courts. How would it be without these courts? In the first place, no *obshchina* of ploughman can live alone. It necessarily must enter a union of agricultural *obshchiny*, which in its turn must be in union with unions of artisans, factory workers, and so forth. It is clear that the *offended obshchina* has to appeal with the complaint to its own union of agricultural *obshchiny*. *How* must this appeal be accomplished, *how* can the union decide the issue? For this there are dozens of methods, each of which is a hundred times better than present ones. The *obshchina* can, for example, immediately summon to the location of the event the elected representatives from all the *obshchiny* of the union, and supposing that every *obshchina* is so interested in its public affairs that it gathers for the resolution of them in several days, the representatives could be on the spot and decide the dispute in about ten days. It is apparent that this is not the time to decide how to do this more conveniently. The important question is whether this method is quicker and whether it leads more truly to the goal than the existing ones.

Every decision must be implemented. Who will implement it if there are no district police officers and neighbouring officials with throngs of troops? We believe that if there were an *obshchina* unreasonable enough to oppose the decision of the union it had joined voluntarily, then the union would always have a very powerful weapon against it—to exclude it and to deprive it, consequently, of the exchange of services for which this *obshchina* joined the union, [while] in addition, informing all the other unions of the reasons for the expulsion. If it did happen that the reasons were erroneous, then the *obshchina* would be accepted in some other union.

It is precisely thus in the disputes among the unions of ploughman and the unions of carpenters, coal miners, ironworkers, and so on. Just as the unions of farmers cannot exist alone, so also the separate *obshchiny* cannot, and they must enter into unions of a second order with other artisans, just as all the groups of workers of a given trade must [unite] among themselves.

In short, we do not see what the legal function of the State could be in such a system nor in what instances the need for it could be found. But one can also find little need in all other matters. For this we will touch upon the main functions of the present day State: taxes (for the needs of this State); an army (for the support of this State and for protection from foreign enemies); institutions for the collection of taxes; institutions for the means of communication, the post and telegraph; institutions for the people's education; institutions for national economy, institutions for the police.

Armies, as the guardians of order, become less necessary the closer the decisions of the government express the interests of the majority. In the absence of a government they become necessary only for protection from foreign enemies. But experience has shown that regular armies have never been sufficient for protection from the invasion of enemies. Still less would they be sufficient if the invasions were accomplished by the will of an entire nation. If the whole nation wished to invade foreign regions, then only an armed populace could oppose it. The German-French war [1870] serves as the best proof. Only an armed nation could stop an army of seven hundred thousand; that is why the Germans were so afraid of a people's war, as much as, if not more than, the French government, and so harshly prevented its inception. The only means of stopping such an invasion would have been the armament of entire unions, the expedient distribution of duties in the unions and so on. Authority and command would be required only for directing a standing army and for providing it with stores and supplies; and with the disappearance of the army the authority disappears.

Means of Communication. Now, when these are located in the hands of private companies which try as much as possible to exploit private persons, it is apparent that their transfer into the hands of the government is an inconvenient measure (England). But if the very construction of railroads is the result of agreement between the producing groups of railroad workers and those *obshchiny* across whose lands the road passes, then it is apparent that such exploitation is out of the question. If the measure of any product is the amount of labour spent on it, and if the railroad association raises the transport fee above this cost, then it would be profitable for all the various unions having business with it (all ploughman who supply the grain) to break their agreement with this association, thus forcing it to return to former relations.

The Posts and Telegraphs. It is clear that this branch presents still fewer reasons for the intervention of the State. At the same time the posts and telegraphs present an excellent example of how much can be achieved by independent development and free agreement. The whole present international system of post offices is the product of such agreement. It would have been considered an absurdity if two hundred years ago it were said to someone that a letter would circle the entire globe in several days, that it would be possible to observe its path almost around the whole globe, that it would pass among scores of sovereign Sates, and that the several kopecks paid for it would be distributed fairly among all these States (the smallness of the unit does not act as an obstacle, for example: the former Germanic customs union), and that all this would be the product of a free union (federal) agreement. But it is in fact so. And here, consequently, we do not see what could constitute the role of the State.

Thus, having touched upon the various functions of contemporary governments, we do not see the necessity for arranging daily life on the social foundations of government and State. Therefore, in connection with the above remarks about every government's inability to act fairly and about its harmfulness, we believe that if the fifth condition of equality is to be realized, it is necessary to recognize the necessity of the abolishment of any government existing now and to give the producing *obshchina* and artels themselves the opportunity to manage absolutely all matters concerning their members, to unite spontaneously in unions on the basis of free agreements as much as necessary, and in these unions, to decide all matters concerning the separate artels and *obshchiny.*

If the positions cited above are acknowledged, then with the total realization of all of these conditions, the ideal is depicted roughly in this way:

The population of a given territory is grouped in the villages and *obshchiny.* In all the *obshchiny* the communal cultivation of the land is gradually introduced.

All the plants, factories, and workshops in the cities, all the raw materials of the owners of these factories are consigned to the use of those who worked in them. Production is on the artel basis. The distribution of occupations among the members of the artel takes place according to the voluntary agreement of the artel members.

All the houses in the cities are consigned to the common use of the whole city. In all quarters, the committees determine the number of apartments needed, lock or alter the worthless ones, and construct new ones. The distribution of apartments is done by categories, depending on the number of families, and within the categories, by lot.

All the capital of urban capitalists in hard cash or valuable items, is declared the property of all members of the territory; all promissory notes are destroyed.

At first, in every factory, work continues as before, let us suppose nine hours a day. Each member of the artel or *obshchina* who works this amount of time according to the assignment of the artel receives in return a receipt from the artel.

All the artels of a given trade are grouped at first in a given city, in one or in several unions, and either these unions or the artels independently enter into unions for the exchange among themselves of the products of their manufacture. Having need of farmers, bakers, herdsmen, shoemakers, and so forth each artel, of necessity, has to enter a union of all the artisans of a given city, which in its turn has to enter a union that possibly has a greater number of agricultural unions. Convinced that each artel's checks for nine hours actually represent nine hours of work of roughly equal difficulty, these unions let each other have their products on the basis of this calculation. If the farmers do not agree to enter these unions and to accept the town checks in exchange for their products, then obviously there has to be a meeting of the elected representatives from all the artels to engage in a sale of their products and in the conversion of them into hard cash. Business with all the other producing groups will proceed on the usual sale and purchase principles exactly as will all foreign trade, for as long as they do not join the union.

All the children receive instructions, vocational and theoretical, from the artel or *obshchina* itself. Since it is necessary to raise the level of education, the artels enter unions and through their combined efforts open institutes for more extensive higher education to be attended by all the youths of the union.

In every agricultural *obshchina*, in every trade artel, exact accounts will be kept. In them will be written the number of working members, the expenses for the purchase and maintenance of the instruments of labour and raw materials, the amount of products manufactured daily; thus, one can determine, on the basis of the simplest calculation, how many measures of rye, wheat, oats, ploughs, shovels, nails, boots, and so on represent one hour of the *obshchina's* labour. This figure serves as the standard in the exchange among the members of the *obshchina*. Guided by this and convinced of the correctness of the calculation, two or several agricultural *obshchiny*, two or several artels of various trades enter a union for the exchange of products among themselves.

According to the rules of the formation of the union, the calculation will be common for the whole union; it is determined by what is equal to one hour of union labour, expressed in nails, pens, hats, grain, wine, and so forth.

Every union will have to receive many items from the outside (for example, tea, kerosene, and so on). Foreign trade is necessary for this. If this union itself exports something, then it has the opportunity by this means to receive hard cash. If not, then it can enter into alliance with the unions of the gold mine owners, in order to receive gold from them according to the same value of production; or, during a time of social upheaval, a union of gold-mine workers can be founded under the supervision of a committee of representatives elected from all the people to manage the working of gold. Clearly, the administration of the exchanges will by no means be entrusted to such a committee, but merely the accurate bookkeeping, the control for the determination of the value of production of a pound of gold. The inventory and custody of all State wealth can be entrusted to other committees, for example, the unemployed capital in the museums, the conversion of jewels into national wealth, the inventory and custody of State weapons of the fleet, battle supplies, gold and silver bars, and the banks and mints, and so on.

It is apparent that all these committees will perform some of the actual or possible functions of the present-day government, but it is no less apparent that they will not at all resemble the present-day government.

One of the difficult problems of the exchange is the following: let us suppose, that the union of Viatka farmers came to the conclusion that their hours of labour, with their soil and climate, amount to ten measures of rye, but the union of Tambov farmers found that ten hours of their labour is equal to eleven measures of rye. And since it seems unprofitable for them to enter in common union, they do not enter a common union where this difference would be equalized. Therefore, the ironworkers and others prefer to exchange their products with the Tambov [farmers] and not with the Viatka [farmers]. Hence, the source of all kinds of dissensions. This difficulty, however, is resolved rather simply by several means.

In the first place, no one ever even supposes that all the difficulties which arise could be settled at once. There is no doubt that it will be possible to solve these and many other difficulties only by means of many trials, failures, redistributions, even quarrels. The question can only be what system gives the most leeway so that ultimately, the correct exchange of the products of labour may be arranged—the present system or the one proposed. But the answer to this question cannot be open to doubt.

In the second place, even now it is possible to foresee some ways out of this difficulty: 1) It is impossible even to suppose that it would be convenient to alter the social system in such vast units as the present States of Russia. There is no doubt that such a State has to be divided into several large unions. Then each of these unions will possess a sum of manufactured riches capable of providing the opportunity to arrange a more equitable exchange. 2) If the value of production in the Viatka province is greater than in Tambov, then the value of iron, firewood, and so on will be greater in the latter. This is already one condition for the restoration of the equality of the value of grain. Finally, if in the Viatka province the production of grain costs more than in Tambov, then it will not even be set aside for export from this province. The grain is expensive here because the cultivation of the land produces so little of it that it cannot be an item of export. Therefore, grain will not even figure in the exchange of the products of the Viatka province with the others. But within the local economy of this province the difficulty in grain production will be balanced by the capacity for the production of other items. Therefore, in sum, the Viatka province will not be poorer than the others. It is well-known that mankind is not, generally speaking, poorer in one district than in another from purely physical conditions (with the exception of some arctic savages.) The differences in the wealth of various provinces now depend more on relative, everyday causes than on natural ones, as do the differences in the wealth of separate persons.

Finally, it is well-known that people now cultivate unprofitable lands and work at the most unremunerative trades only because they are forced to do this, since they cannot pass on to other lands and cannot establish another trade. Therefore, perhaps one must even preserve the inequality in the exchange since it will serve as a reason for people, too attached to the native land by sentimental affection, to abandon it sooner for resettlement to other, more convenient locations.

In general, we are not writing a scheme for the structure of a society many years in the future. If we even speak about how society could be structured in the future it is only in order to show that the destruction of presently existing obstacles will expedite the change for a more equitable structure, only in order to jot down an outline of this future system in the most general terms. We are even deeply convinced that any attempt to define this system more precisely is a fruitless expenditure of time. And here is why. To define a system in which there is absolutely no room for any injustice whatsoever means to jump ahead many thousands of years. Such work is already fruitless, because with the abolition of some injustices that exist now, even the concept of justice, of good and evil, of the good and bad, of the useful and harmful, will be modified. Therefore, there does not even exist now that mind which comprehends all the future moral ideas of mankind. Consequently, any contemporary idea will be a manifestation of present-day conceptions of morality, a manifestation which will be impossible, because before it is realized, in its totality, new conceptions of justice will be created and *begin to be realized.*

Consequently, it is impossible to construct theoretically an ideal which could be realized even approximately.

But no matter how good the theoretical ideal, it has no value whatever if it does not have guarantees of realization. And it can have a guarantee of realization only when it is the expression of the existing aspirations and hopes of the majority. Meanwhile, one can say only that the aspiration of the majority is the realization of the above-mentioned ideals of equality. In what practical form these ideals will be shaped no one can now decide, least of all, of course, the scholar. For this it is necessary to know the quantity and forms of the integral of the total aggregate of the system of ideas, the degree of development, the tendencies of each separate person. We need not speak of the scholar, who cannot know this (for neither statistics nor history is, and for a very long time will not be, the expression of this aspect of life); yet even the man standing closest to the people can determine only in the most general features what could now satisfy mankind.

Our concern is to express this general striving, to elucidate it for those to whom it is still more vague than to us; to show that these hopes can be realized; to encourage this belief in those in whom it is weakening; to show that the main obstacles to the realization of these hopes are not in their vagueness but are external obstacles; to point out the weak aspects of these obstacles, to create around ourselves groups for the ruthless destruction of this whole armour of obstacles, and to fall [in battle] in the breaking of this armour.

But to work out the particulars of these ideals, that is, to work out the fine points of *one's own* dialectic, to exercise *one's mind* with logical rigour—this is the concern of idle parasites. It must not be *our* concern.

In light of all the foregoing, we believe that the realization of the future system must proceed simultaneously in all its aspects, that is, that along with the destruction of the economic nobility must go the destruction of the contemporary State system.

Further, proceeding from the principle that the more clearly defined the goals and character of the revolution, and the more socialist these goals, then the more it will have adherents, we believe that the revolution must strive to realize all these goals at once, as a whole, bearing in mind that limitations and compromises will inevitably be provoked by the activity itself.

Therefore, we would believe it necessary to take the following steps immediately after the disorganization of the present government:

The land should be declared the property of all, of the whole Russian people.

Every village and countryside settlement should receive the use of those lands which they now control.

All the lands taken by the whole countryside or by separate peasants of the village or countryside should become the possession of this village or countryside.

All the landowner's lands which are lying fallow should become the possession of the former peasants of this landowner.

All the lands bought by separate peasants for themselves should become the possession of the whole community of the village where such peasants are registered.

All the workers living off the wages of the landowners or leaseholders should register in the village which formerly was in the possession of the landowner. If there are more than ten of them, they should form a special settlement, having received from the *mir* a strip equal to those of the other members of the village. The landowners who survive should work the land of the *mir* on an equal basis with the other peasants of the village or countryside.

No recompense whatsoever for the expropriated land is due: nothing special from the village community allotment is due. If the *mir* should designate them [the landowners] as incapable of any work it should be empowered to fix them a stipend at its discretion, equal to that of the aged.

All the landowner's farmsteads, gardens, draft animals, instruments, and machines should become the possession of the former peasants of that landowner. If the landowner's land is bought by someone after the emancipation of the peasants, then it is allotted to the workers on the estate.

In every district a committee should be named from the elected peasant representatives, in order to make the lands equal among the peasants of that district, to draw up the boundaries and to place posts.

The subsequent redivision of land should occur in three, five, and ten years.

Every plant or factory should become the possession of the workers in that plant or factory, along with all the machines and supplies of raw materials.

The workers must select from themselves a manager, foremen, and so forth.

In every factory a strict calculation must be made of how many people worked every day and how much was done.

At first, for a certain time, every worker should receive some pay for every hour of work.

From all factories of every region, honest workers must be chosen to ascertain how many people work every day in each factory and how much and what is made.

Everything that is manufactured by every factory should be pooled in stores and for a certain period should not be sold.

The former masters of the factories who survive should be accepted equally with all in any factory—at a post to which they are assigned.

All former officials, from ministers to copyists, should be accepted with equal rights into any artel, given the consent of the artel.

All former soldiers should be dispersed to their homes, having received a certain sum for the journey.

In each village an artel guard of some size should be formed.

All former criminals should return to their homes.

The offenses of each should be judged honestly in that artel where he is registered.

All the houses in the cities should become the possession of the whole city.

In each quarter, committees should be named for the calculation of how many apartments are needed for the inhabitants of this quarter, for the subdivision of them into unmarried, artel, and family [apartments]. All those registered in apartments for the unmarried receive them by lot from those listed in this category. The same holds for the artel and family [categories].

All cash capital of separate persons, institutions, palaces, churches, and monasteries must go into a common treasury into which it must be placed according to schedule. After some time it will be divided among the provinces or districts without exception.

All ships should become the possession of the sailors who work on them.

Committees should be named for appraising the value of transporting [cargo] for a given distance on each ship. All the promissory notes either of individuals or of the State should be destroyed by burning on the square.

All *ownership* records and serf books in the courts must be burned, but all account books in the stores must be preserved.

All wares in the stores must be registered in detail and records made thereof. After a certain time they should be given out to artels selected from among those of the city.

In each city a committee should be named for the purchase of all those provisions the peasants bring to the marketplace. For a certain time, the distribution should be free, but subsequently this committee should make the transaction with hour-receipts.

We move now to the question on which the greatest division exists among the various schools. This question is whether the realization of the stated ideal is possible by peaceful means or whether it will necessarily be achieved by means of revolution, upheaval?

Very many believe that this realization must be achieved by peaceful, gradual means. Very many go further and say that gradual [development] of some aspects of this ideal must take place first, at least in part, and subsequently the remaining (that is, not only each of the aspects of the ideal gradually, but also each one separately).

The most usual way indicated is first of all the acquisition of political rights by the people, that is, the freedom of assembly, freedom of the press, freedom of the composition of societies. And subsequently, the establishment of a government of the people (and even of voting by the people). The origin of this way of thinking is obvious. It has blown over directly from western Europe.

However, there are many extremely weighty objections against this path.

It goes without saying that they [those who favour peaceful means] proceed from the utterly unproven position that every people must inevitably pass through all those phases of development which other peoples have passed through. But what is important for us is not its origin, but the fact that it assumes that the people's use of political rights is a better condition for the acceleration of social upheaval than the absence of these rights. By now one can show *a priori* that this supposition is false. If the question were what condition of the people is more advantageous for peaceful progress, then there is no doubt that it is the one in which the people can freely align themselves, discuss their affairs, and execute their decisions. But the matter takes on quite another aspect if one assumes that the social transformation cannot occur by peaceful means, but inevitably must occur by means of insurrection. If one admits this position as fundamental, then the question becomes this: what condition most hastens social insurrection—the one in which the people enjoy the freedom of meetings and societies, the freedom of speech and of the press, or that in which it enjoys not one of these guarantees, not even individual security? What position most encourages the revolutionary spirit of the people? If that is the way the question is stated there can be no doubt of the answer. Not we, but the very defenders of the acquisition of political rights who assert that the use of these rights is the best guarantee against revolutionary outbreaks, answer the question by themselves. But this position can be corroborated by many other considerations. We are ready to admit that the freedoms of speech and assembly extraordinarily assist the elucidation of all considerations and ideas; it also stands to reason that the clarity of the consciousness in a large measure assists its realization. But we know very well that the intellect and the will operate in every action. And the significance of the latter is incomparably greater than that of the former in all ordinary life and the more so in any unusual action. Indeed, by no conclusions whatever is it possible to convince a man that it pays for him to take up arms at a given moment, since such an appeal is an appeal for self-sacrifice. By no conclusions whatever is it possible to convince a man that it will be best of all for him to risk his life, in order to gain possible prosperity for his neighbours and children, [as] in a lottery (that is, in a gathering of facts where it is impossible to weigh *all the pros and cons)*. Between a clear consciousness and a fervent desire to realize the good (though necessarily vague) ideal, [there is] a terrible abyss. And this abyss explains all those facts which can lead to the corroboration of the stated position.

Indispensable for the beginning of any revolution are, first of all, the realization of dissatisfaction with the present, the consciousness of the endlessness of this condition and of its irreparability by customary means, and finally, a readiness for risk in order to change this condition.

For the success of the revolution, the force of pressure, weakness of the government, and clarity of the aspirations are indispensable.

The people's enjoyment of political rights for all these indispensable elements (not excluding even the last) acts in the reverse direction.

The less secure a person feels in his most sacred rights, the greater is his inclination to revolutionary methods of action, the greater is his animosity towards the contemporary order. Examples: the mass uprisings in China and Spain on the one hand and, [on the other], the obtuse satisfaction of the citizens of the Swiss republic with their condition. In fact, all large-scale uprisings occur when the people can bear it no longer (after hunger, disease, and so forth). The Spaniards declared that if the government began to take drastic measures, this would provoke an uprising of vast dimensions.

The less measures are taken which arouse hopes for further improvements, the less futile prove to be any beginnings on which the hopes at first were placed, the stronger is the readiness for revolutionary action.

It is necessary to keep in mind at this point that the more trivial the reforms, the more clearly evident is their triviality to the entire mass. And the reforms are the more trivial the less they enlist the energies of gifted people. We know what a mass of rather clever people took great interest in the judicial reform in Russia, because this reform was most cleverly arranged; and we also know that the revolutionary attitude of the Russian youth in a large measure is supported by the fact that Russia lags behind contemporary states and that this youth cannot apply its energies to such pursuits which it knows from the life of western Europe. Under the conditions in Germany, they would turn into learned professors trying to solve a question of metaphysics, of science, but not of life.

It goes without saying, finally, that the more precarious the material and political condition of the people, the stronger is the readiness for risk on their part.

We see, consequently, that the possession of political rights acts on all sides as a diminution of revolutionary initiative.

Thus, it is clear that this fact weakens the main condition of the success of a revolution, that is, the force of pressure. Besides, the power of the government is increased. The less the government violates various rights of the individual, the more it assures the protection of property, the better [and] more popular it is, the stronger it is, the more easily it can suppress an uprising. The less popular it is the weaker it is. Soldiers, although tyrannized during the time of Alexander I, were in many places ready to follow their own humane officers. The Muscovite *khoz-halyr*[2] of the good old times would never refuse the government those services which the Petersburg police officer refuses and will refuse.

All these positions are so obvious and their corroborating facts are so generally well-known that there is no need to pause over them. We proceed to the clarification of the views. It is said to us: the more free the discussion of the question, the better will the vague strivings be explained and the easier it will be to realize them. In an abstract form, this is indisputable. But here again is the same everlasting confusion of the idea of the future system with the idea of the present one; the same everlasting habit of thinking in abstract ideas, without hitting upon their real, ordinary forms. Let us suppose that this position is true. But where and when? In the future system—yes! In the present one—absolutely not. Indeed, those maintaining this position forget that the primary condition for the clarification of a view is its certainty, its delineation from others, the truthfulness of those views with which it conflicts. But if the acquisition of political rights gives the socialists the complete freedom to express themselves, then it gives no less a freedom to their opponents; together with the propagation of social ideas goes the propagation of antisocial ones. But still worse: there arises the propagation of whole billions of intermediate opinions, each of which tries to disguise one or another side of the common evils, to cover it with this or that rag, to distract from it with this or that trinket. If all the opinions were stated with something approaching candour, they would be almost harmless. If this whole net of trinkets was proposed through error and not with cunning, if it were proposed with force, with intellectual clarity, then the truth would emerge from the conflict.

But under [present] circumstances it fully achieves its aim; it actually deprives less developed people of the possibility to confront matters squarely. And to this intellectual and cultural superiority, to the general servility before self-imputed knowledge, to all the forces which heighten this servility—to this is added the strength of capital, which provides the opportunity to spread one's ideas by newspaper propaganda, by cajolery, by bribery (direct and indirect) of the gifted and influential individuals from the mass, as well as in other ways. What kind of socialist propaganda can endure competition with newspapers with an initial expenditure of 140 million rubles of capital in two years, issued in a hundred thousand copies (like *The Times* and *Daily News* [of London] and having the powerful support of the entire civilized bourgeois public? It is worthwhile to remember how much each such newspaper corrupts people every day so as to curse this freedom of speech in contemporary society—which provides no opportunity for a socialist counter-balance. And this propagation is terrible, not because of the filth, not because of the abomination of its opinions, but simply because it enfolds a man in the mist of a world foreign to him. This is not the sting of a snake, this is the captivating glance of a boa constrictor, this is the slime which engulfs the helpless man.

And these gentlemen forget still more. They forget the available time and the available brainpower of each man and of each society in total. When tomorrow it is necessary to select a collector of taxes in the *obshchina,* when the day after tomorrow one will have to decide between this and that candidate for the chamber of State or government, when tomorrow it is necessary at a meeting to speak out against the tax on tobacco and in answer to the speech of an agitator to adduce just as many facts, when, even, it is simply necessary to know what the Virginians think about the tax on tobacco, when tomorrow one will have to listen to the lofty speech of a learned orator and so on, and each somewhat honest man will outdo himself on these "issues"—then will there remain much time and ready brainpower to think about the social revolution, about the *future* system, when in the *present one*...[3] and the first ten hours of the working day are spent before the puddling furnace with a very heavy poker in [one's] hands?

And after all this can one still speak about the acquisition of political rights? No, there is no other way for us: here, where there are not these rights—there is no need for us to trouble about them; there, where they are—we must not use them, employing the law of Rostopchin with respect to the French army of 1812: *faire de vide devant eux.*

* * *

We proceed now to the most difficult but at the same time the most essential question of our programme, the question about the practical measures which should be taken for the realization of our ideal.

We have already stated that in our opinion the realization of this ideal must occur by means of social revolution. In this we do not at all flatter ourselves with the hope that with the first revolution the ideal will be realized in all its completeness; we are even convinced that for the realization of the equality we have sketched, many years are still required, and many limited, perhaps even general, outbursts. But we are also convinced that the more completely, the more widely the demands of the masses are established from the very first revolution, the more clearly and practically these demands are expressed—then the more the first step will destroy those cultural forms which hinder the realization of the socialist system, the more disorganized those forces and attitudes to which present-day social and State daily life adhere will be; then, the more peaceful the successive upheavals will be, and the sooner will follow successively large-scale improvements in the attitudes of people.

Therefore, our goal must be to apply our powers to hastening this outburst, so as to elucidate those hopes and aspirations which exist in the vast majority in vague forms, so that in good time one can take advantage of those circumstances under which an outburst could have the most favourable outcome, so that, finally, the outburst itself would occur in the name of clearly expressed demands, and precisely in the name of those cited by us above.

We must, consequently, set forth the sum total of measures by which, in our opinion, these goals can best be reached.

If, with the working out of our ideal, we could proceed largely by logical means, then here our main support will be experience. While speaking about the ideal, we could proceed from the common aspirations and hopes of the masses, and deduce that social structure which could be the best way to use these aspirations (of course, not contradicting the character of the views of our people) and which could be the expression of conceptions about justice that are always inherent in all the masses. Here we cannot be satisfied with the general hopes and aspirations of our people; we must take into account the entire range of private notions, ways of thinking, attitudes, actions, and so forth; it is not possible to foresee in advance which ones; it is possible to find out only by means of experience.

Further, in the general aspirations of the masses of all peoples there is very much in common; that is why the aspirations and hopes expressed by western European workers are, in many respects, accepted sympathetically by ours. But in questions of revolutionary practice the western European examples must be introduced only with extreme caution, since it is extremely difficult to weigh in each given instance the totality of everyday conditions which cause this or that result.

But these considerations also define the one common trait on the whole second half of our programme. On the one hand we now consider our ideals finally settled, we consider the fundamental principles of our ideals invariable, and we will make any particular concession only when we see the final impossibility of realizing some aspect of our ideal in practice, and then, nevertheless, will consider this concession forced and temporary. On the other hand, since the programme of our practical preparatory measures must be determined not only by their expediency in view of the common ideal, but also by the totality of the everyday conditions of the milieu in which we act, then we will not consider this part of our programme something invariable; on the contrary, we will be ready for any change in it, if only life will show us that such methods of action will better and more directly lead to the proposed goal.

There are, however, several fundamental positions which we consider possible and necessary to maintain unchanged in all our practical, preparatory work. This is the rejection within the revolutionary organization of such relations among people, and of such ways of conduct, as directly contradict the ideal for the sake of which they are introduced. Thus, we absolutely reject the introduction into the revolutionary organization of a hierarchy of ranks which enslaves many people to one or several persons; an inequality in the interrelations of the members of one and the same organization; mutual deception and coercion for the attainment of our goals. It goes without saying, of course, that we consider all similar means completely permissable and even necessary in all our relations with the government with which we enter into battle.

We will still return to these questions when we elucidate the character of the organization proposed by us.

First of all, we are deeply convinced that no revolution is possible if the need for it is not felt in the people themselves. No handful of people, however energetic and talented, can evoke a popular insurrection, if the people themselves, in their own best representatives, do not achieve the realization that they have no other way out of the position with which they are dissatisfied except insurrection. Consequently, the business of any revolutionary party is not to call for insurrection, but only to pave the way for the success of imminent insurrection, that is, to unite the dissatisfied elements, to promote the acquaintance of separate units or groups with the aspirations and actions of other similar groups, to assist the people in defining more clearly the true causes of dissatisfaction, to assist them in determining more clearly their actual enemies, removing the mask from the enemies who hide behind some decorous disguise, and finally, to contribute to the elucidation both of the nearest practical goals and the means of their realization.

Therefore, first of all, are there these dissatisfied elements among the Russian people? Does there exist that mood which is necessary for the success of any revolutionary organization?

We can boldly answer that there are. All our personal observations, all the information we receive, irrefutably indicates that among our peasantry and factory workers there is a smouldering discontent; that with the systematic destruction of the masses of people this discontent is growing; that in the first period after the emancipation of the peasants it was weaker than now; that the hope continues to live among the peasants that by some means the landowners and the peasants will be made equal in regard to the land, taxes, and feudal duties; that the hope that this equalization will proceed from above is gradually being lost; that the worship of the person of the tsar is in some places being undermined noticeably; that this worship, about which so many have spoken before, is in general extremely fragile and very easily gives way to completely different attitudes, especially among the peasant youth; that the belief in the fact that the tsar is completely powerless among the lords surrounding him is constantly strengthening and thus leads inevitably to the fact that the people, once their patience is exhausted, will undertake to destroy these lords mercilessly (and without their support the tsar will become a powerless figurehead); that this discontent of the peasantry is noticed not in any one locality, but to a greater or lesser degree everywhere; that only those who have never been closely associated with the peasantry or factory workers deny this, and, on the contrary, all those who have been in some manner close to the peasantry or factory workers confirm it; that the observations of the same people lead to the conclusion that the readiness for insurrection, for risk, is much greater than even the optimists could believe; that finally, this is confirmed by the local uprisings which are constantly recurring. So much for the attitudes in the economic sphere.

As for the State [sphere], we see on one hand the greatest indifference to all reforms of government, on the other—a general hostility towards any representative of State interests: this hostility constantly grows with the increase of State extortions.

Yet there is a divergence between the nobility and the people; the development of senseless luxury among the nobility, the rapid development among the nobility of an unimaginable avidity and depravity which accompanies the decline of creation, talent, and serious thought, and the development of cruelty, of the mad pursuit of easy gain, and so on, all attest that the nobility on its part will not decide in time on the necessary concessions and will not be able to satisfy the people with them.

Finally, the development in Europe of the military-predatory element, the senseless increase of regular armies, and the inevitability of large scale wars in Europe, indicate the inevitability of such a development of State power as must rapidly lead many states of Europe, beginning with the poorest, to complete bankruptcy, and the people to further ruin. In short, all that we see around us leads to the unquestionable conviction that to begin organizing a revolutionary party is quite timely and that the tasks of this party are significantly eased by the assistance it meets everywhere.

For the convenience of survey, the tasks of this party can be subdivided into two branches of activity, which, however, must in fact proceed simultaneously and inseparably: on one hand is the dissemination of its views and the increase in the number of like-minded persons, and on the other hand, the unification of them into one common organization.

For convenience we will examine these two activities separately.

First of all, where must our activity be directed, where must we chiefly spread our views and seek for ourselves like-minded persons— among the student youth and nobility in general or among the peasantry and urban workers?

We answer this question categorically, and we consider this answer the fundamental position in our practical programme: unquestionably among the peasantry and urban workers. Here must we spread our views, here must we seek comrades who would aid the further dissemination of these views; with these comrades we must enter into a friendly, closely united organization. We do not wish to sever any relations with the education milieu and especially not with the milieu of student youth; but, refusing to take upon ourselves the permanent role of tutoring this youth in the stated direction, we will enter into close relations only with those circles or individuals who immediately inspire the confidence or the almost complete hope that they will direct their subsequent activity among the peasantry and urban workers. For the mass of educated youth we are ready to do only one thing: to disseminate, and (if the cause cannot spread without our assistance, and also if we have enough extra energy) to prepare those books that directly assist

the explanation of our ideals and our goals, that make available those
facts which show the complete inevitability of the social upheaval and
the necessity to unite, to organize the people's awakened strengths.

We came to these conclusions by means of experience, by means of
life itself, but we can also confirm them with several considerations. We
will set forth both these and others.

First of all, the insurrection must proceed among the peasantry and
urban workers themselves. Only then can it count on success. But no
less necessary for the success of the insurrection is the existence among
the very insurrectionists of a strong, friendly, active group of people
who, serving as a bond between the separate localities and having
clearly determined *how* to formulate the demands of the people, how to
avoid various traps, how to secure its victory, are agreed on the means
of action. It is clear, moreover, that such a party must not stand outside
the people but among them, must serve not as a champion of some
alien opinions worked out in isolation, but only as a more distinct, more
complete expression of the demands of the people themselves; in short,
it is clear that such a party cannot be a group of people alien to the
peasantry and workers, but must be the focus of the most conscious
and decisive forces of those peasants and urban workers. Any party
standing outside the people—especially one of the nobility—however
it be inspired with a desire for the well-being of the people, however
well it expresses the demands of the people, will inevitably be doomed
to ruin, together with all the rest, as soon as the rebelling people with
their first deeds lay open the chasm between the nobility and
peasantry. And we see in this only an entirely justified retribution for
the fact that those of this party were earlier not able to become comrades among the people but rather remained supreme guides. Only
those whose former way of life, whose previous deeds are wholly of a
character which merits the faith of the peasantry and workers will be
heeded by them; and this will be only the activists of the peasantry itself and those who will wholeheartedly surrender themselves to the
people's affairs and prove themselves not with heroic deeds in a moment of enthusiasm, but with all their previous ordinary life; those
who, having cast off any shade of nobility in life, now will enter into
close relations with the peasantry and urban workers, tied by personal
friendship and confidence. Finally, once the necessity of the unification
of the people's awakened forces is recognized, then we definitely can
not understand how it would be possible to avoid the conclusion that
the only possible place is one among the peasantry and workers themselves. Such a way of life serves as direct proof to one's associates that

professed convictions are not simple verbiage, but a matter of one's whole life. Such is the main reason which prompts us to transfer our activity to the midst of the peasantry and urban workers. But there are still several secondary considerations which lead to the same conclusion.

Most important is the relatively mild acceptance by our students of the propagation of the socialist revolution and of an active participation in this direction. Moreover, it is clear that such a rejection is evoked not by a deficiency of those facts which might lead to a belief in the intolerable nature of today's social order—these facts are too generally known—nor by the impossibility of being convinced that any useful reform in this direction cannot be peaceful—in this respect as well, contemporary history is too rich in facts. [It arises] simply from not being receptive to any sort of extreme views, an inability to renounce the tradition of scholarly learning and, finally, simply an unwillingness to accept in theory that sort of conclusion whose fulfilment in life is by no means desired. Besides that, all the educated youth is so infected by an awe of authority, so corrupted by the habit of demanding hundreds of facts to be convinced, facts twisted and presented in all sorts of ways, dug out from the same various, authoritative sources, when there already exists a whole aggregate of facts illustrating the argument (just like those scholars who maintain that the variability of species *still* is unproven). Finally, they are so accustomed to demanding that the path of the future development of mankind be scientifically deduced for them, when to deduce this scientifically is not possible either now or in the very distant future—that, generally speaking, any propagandizing among the educated youth requires so much erudition and dialectics that it involves a terribly unproductive waste of time, and a distraction of energy from incomparably more urgent matters. Moreover, those of the young who sincerely seek a way out of their doubt, will, on finding out the necessary facts, inevitably come to the same conclusion themselves concerning the necessity of revolutionary activity.

For this reason, our responsibility regarding these individuals should only be to give them the opportunity to learn certain facts, that is, to acquaint them with the main events of the most recent history of the working-class movement in the West and at home; with the relation of the nobility and the government to this movement; and, finally, with the results which we ourselves are approaching in our activity—but even here only as much as our assistance can promote the appearance and distribution of such books. Thus, we, of course, will keep up an acquaintance with such circles where it is possible to meet with people who, uncorrupted by the aristocratic-scholastic spirit, willingly agree with the necessity of transferring their activity to the worker's milieu; and we will try not to miss the opportunity of drawing near such people and arranging things with them. But to take on oneself the role of tutor, to concern oneself with the education and training of the individuals working among the people—this we positively decline, since we can always find like-minded people of much greater reliability, in many respects more useful, and in any case more deserving if we turn directly to the milieu of the peasantry and the urban workers. Finally, we must acknowledge that even the very best representatives of civilized society, once they have managed to get used to its corroding conditions, never provide such solid representatives of propaganda among the people as one would wish. They are so accustomed to the accepted form of life and thought, and to a certain type of world view, that [few] isolated individuals ever completely give them up.

Finally, there is one other feature of activity among the peasants and urban workers which should not be left without comment. The necessary and primary condition of any success whatsoever among the peasants and the workers is the full renunciation of any signs of nobility, the lowering of one's material circumstances almost to the level of that of the milieu where one intends to act. And one must work, do actual work, which each worker and each peasant can understand precisely as work. On the other hand, we know that every revolutionary activist is required to have a moral strength, a stubborn, steadfast strength of will. And every party actually always did strive to instill this quality in its members, but for the most part, they strove to achieve this largely by mutual moral influences. Without denying the effectiveness of the latter, we consider it insufficient, and believe that a better school for instilling this will is the voluntary assumption of pleasant, useful (though not easy) persistent labour and the rejection of material well-being. A person unable to renounce these comforts, when he sees the usefulness of such renunciation, is not capable of persistent, tedious labour, and never will be capable of persistent revolutionary activity. He might be the hero of a moment, but we have no need of heroes; in moments of passion, they appear of themselves, from among the most ordinary people. We need people who, once having come to a certain conviction, are for its sake ready to withstand all possible deprivations day in and day out. But activity among the peasants and workers demands precisely this rejection of every comfort of life, a lowering of one's prosperity to a level attainable by the worker, and—work, without fail, work. Thus, we see in the activity indicated by us both an unavoidable educational significance and beyond that, the best means of testing people. If any sort of deprivation was to be regarded as expiatory penance or exclusively a means of education, then we, of course, would not consider it; we are not a monastic order. But in our century of lying and deceit by others and ourselves, we consider it not superfluous to note that activity among the peasants and the workers, though provoked by entirely different considerations, does have, coincidentally, this meaning and this significance.

On the other hand, we see that the search among the peasantry and the urban workers for individuals who might serve as centres for further propagandizing the idea of the necessity of a socialist upheaval (in the direction indicated above) gives results far better than even the most daring innovator could have expected several years ago. We could draw a picture here of the results achieved in several corners of Russia, but in order not to give a fuzzy, incomplete picture instead of the one it would be appropriate to trace we will restrain ourselves once and for all. Anyone sincerely desiring to learn these results can always find the opportunity to do so orally, from us or from our friends.

Here is why we set forth the basic position of our practical programme—we intend to disseminate our views and to search out those who think as we do almost exclusively among the peasantry and the industrial workers.

We now pass to the possible objections to this position. It may be pointed out to us; it is too soon to undertake such activity. We are few; when we gather a number sufficient so that our activity among the people might have noticeable results, then we, of course, will set out to the peasantry and the workers' milieu. Till that time, let us gather friends from among the educated youth.

In part we have already answered this objection by pointing out that we will sooner find like-minded people in the peasant and working-class milieu that in the students' milieu. But we could introduce even more particular arguments against this objection.

First of all, this objection assumes as proved one proposition which, however, is not proved, and indeed is not true. This is that the most productive propagandists and organizers among the people apparently are, and will be, the so-called intelligentsia. We consider this position completely false. Even if a man from the intelligentsia is better educated, more skilled in argumentation, more capable of finding in each fact a particular side, then it still by no means follows that such a person is necessarily a better agitator than a person from the milieu of the people. Experience up to now leads to the conclusion that agitators as devoted to the task can arise from the milieu of the people as arose from the intelligentsia. As concerns the persuasiveness of the arguments of these [educated] agitators, it must be remembered that they will have dealings not with scholars, who are always ready to hide behind every barrier, behind every bush, if only to uphold some traditional idea, but with people not prejudiced against the truth of social views. If the argument of such agitation could not persevere against the argument of some philosopher, then this is proof of the idea that the existing structure is so bad and so inflexible that it is necessary, and possible, to change it only through revolution—[an idea] which, once instilled, transforms itself into belief among these agitators, and does not give way before any argument; after this person sooner seeks the motivation of what is being said to him than the logical proof of what is being asserted. Thus, we are convinced that to be persuaded of the injustice of the present system, of its inability to alter itself without pressure on the part of the oppressed, and, finally, of the possibility of its change by this means, in no way requires the extensive preparation which the civilized youth supposes. But once having acknowledged that the preparation of the social revolution requires incomparably less training than that which we receive, if only it be directed expediently—and that the training of such people who are not at all prejudiced requires no great amount of time—we must accordingly acknowledge further that, because of the range and type of his activity, an agitator from the people will be incomparably more useful than an agitator from the civilized milieu. This last assertion is already so clear that we will not enlarge on it.

Further, we consider it a central mistake to set up a goal of creating agitators among the people who hold themselves at a distance from the people and move in the circle of their own intelligentsia comrades. It is impossible to suddenly cross at some given moment from the spheres of the intelligentsia to the milieu of the people, just as one pleases. The spheres of the intelligentsia pervasively place on the people who move in them a characteristic stamp, which it is first necessary to renounce in order to have success among the people. To become a populist agitator in several days is impossible; it is necessary to be trained in this activity. For this reason, we consider the best means for the achievement of *this* aim of ours to be to proceed immediately to activity among the people, no matter how small the circle of individuals who have arrived at this same conclusion. We are also convinced that rallying people in the name of a future activity is impossible, or at least, extremely inconvenient, and that it is much easier to rally people in the name of an activity in whose possibility and appropriateness everyone can believe now, and in which one can immediately engage oneself. By showing the results achieved and acting on people not merely by words, but by words and deeds, it is considerably easier to convince them of that of which one is oneself convinced. Since it is necessary to have dealings with the most ordinary people, and since any undertaking must be built bearing in mind that any unification in the name of an activity proposed for the future, in which it is not possible to be immediately engaged, will lead to the formation of a circle of such people whose mutual inclination and influence on one another will more quickly provide the main business, and they will soon completely forget about their future goal. Finally, in immediately setting off for activity among the people (and we suggest that the educated youth with whom we are in agreement do this), we at once give them the opportunity to test and prove their strengths in that endeavour which demands the rejection of many previous traditions. Moreover, this is at the same time an act in the service of the future revolution, for each one of the educated youth, even though he might not consider himself prepared for agitation among his educational fellows, always has so many facts already in reserve that he can share them with the people of the peasantry and the workers. Even if his ideals about the future are not so clearly understood by them as to serve as an object of dissemination, he always can assist the development among the workers and peasants of a criticism of existing conditions and the elucidation of the reasons for all the evils of contemporary life. Such contact with the peasants and workers not only does not hinder the development of ideals of the future in him [the educated youth] but even will promote the development of precisely those ideals which result directly from a rejection of the falsity of all aspects of existing conditions.

In short, we believe that: 1) to unite in order to proceed immediately to activity among the people is the most direct route; 2) to unite in the name of some future enterprise is extremely inconvenient; 3) to unite in the name of an enterprise already under way is considerably more expedient and useful; 4) any result achieved in activity among the people is already a result achieved in the cause of the social revolution; 5) activity among the people is activity which gives the opportunity to every honest person to apply his strengths; 6) this activity offers the most satisfactory conditions for his further personal development and excludes the possibility of being distracted from his ultimate aims; 7) finally, such activity, conducted jointly, is the best means of harmoniously encompassing the varied shades of opinions, which will always exist, and to bring them to a more direct expression of the aspirations for equality which are inherent in the people.

For this reason, we consider as a definite mistake a programme which demands full agreement among the participants of all details of the ideal and, besides that, the organization of an extensive group of participants before proceeding to activity among the people.

For this reason, we say to each honest man, no matter how isolated he might be in some corner of Russia: assume that position in which it will be possible for you to come together with the peasants and urban workers on an equal level; begin to gather like-minded people from among them, and try to train populist agitators devoted to the undertaking from among the better people of this milieu; then, in the name of the incipient undertaking, gather around yourself friends from the intelligentsia who have not been contaminated by the nobility.

This is the direct expression of our views on this question. We can only add that daily experience indicates that a very great number of activists in all parts of Russia have come to the same conclusion, completely independent of one another.

The question arises, then, in what situation can activity among the people be most useful? In what situation should the populist activist begin?

To these questions we can give one general, categorical answer. Most important is that the [situation] in which a man lives in these circumstances be such that any worker or peasant entering his house and speaking with him sees in his form of life a worker or peasant just like himself and the other and if he [the worker] feels a difference between him and the other, it is only in the degree of development. Thus, any such situation in which a person in order to retain his place is required to live in the manner of the nobility, we consider definitely disadvantageous.

We, therefore, positively reject the possibility [that persons] in the positions of government officials, landholders, and so on will have success. We believe, then, that the most advantageous situation is the situation of the peasant or the industrial factory worker. But we believe that there are also many other situations which do not exclude the possibility of activity in certain cases, as, for example, a village doctor's assistant, sometimes a teacher, even perhaps a district clerk, and so forth. This would not be the place to go into an analysis of the relative advantages of these situations; guided by a self-established aim, each can weigh the advantages and disadvantages of any situation better than we.

We now pass to the most immediate definition of what must properly comprise, in our opinion, the activity of everyone placed in such a situation. In its general features this activity is clear. It is: 1) to elucidate to one's associates the central deficiencies of the existing system; 2) to elucidate that masked and obvious exploitation to which the worker is subjected by all the higher strata of the society and the State; 3) to point out the means of escaping this condition, that is, to convince others that this system of society will not change without strong pressure from the oppressed, that any concession from the nobility can be forced only by strength; finally, that to strive to achieve, even [successfully] to achieve, some one particular concession would not have any significance, given the solidarity of the economic and State exploitation; 4) to convince others that the forceful appropriation of the nobility's and the State's means of exploitation is possible, and that there are facts to confirm [the view] that an agreement will be established between the peasants and the workers of various localities when this results; 5) finally, to unite the most active individuals into one general organization, that is, to present the opportunity for activists of different localities to become personally acquainted, to find out, in this way, about the course of affairs in different places, to confer and to arrange among themselves relatively general measures.

If it is agreed that this must be the character of any activity which is located among the peasants and urban workers, then one disputed issue is resolved: should propaganda be directed at the separate individual or at the masses? In other words, what sort of propaganda should be conducted—*personal* or *mass*? We do not now have sufficient experience to decide this question definitely, but we will propose here several considerations regarding both possibilities.

We believe that if the uprising does not occur immediately, in a very short interval of time, then conducting propaganda which is overt, ubiquitous, and directed to one and all is impossible and useless. Going among the villages, sowing on the run ideas about the necessity of an uprising, creating momentary impressions (granting that a person is in such a position that the peasantry listens to him), we consider useless, and, most important, relatively ineffective at the present moment. Any momentary influence in this direction will not endure; it will very soon fade if the same idea is not subsequently enforced constantly by local populist agitators. Finally, to produce a coordinated impression of some strength on the immense expanse of Russia would require considerably more activists than could be gathered now.

For this reason we would consider a permanent influence more useful, and given this, an influence both on opinion in general in a given village or even neighbourhood, and an influence on separate individuals. But in this [latter] case the influence [must be] so strong and complete that, with the departure of the activists from the village, those separate individuals who remain would continue to explain to their fellow villagers the same views and would continue to gather the better individuals for the expansion of the undertaking. Moreover, we consider it necessary, of course, that this village or rural area should subsequently be visited constantly (and the oftener the better) by the one who previously lived in it, or by those who through him acquire an acquaintance with a circle of selected people of that village. We consider it no less necessary, then, that the circle of this village should be acquainted not only with that agitator who lived there, but with people from circles formed in other villages. Perhaps periodic meetings will be necessary for this, which we consider completely feasible. If these meetings had to be limited only to delegates, stories of what was happening in the various places, they would still be useful. But it is more likely that at those meetings some general questions concerning the general undertaking will be raised.

We believe, then, that it would be useful for every village circle to create some similar organization, that is, it should meet for the discussion of the general business of the circle (and there always is such general business, and the more zealous the agitator, the more there will be), it should create some division of responsibilities according to general agreement, and should communicate with other village circles with which it is familiar. We would suggest that it is never necessary to stop because of the possible insignificance of a circle's composition or of the issues available at a given moment. A circle might consist of only three people, but if these people should united by a close, personal friendship, then they would find general issues; and once having acknowledged themselves mutually bound by the general enterprise, they would have more inclination to activity. If a meeting consisted only of representatives from four to five circles and if the result was only a realistic, graphic description by each of these four to five people, assembled from different places, that this and that was being done in this and that place—then, still, this result might be worth a certain expenditure of time and means, if only its significance not be exaggerated.

Such are our reasons for a united propaganda and organization. But if a circle is formed only to engage in personal development and indoctrination, if new friends are acquired only to conduct idle talk about important matters safely in a large group, then it is clear that this turns into the worst and most harmful inactivity. Moreover, an exclusive circle, if it intends to reach decisions merely within itself, unavoidably comes to this if its members have not sufficiently developed any worthwhile features; but one must always expect precisely that in the majority. It is just here, in our opinion, that what we have called mass propaganda, offers assistance. If the aim of such a circle is the further dissemination of its views not only among the circle of adherents, but rather among all inhabitants of the same village, then such a circle will be incomparably better insured against disintegration and against moral corruption, and moreover it will be preparing for the undertaking of the populist movement.

Indeed, if the more intelligent individuals (honest and sincere—these conditions we consider to be recognized as the most important requisites) will constantly remember to read today such and such a book and to conduct such and such a conversation concerning it, to provoke talk about it tomorrow at a gathering and so on—then they will achieve three goals at once: they will better discover the attitude of separate individuals and their own ability to advocate their beliefs to the people; encourage certain attitudes of the majority; and, besides, protect themselves against idleness and empty chatter. We confess we somehow do not always believe those people who acquire beliefs for themselves alone or to share them with special individuals. Thus, we come to the conclusion that in order for individual propaganda and organization to proceed somewhat successfully in peasant and workers' milieus, it is necessary that the populist agitators who come from the intelligentsia, or from the peoples' milieu itself, should by no means limit themselves to communication among adherents; rather they should also try to influence the general opinion of all the masses by any means considered useful. Thus, the proponents of propaganda and organization directed at individuals will acknowledge that mass propaganda is useful even for the most individually oriented propaganda and agitation.

But mass propagation has a tremendous significance in itself. Indeed, if a fleeting influence cannot seriously be acknowledged as useful, then no one will begin to deny that an influence and activity constantly repeated on a large scale and in a definite direction could achieve a definite result, modifying general opinion in a definite direction. Thus, it cannot but be acknowledged that such a modification is not only useful but highly desirable, and this for many reasons.

First of all, though it is doubtless true that the social viewpoints are so just and follow so easily from very simple considerations that they are inherent in all people, nevertheless we know that it is still very far from a vague comprehension—and it is of course vague—to a comprehension so clear that the village would agree with those measures proposed by the better, energetic individuals. It is still further to immediate action. Therefore, let us grant that in the village a circle could be formed from the better people, that they could be esteemed by society, and that they could convince the village—considering it in the totality of its present unpreparedness—to take up arms (once it is clear to the village that other villages as well have taken this course.) Nevertheless, it cannot be asserted that the village—considering the unpreparedness of the masses—definitely would take those ultimate measures which would ensure and secure victory for it. But not only that; it cannot even be guaranteed that, taking up arms, it would begin to destroy precisely that (and precisely to that degree) which requires destruction. Therefore, besides the training of separate people, it is extremely necessary not only that *certain* conscious ideas about the totality of general relations and about the possible means of restructuring them should reach the masses, but as many as possible, as clearly as possible.

In saying this, we, of course, do not at all wish to state that it is necessary that the social revolution wait while these clear, conscious ideas penetrate the masses. But we do say that the more of these that penetrate, the better, and that, consequently, it would be extremely strange and inconsistent to let pass any occasion for disseminating these ideas to the masses. It is precisely among the masses that it is necessary to develop the spirit of criticism, the spirit of dissatisfaction, an understanding of the hopelessness of peaceful reforms, the spirit of courage and faith in the possibility of united activity. The more developed this spirit is in every person, the more united with others each separate individual who enters into an organization of the people will feel, the stronger his faith in the possibility of a transformation will be, and the more clearly will his view of the future system take form. Finally, every individual is a product of the views surrounding him, and the more that certain opinions reach the masses, the more there will stand out from the masses new people who devote themselves to the common undertaking, and the more radical will these people be.

This is why we think that any populist activist must utilize every occasion, and even must seek out all occasions, to influence one and all in the understood direction. He must never forget this goal, not in a single conversation, not in a single act, and, in fact, he cannot forget it if he but applies himself with enthusiasm to his work. Suppose a man is oppressed, not educated, capable of considering only the most immediate events and totally incapable of discussing their causes. But even here it will always be possible, by assuming the point of view of this man, to analyze phenomena in a more general way and to lead him to consideration of general causes. With each separate individual it will be necessary to develop social views and the inferences from them forcefully, to another, in the most primitive form. But, at least, all these conversations should be aimed at developing a receptivity for these views, a sensitivity for feeling the yoke, and the realization of the necessity of counterposing peasant unity against it.

How to proceed with each person, what chord to touch, how openly to state your ultimate ideas, all this will depend on the training of that person, of that society with which you are dealing, and the caution which is necessary in this or that instance. One thing, however, should be remembered: a receptivity to these ultimate goals must be prepared in one and all; consequently, it is necessary to act in this direction. Of course, people will be found everywhere in whom personal egotism is stronger than anything else, and to bother with them, even in passing, would mean to spend time and energy fruitlessly. But we are not speaking of them; we are speaking of all the masses who have neither the occasion nor the time to be consciously concerned with their surroundings, but who, precisely, will be required to act at some time. Not to try to influence these masses would be simply a mistake.

In the light of what has been said, we consider that efforts directed at individuals and efforts directed at masses must proceed simultaneously, hand in hand; to try to influence only the general opinion of the masses, without creating an intimate circle of several people which could be made into a general organization, would be just as much of a mistake as to try to form only an intimate circle but to let pass the opportunity to influence the general attitude of the masses. The interests of the whole undertaking demand both the one and the other influences simultaneously.

It is clear that all that has been said applies completely to the urban workers as well. We note, in addition, that our urban workers present several essential differences from those of western Europe, and that these differences explain why activity among urban workers, despite their small number in Russia, has serious significance. The fact is that alongside the workers who are turned into constant city dwellers and have a defined trade, that is, skilled workers, there exists a considerably more extensive class of workers, so-called unskilled workers. This is made up entirely of peasants, mostly youths, who have not mastered a defined labour trade and who go to work at all sorts of textile factories.

They all have a land allotment in their native district and are closely tied to their fellow villagers; none live in the city constantly, but gather from the various corners of Russia for a time, and then, once again, after some two years, and often every year in times of unemployment, they return to their villages to do peasant labour.

This mobile element from the peasant milieu in most cases represents both a highly receptive ground and means for the dissemination of social ideas; they are free of the conservative influence of the family, somewhat more observant of various relations in life and, moreover, they continually return to the village. Furthermore, they all live not in isolation, as the skilled workers do, but in artels, which considerably facilitates an acquaintance with a large circle of people. The culling out from them separate individuals capable of further agitation is facilitated, moreover, by the wide range available for the selection of the best people; and the aid of the educated youth who conduct studies with these workers significantly facilitates the choice, since it provides the possibility of maintaining an acquaintance with very many workers. Since these workers in no way sever their ties with the village and do not in the least alter their previous, peasant form of life, it is easiest of all to train from among them the people who will later serve as the nuclei of peasant circles in the villages.

This is not the place to set forth the practical methods of this propaganda, but we will pause over one circumstance which, in our opinion, many treat too lightly. This is that we consider it necessary and useful to impart to the workers information regarding the field of scientific knowledge. We were often asked before, as a favour, to concern ourselves with the teaching of reading and writing and arithmetic. If this is a natural means to become acquainted with an artel and if it is to be expected that people will be found in this artel who will become rather interested in social propaganda then we, of course, will not refuse such lessons; or, if there are other, more productive studies, then we will try to seek out people who, though not wishing to concern themselves with social propaganda, would, however, concern themselves with [these studies]—knowing the aim with which these lessons are conducted. When we see, on reading some book in the course of these studies and conducting a general discussion about the reading, that separate individuals take the common interest to heart, we will try, by more frequent conversations, to lead these people to the idea that the study of arithmetic or writing does not at all lead to the goal; we will then begin to acquaint them with the totality of the social viewpoint and will try to enter into personal, friendly relations with them. Those who see the study of arithmetic as their exclusive goal, we will, of course, leave in a certain time, as we understand very well that it is impossible to teach arithmetic to all those who want to learn it, and that there are things more important. If we must meet a person who is receptive, energetic and gives promise of becoming a useful agitator, who does not even know how to read, we, of course, will unfailingly consider it a *necessity* to teach him reading and writing, understanding very well that a literate person can more easily conduct agitation than can an illiterate; so that those things about which there was no time to talk, he will discover both from the proper books and from the personal reflections about what was read.

, We also consider it necessary to impart to those better people who will become populist agitators more detailed information about history (that, of course, which serves as the basis of our conclusions) concerning so-called political economy, that is, a criticism of existing relations between labour and capital. We know it takes more than a day or two to transform a peaceful worker, who for a decade has stood behind a machine revealing his energy, honesty and lack of egotism solely in personal or artel relations—into a convinced, active, populist agitator. We know further that the transformation is the more durable and the guarantee of ultimate success is the greater, the larger the accumulation of facts which a man possesses and the more the sphere of phenomena provides him with arguments to strengthen his ideas. For this reason, we must impart to such a person the material he requires and we must attempt to sharpen his capability to use any fact to strengthen his views. Since in a three to four month period there will always be found more than enough time for such conversations, and since an exposition of necessary historical facts or an elucidation of economic relations is often more convenient in continuous form, we consider it positively necessary to impart this information by reading them a course of history and political economy (of one can designate as a course a score or serialized stories in which every fact supports a particular set of views, and every conclusion serves as an object of general discussion on a particular topic.) For this reason, we affirm that it is necessary to train populist agitators. To train them in a period of weeks is impossible if one wishes to leave anything which endures after one departs. During a period which lasts several months, time will always be found to familiarize them in detail with those facts which later will be very useful to them in their agitational activities.

Consequently, it is necessary to conduct these discussions, and it is necessary to be concerned about the more extensive education of these agitators, always strictly avoiding, of course, burdening their minds with any superfluous ballast whatsoever.

It is clear that in any undertaking no specific boundaries can be set. It is only necessary that each activist should clearly understand his goal and not deviate from it because of irrelevant inducements.

From all that has been said, it is already clear that we set aside the main position in our propaganda for personal, *oral* and not *written* propaganda, both in view of the goals and in view of the illiteracy of the Russian people. But by this we by no means deny the necessity of written propaganda, and we consider it necessary for the very same goals.

About the character of written propaganda in the so-called civilized milieu we have already spoken above; the possibilities of our relations to [this milieu] were defined. But far more necessary is the appearance and dissemination among the workers and peasantry of such books as would satisfy the aims set forth above. Books of this type we consider positively necessary.

Those books are necessary which would give those who are unable to raise and formulate certain questions easily the opportunity to broach these questions nevertheless. A book especially written for this purpose provides the opportunity to raise and subject to general discussion such questions. Further, those books are necessary which would give the populist agitator the material and facts with which to convince his interlocutors. Such facts are provided by books about the history of the people, by books which explain the means by which capital has accumulated in private hands, the seizure of land, the seizure by the government of the people's rights, and so forth. Moreover, those books are necessary which arouse the spirit of independence, the consciousness in the people of its strength and of the impotence of the nobility; and those which enforce the feeling of world unity, a consciousness of the common interests and the common enemies of all the separate parts of the Russian land, of all the separate classes of the people; and those which make clear the mutual interests of the tsar, nobility, merchants, extortionists and clergy. In short, fictional stories are needed as occasions for discussion; stories are needed about the strong personalities who emerge from the peasant milieu; historical and realistic stories are also needed which elucidate all the desperation of the contemporary way of life, which arouse a consciousness and spirit of strength, elucidating the necessity, the possibility, and the means of preliminary organization. For this reason, we set as our essential task the preparation and dissemination of such books. We are certain that everyone occupied with propaganda in the peasant and workers' milieu who possesses creativity and talent can always find time to write such books, without interrupting personal propaganda; and we are always ready to apportion a part of our energies to the printing and dissemination of these books.

It is clear that almost all such books be uncensored. We also need, however, short, censored stories touching on various aspects of social life, since it is impossible to appear before an unknown group of peasants or workers for the first time with an uncensored book; for this reason we will always try to get our writers to produce—and we will always try to find in earlier publications—those stories, which, since they are at least not harmful, could provide the basis for necessary discussions. It is clear that all this requires the most insignificant expenditure of time; and means always can be found even from outside sources.

Finally, we believe that it would be highly useful to have a periodical publication, not large, written in language understood by the peasants and workers, which would act in this same direction, while introducing a contemporary element into it.

It remains for us, finally, to examine one type of propaganda which we call *factual.*

Here we place all those activities which promote, in our and others' opinion, the spread of the views stated by us, as well as the organization of a revolutionary party of the people. Here we will examine, consequently, all such institutions which propagandize the social viewpoint, as for example, local disturbances in the factories or the towns with some particular aim, directed against some local abuses; finally, local, popular movements with a broad, socialist goal.

We begin with the *artel.* After everything stated above, it hardly needs mention that as a means of improving the social mode of life we consider the artel to be completely inapplicable and inexpedient. As an educational measure for the preparation of the social revolution we consider it not only not useful, but even completely harmful. Any temporary improvement of the material mode of life of a small group of people in the present, criminal society unavoidably leads to a strengthening of their conservative spirit. All their further activity is directed to preserving, to holding this, *their* privileged position, and for just this reason they must, as if fated, dissipate any impulse and in part even the actual possibility of spreading this improvement to others. Absorbed in matters of their artel, they are occupied with them first and foremost, and become less capable of using their time for active social propaganda. Then, little by little, they lose any desire to concern themselves with this undertaking; the improvement of circumstances leads only to the effort to retain these circumstances, to preserve them from the hazard of any movement, of any political interference, and so forth; it leads to self-aggrandizement and a supercilious attitude to one's other less-fortunate brothers; that which in significant measure is the result of fortunate accidents is ascribed to one's personal energy, and so on. In short, we are convinced that any artel, no matter how successful, is the best means of attracting the most intelligent workers to a semi-bourgeois situation, and, often of taking useful energy from the revolutionary agitation. For this reason, we do not consider the artel a means of social propaganda.

Such are the most natural, general conclusions; but each of them can be supported and developed by scores of proofs taken from experience. All the procedures in western Europe and to some extent in Russia provide rich material for this. Naturally, we attribute just as little educational significance to consumer artels. Those of the German agitators who are delighted by the results of low prices in some communal kitchens and attribute an educational significance to the common management of kitchens could be convinced, precisely in Russia, where each artel of unmarried factory workers represents such a consumer union, how simple and comprehensible this principle is, apart from any propaganda, and how easily it is realized in practice, if it does not encounter some external or historical obstacles. They would similarly be convinced of how slow is the path they have chosen, if they consider the establishment of consumer societies a step towards revolutionary activity. We view mutual-aid funds, mutual assistance, and so on in the same way we view consumer artels. All previous considerations apply unconditionally to them, and all of these could be supported by a still greater quantity of facts, proving both their impotence and their harmful influence. We would even consider personal help by means of collections each time it is necessary (for example, a friend suffering from an accident) is more moral than a fund which becomes some sort of tax for the poor. For this reason, we will never advocate these funds and are always ready to dissuade our friends.

But, nevertheless, we do consider useful any *fund for social propaganda,* for the acquisition of books which provoke criticism of the existing situation and a realization of one's own strengths; for assistance to agitators who give up their jobs in exchange for a life devoted to the aim of propaganda; for the maintenance of apartments, and so on. Of course, we very well understand the insufficiency of such funds (except for the exceptional workers with means) and thus would not begin to exaggerate their significance. Clearly it would be most desirable if these funds were to be established in accordance with the necessities of propaganda and organization. Finally, among a number of similar educational methods, we consider as positively useful the *community of workers built on communistic principles,* that is common ownership of all earnings. But we know very well how great the difficulties are which attend any such institution, due to the impossibility of building a communist spirit in present society, and partly because of local conditions (the sending off of one's earnings to the village, and so on). We believe, for this reason, that one ought to recommend this measure as an excellent educational means for agitators, but that to bring it to fulfilment will be possible only to a limited degree and with special individuals; and [that] only, in large part, when the workers live with those members of the young intelligentsia who have been educated in this spirit. In any case, if persons of such similar inclinations do build such a community, then, in our opinion, they should not be disregarded.

We regard any local disturbances with some particular aim (for example, a demonstration against a foreman or manager at a factory, a demonstration against some restraining measure, a disturbance in a village with the aim of removing the foremen, the clerks, the middlemen, and so on) as a means of educating the masses and as a means for the populist agitators to get to know the people better, to know the outstanding individuals and finally, for these individuals to acquire local influence and, in part, to be educated in the spirit of opposition, of more or less dangerous protest. The significance of particular movements, of course, is impossible to deny, and since they always occur apart from the will of separate individuals, it remains for the agitator merely to utilize them in order to know the people better. It is impossible not to acknowledge that such disturbances, if they do not lead to cruel suppression, always reinforce the spirit of dissatisfaction and irritation in the masses.

Acknowledging this usefulness, however, we clearly must decide whether it is in the interests of organization to provoke and support such disturbances. We believe that a general answer to this question cannot be given. It is only necessary to have in mind, in each particular case, how much each disturbance can promote or hinder the success of organization and propaganda. If it is possible to foretell that such a disturbance will provide the opportunity to know the people better, while not entailing the removal of agitators from the area with which they have already familiarized themselves and where they have already gained a certain confidence—and if along with this it gives the masses an opportunity to feel the strength of comradely protest—then, of course, it is necessary to support and call forth such disturbance; it is possible to foretell that, though gaining its particular goal, the disturbance may entail the removal of the agitators from the area where it would be desirable for them to remain, then it would be appropriate to avoid such a disturbance. It is appropriate for activists, in our opinion, to protect their efforts and not to expose themselves to risks for trifles or for results which will be useful to no one. It is necessary to remember, besides, that all the governments of the West, and ours as well, will not hesitate to adopt the same programme, namely, always trying to provoke these local disturbances in order to seize the better people, tear them from their places, or shoot them and plant terror among the populace. For this reason, such a movement becomes a two-edged sword. On the one hand, the relations between the government and the people are made clear; on the other hand, it draws too heavily on the strengths of the revolutionary party and on the better people of a given district.

There is one more consideration, concerning, however, only people from the so-called civilized milieu. This is that in many disturbances they will by no means suffer all those consequences which such a disturbance inflicts on the peasantry and the urban workers. No matter how morally heavy the punishment is which befalls a person from the intelligentsia in such a case, it is incomparably lighter materially than the punishment which befalls the others (and appropriately so, in the eyes of the people). Though it be in the name of general principles, this circumstance, however, obviously undermines for the future the credibility of agitation in certain localities by a person from the intelligentsia. Finally, any means not leading directly to an end, becomes very quickly itself an end of a new undertaking, and we would consider it necessary in any similar undertaking always to consider prevalent, general opinion concerning a particular question in formulating a decision. Not less essential is that any [misdirected] agitation detracts attention and time from the more essential agitation.

But there can also appear another consideration. Any agitation not reinforced by action soon ceases to sustain the courage of the activists. Activists cannot so calmly bear the injustice surrounding them, and they inevitably strive to enter the battle against this injustice, in whatever form it appears. To try to abstain from protest when it insistently suggests itself means to develop an indifference to surroundings, and even a type of Jesuitism. We think, however, that such an objection would be incorrect. First of all, it would be very desirable if the propaganda and the organization of agitators were looked on precisely as a business, and that a battle with a manager or foreman would not be considered a more serious "enterprise." Any person looking at any fact presented to him just from the point of view of propaganda and organization will always be able to utilize it in order to explain it to those around him as a particular manifestation of the whole, and to transfer to the common enemy the passionate abhorrence aroused by it. Further, any activist and sensitive man is, even without external interference, sufficiently inclined to protest against any particular outrage, and with such people it is sooner necessary to restrain outbursts of passion against a particular event, pointing out the opportunity to use it for organizing the people, than it is to inflame this passion against the actual event. Finally, as concerns that fact which [is true] of any effected protest, no matter how clear its damage and no matter what might be said against it at the time of preliminary discussion—in any risk the agitator must be in the forefront; there is no need to discuss this elementary fact. All that has been said also applies completely to the question of *strikes*. So much has been written and said about them already that we can limit ourselves only to general conclusions.

First of all, it is clear that strikes, just as any palliative measures, cannot essentially improve the position of the workers. That small improvement which a strike sometimes achieves in either a shortening of the workers' hours or in an increase of the workers' pay is always temporary and is very soon wiped out. Further, one can adduce the fact that a strike in western Europe is always the sole means of raising the income somewhat, when, with the increase in the cost of living, this becomes absolutely inadequate for existence. For this reason, in western Europe the strike became a common weapon in the fight between labour and capital, both in the industrial and in the agricultural spheres, and the organization of the strike was for a long time the sole goal which occupied (and till this time occupies) a great many workers' societies and a great many agitators. In Russia, a strike is a manifestation incomparably more rare for a great many reasons, about which this is not the place to speak. Must the strike, consequently, be propagandized here in the same way it has been propagandized for the past twenty to thirty years in western Europe? Can we not achieve with its help the same results as were achieved by western European workers and which indisputably promoted social propaganda in several respects?

It would be extremely improper to compare our position in this respect with that of western Europe. In western Europe strikes are not a phenomenon of recent years, nor even of the last century. In England, that is, precisely in that country where they [strikes] have achieved both the highest wage and the lowest number of working hours, they were already begun and organized in the thirteenth century. Workers' unions were already so widespread and so strong in the last century thanks to the strike that whole decades would be necessary for the development of such unions now [in Russia]. That is why England could outstrip other countries in the rate of raising wages and decreasing working hours, which, however, is noticeable everywhere in the last century, although to a lesser degree than in England. The power of the workers' unions for strikes cannot be acquired quickly—it requires long years of strikes unimpeded by the government and long years of training.

Now new ideals, new goals, new aspirations are appearing among the workers. The problem of the labour question has already become not the partial improvement of daily life, but the question of the transfer of the instruments of labour to the workers themselves. In this form, the problem also has arisen in Russia. Consequently, the question about the organization for strikes also becomes the question of whether or not we must now, when this problem is so widespread, work to create an organization which was established in the West at the time when the problem was raised about the [partial] improvement of daily life, and not about radical change. The answer is inevitable and clear: *no!* Can it really be useful to oppose evil in its particular form when the general cause of evil is already known? Do we really have the right to hide this general cause? Indeed, once the general cause of evil is known, once hope and belief in its eradication have appeared, can we and the workers introduce into the propaganda of the organization for strikes that belief which was introduced into this propaganda by those who saw in the strike the sole possible weapon of the struggle with capital? It is clear, consequently, in Russia, where the workers' movement is beginning at this time, that the strong organization for strikes which exists in many places of western Europe cannot be created. It is clear that if the workers' movement retains its faith in the attainment of the ultimate goal, it will not apply itself to strikes with that energy applied up to recent times in western Europe.

But if the strike cannot be a goal in itself for us, might it nevertheless be a useful means towards the attainment of a given goal? Offering a practical impetus for organization accessible to all, cannot the strike lead those into the organization who would not join without this impetus? Will it not serve as a good opportunity for social propaganda?

But here, in turn, we again encounter the same question: how useful for the attainment of a given goal is it to place some secondary goal in the forefront? Or, in other words, how useful is it to attract to an organization which seeks a social transformation people who still do not agree with the necessity of a transformation? But the answer to the question in such a form cannot be open to doubt. Of course it is not useful because these people will only obstruct the organization in the attainment of its goals; consequently, it is necessary to act on them by other means. In general, we consider it not only careless but quite impractical to recruit people for one goal while presenting them with another. As to the fact that the strike can serve as a good occasion for social propaganda, it is necessary to remark that there is always an opportunity for criticism of the mode of daily life, and the strike is not the most opportune. The strike serves as a good method for arousing the consciousness of one's power only when it ends in victory. Speaking about the form which has attained the greatest development in the West we will refer here to the example of western Europe. All who have dealings with strikes confirm exactly this. But the strike is only crowned with success when the workers have other funds beforehand (disregarding for the time being the interference of the government, and even supposing that it does not exist). We have already stated above why we think that we do not now intend to form another organization for strikes.

As to the consciousness (of solidarity) of unity, of community, which mutual assistance during strikes so promotes, we think that the same consciousness is achieved in the same degree by the constant intercourse of the groups which are indispensable for an organization; and the more lively and intimate the intercourse, the more homogenous their composition. An extensive organization for the sake of strikes does not at all assist this last condition but rather hinders it by introducing the extreme heterogeneity of agitational training into the structure of circles which are necessary for these goals. This is why we think that for us an extensive organization for strikes would not be an expedient means for attaining goals.

There remains, then, the educational element of the strike, which is unquestionable in many respects. Any strike trains the participants for a common management of affairs and for the distribution of responsibilities, distinguishes the people most talented and devoted to a common cause, and finally, forces the others to get to know these people and strengthens their influence. For this reason we assert that it would not be appropriate if forces were available to let one strike pass without the populist activists taking the opportunity of active participation in it. But for the sake of this, to provide strikes purposely, with all their terrible consequences for the workers in the case of failure (deprivations, hunger, the spending of the last meagre savings), we consider positively inadvisable.

Finally, we move to the last category of instances for factual propaganda. This is the local movement with a definite, common socialist goal. Let us suppose that there is a basis for thinking that in some province an insurrection could arise *with a clear goal to expropriate all the lands, factories, houses, and capital in the possession of the mir, and to organize itself in its own way.* But also, it is expected that this movement will not be supported and will be crushed by the troops. Should one assist this movement, should one support morally and physically those who gather to begin this movement, or should one make all efforts in order to refrain from this? It is evident that many considerations arise here. Let us disregard the fact that such disturbances, begun with goals clear to all, can lead also to arousing the neighbouring districts. Even when all the determining circumstances are apparently known, no one can guarantee the outcome of such a movement, especially when everywhere there are some dissatisfied elements. History is full of such surprises, which not one of the most gifted and knowing contemporaries foresaw at all. Therefore, we would never take it upon ourselves to decide this question except as we are acquainted with the local conditions of a given case and according to a discussion of them at a full meeting of the populist activists. But we point out this question now because it determines the party's plan of action. If it were decided that *such* a local movement were desirable, then the choice of the locality would make it possible to direct all the available forces there, instead of scattering them across all of Russia. Therefore, we will state only several considerations which might appropriately motivate one to ask this question, since a knowledge of the local conditions of different parts of Russia will allow us to talk about it.

What the oppressed, local socialist movement consists of is well-known. What bacchanalia are played out by the eternal predators of the people over the corpses of all that is honest, bold, intelligent in a defeated locality—all this is scorched with shameful marks on the bestial faces of these predators. That this devastation overwhelmingly oppresses even the largely indifferent majority is also well-known. But something else is clear as well: those of the survivors in whom the spark of the human spirit is not extinguished by bestial needs will be driven to curse all of life with enmity. It is clear that the eyes of anyone not blind will be opened by this drama when the masks are removed and frenzy drives the impotent and base to wreak their anger on the strong and honest caught in the trap. Let the nobility and the tsar be displayed at least once in all their bestial nakedness, and the rivers of blood spilled in one locality will not flow without consequence. Without the rivers of blood the social upheaval will not be accomplished; subsequent [upheavals] will replace the first ones, if only the first will let loose the flood for the future ones. But, nevertheless, these first rivers, perhaps streams, are already flowing now, and they flow, trickle, uninterrupted through all the recent decades. Perhaps it would be folly on our part even to dream about how to hold them back, and perhaps there is no better outcome for us than to drown ourselves in that first river which bursts the dam.

Our relations to all parties are quite clearly defined in what has been said. We will state them, however, in a few words.

First of all our relations to the International. To unite with the International, not in principle but in fact, we consider impossible to discuss now. As long as we have no strong organization among the peasantry and workers, our relations will only be personal and not businesslike; it is hardly worthwhile to discuss such relations. Consequently, [the question] of whether to join the International or not is still in the future. We can only say that due to the vast difference [between] the way we think (the character of our ideas and aspirations) and the characteristics of the western European workers, due to the difference of language and to our economic isolation, we do not think that in the near future our relations could be in any way intimate and active, except among separate individuals. No doubt every socialist movement in the West will be quickly echoed in our people, any large scale success of Western International organizations will be received with sympathy and interest by us and will encourage us. It is also highly probable that the decisions of the International will be discussed here not only by educated youths, but also by workers' groups. All this however does not yet constitute that intercourse which must exist among the parts of *one* party. And this can hardly be arranged quickly. Therefore, we limit ourselves only by the declaration that in principle (as evident from all that has been said), we fully agree with the branch of federalists in the International and we deny the Statist principles of the other branch.

As to our Russian parties abroad (since we agree in principle with the Russian representatives of the federalist division of the International), we completely remove ourselves from any interference in their dissensions because they have a personal character and because, living here, we cannot have any precise understanding of the character of these dissensions. We must say in regard to their periodical publications that we cannot recognize any of them as the organ of our party.

Deeply respecting some representatives of our Russian emigration and their activity in the International, we nonetheless do not intend to enter into a close organized union with any of them, because we see no possibility whatever to make this union functional. We intend to develop here autonomously, without any guidance from foreign parties, since we believe that the emigration can never be the exact expression of the needs of our people, except in their most general features: a necessary condition for this is a stay among the Russian peasantry and urban workers. Finally, a necessary condition for the full unification of individuals is the opportunity to engage in uninterrupted, intimate relations—which is impossible at the present moment.[3]

NOTES

1. *Obshchina:* the traditional Russian peasant commune. The artel was the traditional artisans' co-operative. Ed.
2. *khozhalyr:* military policeman. Ed.
3. The text breaks off here in the manuscript. Ed.

Anarchist Communism:

Its Basis and Principles

Preface

ON Kropotkin's first visit to England, after his flight from a Russian prison in 1876, he lived somewhat furtively, in fear of the Tsarist agents who were searching Europe for him. Unobtrusively he made his scientific contacts to assure himself a meagre living, but he would find very little in the way of revolutionary activity going on among the English and encountered only a few foreign expatriates whose ideas interested him. He soon set off to Switzerland, where he re-established contact with the expatriate Russians and the anarchists of the Jura towns, and in Geneva established *La Révolte* as a journal of the libertarian section of the dying International.

Kropotkin was brought back to England in July 1881 to attend the anarchist international congress which was held in London, and was attended by such revolutionary luminaries as Errico Malatesta, Louise Michel, back from her exile in New Caledonia, and Kropotkin's old comrade, Nicholas Chaikovski, as well as by the notorious French police spy, Serreaux. After the congress ended, Kropotkin — now a minor celebrity — stayed on for some time in England before he returned to the continent; he had been expelled from Switzerland at the insistence of the Tsarist authorities after the assassination of Alexander II (in which he was in no way involved) and moved to Thonon over the frontier in France, where he started up *Le Révolté* as a successor to the suppressed *La Révolte*.

A native socialist movement was at last emerging in England, and Kropotkin met some of its leading figures, including H.M. Hyndman, leader of the Social Democratic Federation and the dean of English Marxists. Despite their differing views, the two men established an affectionate friendship that lasted the rest of their lives. And Hyndman at this time initiated one of the most important relationships in Kropotkin's later life when he introduced him to the enterprising and radically inclined editor of *The Nineteenth Century,* James Knowles. It was Knowles, more than any other individual, who increased and diversified Kropotkin's audience by introducing him to the middle classes of England and to a series of periodicals and publishing houses that extended far beyond the tiny local core of anarchists. He immediately saw the interest in Kropotkin's experiences as a commissioner investigating prisons in Siberia and later an actual prisoner in the Russian penal system. He commissioned him to write a series of essays on prisons in action and prison reform. The first of these appeared in *The Nineteenth Century* in 1882, but the project was delayed and at the same time enriched by the period of more than three years which, from early 1883, Kropotkin spent in French prisons. After publication of Kropotkin's essays was completed by *The Nineteenth Century*, the collection of them — *In Russian and French Prisons* — appeared as Kropotkin's first book addressed to a general public, and established him in the eyes of that public as a man of letters as well as an agitational writer.

Knowles would play a similar role in connection with some of Kropotkin's later major works. It was he, together with the evolutionist Henry Walter Bates, who encouraged Kropotkin to develop his ideas about mutual aid as a factor in evolution; the essays representing various facets of his thoughts on these subjects appeared in *The Nineteenth Century* before they were actually published in the book, *Mutual Aid*, and the same applied to other books addressing a more general readership than the anarchist converted, such as *Fields, Factories and Workshops* and *Ethics*.

Knowles never declared himself an anarchist, and it is possible that he was not much more than an enterprising editor who saw Kropotkin's ideas as interesting ones that deserved to be placed before a general public. It certainly broke the narrow circle of the English anarchists when the two articles that formed the actual substance of *Anarchist Communism: Its Basis and Principles* were written for *The Nineteenth Century* and published there in 1887. Freedom Press eventually did publish the two essays as a pamphlet in 1891.

Reading *Anarchist Communism...* and the other pamphlets here reproduced, one realizes how unified Kropotkin's work actually was, how much his concepts echo from book to book, so that in the proposals of economic arrangement in *Anarchist Communism* one can pick up the links connecting this relatively simple exposition with the more elaborate arguments of *Mutual Aid* and *Ethics*. The virtue of these pamphlets lies largely in their combination of clarity with conciseness. They are exposition rather than propaganda, and at its best.

G.W.

Anarchist Communism: Its Basis and Principles

I

ANARCHISM, the no-government system of socialism, has a double origin. It is an outgrowth of the two great movements of thought in the economic and the political fields which characterize the nineteenth century, and especially its second part. In common with all socialists, the anarchists hold that the private ownership of land, capital, and machinery has had its time; that it is condemned to disappear; and that all requisites for production must, and will, become the common property of society, and be managed in common by the producers of wealth. And in common with the most advanced representatives of political radicalism, they maintain that the ideal of the political organization of society is a condition of things where the functions of government are reduced to a minimum, and the individual recovers his full liberty of initiative and action for satisfying, by means of free groups and federations—freely constituted—all the infinitely varied needs of the human being.

As regards socialism, most of the anarchists arrive at its ultimate conclusion, that is, at a complete negation of the wage-system and at communism. And with reference to political organization, by giving a further development to the above-mentioned part of the radical programme, they arrive at the conclusion that the ultimate aim of society is the reduction of the functions of government to *nil*—that is, to a society without government, to an-archy. The anarchists maintain, moreover, that such being the ideal of social and political organization, they must not remit it to future centuries, but that only those changes in our social organization which are in accordance with the above double ideal, and constitute an approach to it, will have a chance of life and be beneficial for the commonwealth.

As to the method followed by the anarchist thinker, it entirely differs from that followed by the utopists. The anarchist thinker does not resort to metaphysical conceptions (like "natural rights," the "duties of the State," and so on) to establish what are, in his opinion, the best conditions for realizing the greatest happiness of humanity. He follows, on the contrary, the course traced by the modern philosophy of evolution.

He studies human society as it is now and was in the past; and without either endowing humanity as a whole, or separate individuals, with superior qualities which they do not possess, he merely considers society as an aggregation of organisms trying to find the best ways of combining the wants of the individual with those of co-operation for the welfare of the species. He studies society and tries to discover its *tendencies*, past and present, its growing needs, intellectual and economic, and in his ideal he merely points out in which direction evolution goes. He distinguishes between the real wants and tendencies of human aggregations and the accidents (want of knowledge, migrations, wars, conquests) which have prevented these tendencies from being satisfied. And he concludes that the two most prominent, although often unconsciousness, tendencies throughout our history have been: first, a tendency towards integrating labour for the production of all riches in common, so as finally to render it impossible to discriminate the part of the common production due to the separate individual; and second, a tendency towards the fullest freedom of the individual in the prosecution of all aims, beneficial both for himself and for society at large. The ideal of the anarchist is thus a mere summing-up of what he considers to be the next phase of evolution. It is no longer a matter of faith; it is a matter for scientific discussion.

In fact, one of the leading features of this century is the growth of socialism and the rapid spreading of socialist views among the working classes. How could it be otherwise? We have witnessed an unparalleled sudden increase of our powers of production, resulting in an accumulation of wealth which has outstripped the most sanguine expectations. But owing to our wage system, this increase of wealth— due to the combined efforts of men of science, of managers, and workmen as well—has resulted only in an unprecedented accumulation of wealth in the hands of the owners of capital; while an increase of misery for great numbers, and an insecurity of life for all, have been the lot of the workmen; the unskilled labourers, in continuous search for labour, are falling into an unheard-of destitution. And even the best paid artisans and skilled workmen labour under the permanent menace of being thrown, in their turn, into the same conditions as the unskilled paupers, in consequence of some of the continuous and unavoidable fluctuations of industry and caprices of capital.

The chasm between the modern millionaire who squanders the produce of human labour in a gorgeous and vain luxury, and the pauper reduced to a miserable and insecure existence, is thus growing wider and wider, so as to break the very unity of society—the harmony of its life—and to endanger the progress of its further development.

At the same time, workingmen are less and less inclined to patiently endure this division of society into two classes, as they themselves become more and more conscious of the wealth-producing power of modern industry, of the part played by labour in the production of wealth, and of their own capacities of organization. In proportion as all classes of the community take a more lively part in public affairs, and knowledge spreads among the masses, their longing for equality becomes stronger, and their demands for social reorganization become louder and louder. They can be ignored no more. The worker claims his share in the riches he produces; he claims not only some additional well-being, but also his full rights in the higher enjoyments of science and art. These claims, which formerly were uttered only by the social reformer, begin now to be made by a daily growing minority of those who work in the factory or till the acre. And they so conform to our feelings of justice that they find support in a daily growing minority among the privileged classes themselves. Socialism becomes thus *the* idea of the nineteenth century; and neither coercion nor pseudo-reforms can stop its further growth.

Much hope of improvement was placed, of course, in the extension of political rights to the working classes. But these concessions, unsupported as they were by corresponding changes in economic relations, provided delusions. They did not materially improve the conditions of the great bulk of the workmen. Therefore, the watchword of socialism is: "Economic freedom as the only secure basis for political freedom." And as long as the present wage system, with all its bad consequences, remains unaltered, the socialist watchword will continue to inspire the workmen. Socialism will continue to grow until it has realized its programme.

Side by side with this great movement of thought in economic matters, a like movement has been going on with regard to political rights, political organization, and the functions of government. Government has been submitted to the same criticism as capital. While most of the radicals saw in universal suffrage and republican institutions the last word of political wisdom, a further step was made by the few. The very functions of government and the State, as also their relations to the individual, were submitted to a sharper and deeper criticism. Representative government having been tried by experiment on a wide field, its defects became more and more prominent. It became obvious that these defects are not merely accidental but inherent in the system itself.

Parliament and its executive proved to be unable to attend to all the numberless affairs of the community and to conciliate the varied and often opposite interests of the separate parts of a State. Election proved unable to find out the men who might represent a nation, and manage, otherwise than in a party spirit, the affairs they are compelled to legislate upon. These defects become so striking that the very principles of the representative system were criticized and their justness doubted.

Again, the dangers of a centralized government became still more conspicuous when the socialists came to the front and asked for a further increase of the powers of government by entrusting it with the management of the immense field covered now by the economic relations between individuals. The question was asked whether a government entrusted with the management of industry and trade would not become a permanent danger for liberty and peace, and whether it even would be able to be a good manager?

The socialists of the earlier part of this century did not fully realize the immense difficulties of the problem. Convinced as they were of the necessity of economic reforms, most of them took no notice of the need of freedom for the individual. And we have had social reformers ready to submit society to any kind of theocracy, or dictatorship in order to obtain reforms in a socialist sense. Therefore, we have seen in England and also on the Continent the division of men of advanced opinions into political radicals and socialists—the former looking with distrust on the latter, as they saw in them a danger for the political liberties which have been won by the civilized nations after a long series of struggles. And even now, when the socialists all over Europe have become political parties, and profess the democratic faith, there remains among most impartial men a well-founded fear of the *Volksstaat* or "popular State" being as great a danger to liberty as any form of autocracy if its government be entrusted with the management of all the social organization including the production and distribution of wealth.

Recent evolution, however, has prepared the way for showing the necessity and possibility of a higher form of social organization which may guarantee economic freedom without reducing the individual to the role of a slave to the State. The origins of government have been carefully studied, and all metaphysical conceptions as to its divine or "social contract" derivation having been laid aside, it appears that it is among us of a relatively modern origin, and that its powers have grown precisely in proportion as the division of society into the privileged and unprivileged classes was growing in the course of ages.

Representative government has also been reduced to its real value—
that of an instrument which has rendered services in the struggle
against autocracy, but not an ideal of free political organization. As to
the system of philosophy which saw in the State a leader of progress, it
was more and more shaken as it became evident that progress is the
most effective when it is not checked by State interference. It has thus
become obvious that a further advance in social life does not lie in the
direction of a further concentration of power and regulative functions
in the hands of a governing body, but in the direction of decentralization, both territorial and functional—in a subdivision of public functions with respect both to their sphere of action and to the initiative of
free constituted groups of all functions which are now considered as
the functions of government.

This current of thought has found its expression not merely in
literature, but also to a limited extent in life. The uprise of the Paris
Commune, followed by that of the Commune of Cartagena—a movement of which the historical bearing seems to have been quite over-
looked—opened a new page of history. If we analyze not only this
movement in itself, but also the impression it left in the minds and the
tendencies manifested during the communal revolution, we must
recognize in it an indication showing that in the future human agglomerations which are more advanced in their social development
will try to start an independent life; and that they will endeavour to
convert the more backward parts of a nation by example, instead of imposing their opinions by law and force, or submitting themselves to the
majority-rule, which always is a mediocrity-rule. At the same time, the
failure of representative government within the Commune itself
proved that self-government and self-administration must be carried
further than in a merely territorial sense. To be effective they must also
be carried into the various functions of life within the free community.
A merely territorial limitation of the sphere of action of government
will not do—representative government being as deficient in a city as it
is in a nation. Life gave thus a further point in favour of the no-government theory, and a new impulse to anarchist thought.

Anarchists recognize the justice of both the just-mentioned tendencies towards economic and political freedom, and see in them two
different manifestations of the very same need of equality which constitutes the very essence of all struggles mentioned by history. Therefore, in common with all socialists, the anarchist says to the political
reformer: "No substantial reform in the sense of political equality and
no limitation of the powers of government can be made as long as

society is divided into two hostile camps, and the labourer remains, economically speaking, a slave to his employer." But to the State socialist we say also: "You cannot modify the existing conditions of property without deeply modifying at the same time the political organization. You must limit the powers of government and renounce parliamentary rule. To each new economic phase of life corresponds to a new political phase. Absolute monarchy corresponded to the system of serfdom. Representative government corresponds to capital-rule. Both, however, are class-rule. But in a society where the distinction between capitalist and labourer has disappeared, there is no need of such a government; it would be an anachronism, a nuisance. Free workers would require a free organization, and this cannot have any other basis than free agreement and free co-operation, without sacrificing the autonomy of the individual to the all-pervading interference of the State. The no-capitalist system implies the no-government system."

Meaning thus the emancipation of man from the oppressive powers of capitalism and government as well, the system of anarchism becomes a synthesis of the two powerful currents of thought which characterize our century.

In arriving at these conclusions anarchism proves to be in accordance with the conclusions arrived at by the philosophy of evolution. By bringing to light the plasticity of organization, the philosophy of evolution has shown the admirable adaptability of organisms to their conditions of life, and the ensuing development of such faculties as render more complete both the adaptations of the aggregates to their surroundings and those of each of the constituent parts of the aggregate to the needs of free co-operation. It has familiarized us with the circumstance that throughout organic nature the capacities for life in common grow in proportion as the integration of organisms into compound aggregates becomes more and more complete; and it has enforced thus the opinion already expressed by social moralists as to the perfectibility of human nature. It has shown us that, in the long run of the struggle for existence, "the fittest" will prove to be those who combine intellectual knowledge with the knowledge necessary for the production of wealth, and not those who are now the richest because they, or their ancestors, have been momentarily the strongest.

By showing that the "struggle for existence" must be conceived not merely in its restricted sense of a struggle between individuals for the means of subsistence but in its wider sense of adaptation of all individuals of the species to the best conditions for the survival of the species, as well as for the greatest possible sum of life and happiness for each and all, it has permitted us to deduce the laws of moral science from the social needs and habits of mankind. It has shown us the infinitesimal part played by positive law in moral evolution, and the immense part played by the natural growth of altruistic feelings, which develop as soon as the conditions of life favour their growth. It has thus enforced the opinion of social reformers as to the necessity of modifying the conditions of life for improving man, instead of trying to improve human nature by moral teachings while life works in an opposite direction. Finally, by studying human society from the biological point of view, it has come to the conclusions arrived at by anarchists from the study of history and present tendencies as to further progress being in the line of socialization of wealth and integrated labour combined with the fullest possible freedom of the individual.

It has happened in the long run of ages that everything which permits men to increase their production, or even to continue it, has been appropriated by the few. The land, which derives its value precisely from its being necessary for an ever-increasing population, belongs to the few, who may prevent the community from cultivating it. The coal-pits, which represent the labour of generations, and which also derive their value from the wants of the manufacturers and railroads, from the immense trade carried on and the density of population, belong again to the few, who have even the right of stopping the extraction of coal if they choose to give another use to their capital. The lace-weaving machine, which represents, in its present state of perfection, the work of three generations of Lancashire weavers, belongs also to the few; and if the grandsons of the very same weaver who invented the first lace-weaving machine claim their right to bring one of these machines into motion, they will be told "Hands off! This machine does not belong to you!" The railroads, which mostly would be useless heaps of iron if not for the present dense population, its industry, trade, and traffic, belong again to the few—to a few shareholders, who may not even know where the railway is situated which brings them a yearly income larger than that of a medieval king. And if the children of those people who died by thousands in digging the tunnels should gather and go— a ragged and starving crowd—to ask bread or work from the shareholders, they would be met with bayonets and bullets.

Who is the sophist who will dare to say that such an organization is just? But what is unjust cannot be beneficial to mankind; and *it is not*. In consequence of this monstrous organization, the son of a workman, when he is able to work, finds no acre to till, no machine to set in motion, unless he agrees to sell his labour for a sum inferior to its real value. His father and grandfather have contributed to drain the field, or erect the factory, to the full extent of their capacities—and nobody can do more than that—but he comes into the world more destitute than a savage. If he resorts to agriculture, he will be permitted to cultivate a plot of land, but on the condition that he gives up part of his product to the landlord. If he resorts to industry, he will be permitted to work, but on the condition that out of the thirty shillings he has produced, ten shillings or more will be pocketed by the owner of the machine. We cry out against the feudal barons who did not permit anyone to settle on the land otherwise than on payment of one quarter of the crops to the lord of the manor; but we continue to do as they did—we extend their system. The forms have changed, but the essence has remained the same. And the workman is compelled to accept the feudal conditions which we call "free contract," because nowhere will he find better conditions. Everything has been appropriated by somebody; he *must* accept the bargain, or starve.

Owing to this circumstance our production takes a wrong turn. It takes no care of the needs of the community; its only aim is to increase the profits of the capitalist. And we have, therefore, the continuous fluctuations of industry, the crisis coming periodically nearly every ten years, and throwing out of employment several hundred thousand men who are brought to complete misery, whose children grow up in the gutter, ready to become inmates of the prison and workhouse. The workmen, being unable to purchase with their wages the riches they are producing, industry must search for markets elsewhere, amidst the middle classes of other nations. It must find markets, in the East, in Africa, anywhere; it must increase, by trade, the number of its serfs in Egypt, in India, on the Congo. But everywhere it finds competitors in other nations which rapidly enter into the same line of industrial development. And wars, continuous wars, must be fought for the supremacy in the world-market—wars for the possession of the East, wars for getting possession of the seas, wars for the right of imposing heavy duties on foreign merchandise. The thunder of European guns never ceases; whole generations are slaughtered from time to time; and we spend in armaments the third of the revenue of our States—a revenue raised, the poor know with what difficulties.

And finally, the injustice of our partition of wealth exercises the most deplorable effect on our morality. Our principles of morality say: "Love your neighbour as yourself"; but let a child follow this principle and take off his coat to give it to the shivering pauper, and his mother will tell him that he must never understand moral principles in their direct sense. If he lives according to them, he will go barefoot, without alleviating the misery around him! Morality is good on the lips, not in deeds. Our preachers say, "Who works, prays," and everyone endeavours to make others work for him. They say, "Never lie!" and politics are a big lie. And we accustom ourselves and our children to live under this double-faced morality, which is hypocrisy, and to conciliate our double-facedness by sophistry. Hypocrisy and sophistry become the very basis of our life. But society cannot live under such a morality. It cannot last so: it must, it will, be changed.

The question is thus no more a mere question of bread. It covers the whole field of human activity. But it has at its bottom a question of social economy, and we conclude: The means of production and of satisfaction of all needs of society, having been created by the common efforts of all, must be at the disposal of all. The private appropriation of requisites for production is neither just nor beneficial. All must be placed on the same footing as producers and consumers of wealth. That will be the only way for society to step out of the bad conditions which have been created by centuries of wars and oppression. That will be the only guarantee for further progress in a direction of equality and freedom, which have always been the real, although unspoken goal of humanity.

II

The views taken in the above as to the combination of efforts being the chief source of our wealth explain why most anarchists see in communism the only equitable solution as to the adequate remuneration of individual efforts. There was a time when a family engaged in agriculture supplemented by a few domestic trades could consider the corn they raised and the plain woollen cloth they wove as productions of their own and nobody else's labour. Even then such a view was not quite correct: there were forests cleared and roads built by common efforts; and even then the family had continually to apply for communal help, as is still the case in so many village communities. But now, in the extremely interwoven state of industry of which each branch supports all others, such an individualistic view can be held no more. If the iron trade and the cotton industry of this country have reached so high a degree of development, they have done so owing to the parallel growth of thousands of other industries, great and small; to the extension of the railway system; to an increase of knowledge among both skilled engineers and the mass of the workmen; to a certain training in organization slowly developed among producers; and, above all, to the world-trade which has itself grown up, thanks to works executed thousands of miles away. The Italians who died from cholera in digging the Suez Canal or from "tunnel-disease" in the St. Gothard Tunnel have contributed as much towards the enrichment of this country as the British girl who is prematurely growing old in serving a machine at Manchester; and this girl as much as the engineer who made a labour-saving improvement in our machinery. How can we pretend to estimate the exact part of each of them in the riches accumulated around us?

We may admire the inventive genius or the organizing capacities of an iron lord; but we must recognize that all his genius and energy would not realize the one-tenth of what they realize here if they were spent in dealing with Mongolian shepherds or Siberian peasants instead of British workmen, British engineers, and trustworthy managers. An English millionaire who succeeded in giving a powerful impulse to a branch of home industry was asked the other day what were, in his opinion, the real causes of his success? His answer was: "I always sought out the right man for a given branch of the concern, and I left him full independence—maintaining, of course, for myself the general supervision." "Did you never fail to find such men?" was the next question. "Never." "But in the new branches which you introduced you wanted a number of new inventions." "No doubt; we spent thousands in buying patents." This little colloquy sums up, in my opinion, the real case of those industrial undertakings which are quoted by the advocates of "an adequate remuneration of individual efforts" in the shape of millions bestowed on the managers of prosperous industries. It shows in how far the efforts are really "individual." Leaving aside the thousand conditions which sometimes permit a man to show, and sometimes prevent him from showing, his capacities to their full extent, it might be asked in how far the same capacities could bring out the same results, if the very same employer could find no trustworthy managers and no skilled workmen, and if hundreds of inventions were not stimulated by the mechanical turn of mind of so many inhabitants of this country.

The anarchists cannot consider, like the collectivists, that a remuneration which would be proportionate to the hours of labour spent by each person in the production of riches may be an ideal, or even an approach to an ideal, society. Without entering here into a discussion as to how far the exchange value of each merchandise is really measured now by the amount of labour necessary for its production—a separate study must be devoted to the subject—we must say that the collectivist ideal seems to us merely unrealizable in a society which has been brought to consider the necessaries for production as a common property. Such a society would be compelled to abandon the wage-system altogether. It appears impossible that the mitigated individualism of the collectivist school could co-exist with the partial communism implied by holding land and machinery in common—unless imposed by a powerful government, much more powerful than all those of our own times. The present wage-system has grown up from the appropriation of the necessaries for production by the few; it was a necessary condition for the growth of the present capitalist production; and it cannot outlive it, even if an attempt be made to pay the worker the full value of his produce, and hours-of-labour-checks be substituted for money. Common possession of the necessities for production implies the common enjoyment of the fruits of the common production; and we consider that an equitable organization of society can only arise when every wage-system is abandoned, and when everybody, contributing for the common well-being to the full extent of his capacities, shall enjoy also from the common stock of society to the fullest possible extent of his needs.

We maintain, moreover, not only that communism is a desirable state of society, but that the growing tendency of modern society is precisely towards communism—free communism—notwithstanding the seemingly contradictory growth of individualism. In the growth of individualism (especially during the last three centuries) we see merely the endeavours of the individual towards emancipating himself from the steadily growing powers of capital and the State. But side by side with this growth we see also, throughout history up to our own times, the latent struggle of the producers of wealth to maintain the partial communism of old, as well as to reintroduce communist principles in a new shape, as soon as favourable conditions permit it. As soon as the communes of the tenth, eleventh, and twelfth centuries were enabled to start their own independent life, they gave a wide extension to work in common, to trade in common, and to a partial consumption in common. All this has disappeared. But the rural commune fights a hard struggle to maintain its old features, and it succeeds in maintaining them in many places of eastern Europe, Switzerland, and even France and Germany; while new organizations, based on the same principles, never fail to grow up wherever it is possible.

Notwithstanding the egotistic turn given to the public mind by the merchant-production of our century, the communist tendency is continually reasserting itself and trying to make its way into public life. The penny bridge disappears before the public bridge; and the turnpike road before the free road. The same spirit pervades thousands of other institutions. Museums, free libraries, and free public schools; parks and pleasure grounds; paved and lighted streets, free for everybody's use; water supplied to private dwellings, with a growing tendency towards disregarding the exact amount of it used by the individual; tramways and railways which have already begun to introduce the season ticket or the uniform tax, and will surely go much further in this line when they are no longer private property: all these are tokens showing in what direction further progress is to be expected.

It is in the direction of putting the wants of the individual *above* the valuation of the services he has rendered, or might render, to society; in considering society as a whole, so intimately connected together that a service rendered to any individual is a service rendered to the whole society. The librarian of the British Museum does not ask the reader what have been his previous services to society, he simply gives him the books he requires; and for a uniform fee, a scientific society leaves its gardens and museums at the free disposal of each member. The crew of a lifeboat do not ask whether the men of a distressed ship are entitled to be rescued at a risk of life; and the Prisoners' Aid Society does not inquire what a released prisoner is worth. Here are men in need of a service; they are *fellow* men, and no further rights are required.

And if this very city, so egotistic today, be visited by a public calamity—let it be besieged, for example, like Paris in 1871, and experience during the seige a want of food—this very same city would be unanimous in proclaiming that the first needs to be satisfied are those of the children and old, no matter what services they may render or have rendered to society. And it would take care of the active defenders of the city, whatever the degrees of gallantry displayed by each of them. But, this tendency already existing, nobody will deny, I suppose, that, in proportion as humanity is relieved from its hard struggle for life, the same tendency will grow stronger. If our productive powers were fully applied to increasing the stock of the staple necessities for life; if a modification of the present conditions of property increased the number of producers by all those who are not producers of wealth now; and if manual labour reconquered its place of honour in society, the communist tendencies already existing would immediately enlarge their sphere of application.

Taking all this into account, and still more the practical aspects of the question as to how private property *might* become common property, most of the anarchists maintain that the very next step to be made by society, as soon as the present regime of property undergoes a modification, will be in a communist sense. We are communists. But our communism is not that of the authoritarian school: it is anarchist communism, communism without government, free communism. It is a synthesis of the two chief aims pursued by humanity since the dawn of its history—economic freedom and political freedom.

I have already said that anarchism means no-government. We know well that the word "anarchy" is also used in current phraseology as synonymous with disorder. But that meaning of "anarchy," being a derived one, implies at least two suppositions. It implies, first, that wherever there is no government there is disorder; and it implies, moreover, that order, due to a strong government and a strong police, is always beneficial. Both implications, however, are anything but proved. There is plenty of order—we should say, of harmony—in many branches of human activity where the government, happily, does not interfere. As to the beneficial effects of order, the kind of order that reigned at Naples under the Bourbons surely was not preferable to some disorder started by Garibaldi; while the Protestants of this country will probably say that the good deal of disorder made by Luther was preferable, at any rate, to the order which reigned under the Pope. While all agree that harmony is always desirable, there is no such unanimity about order, and still less about the "order" which is supposed to reign in our modern societies. So that we have no objection whatever to the use of the word "anarchy" as a negation of what has been often described as order.

By taking for our watchword anarchy in its sense of no-government, we intend to express a pronounced tendency of human society. In history, we see that precisely those epochs when small parts of humanity broke down the power of their rulers and reassumed their freedom were epochs of the greatest progress, economic and intellectual. Be it the growth of the free cities, whose unrivalled monuments—free work of free associations of workers—still testify to the revival of mind and the well-being of the citizen; be it the great movement which gave birth to the Reformation—those epochs when the individual recovered some part of his freedom witnessed the greatest progress. And if we carefully watch the present development of civilized nations, we cannot fail to discover in it a marked and ever-growing movement towards limiting more and more the sphere of action of government, so as to leave more and more liberty to the initiative of the individual. After having tried all kinds of government, and endeavoured to solve the insoluble problem of having a government "which might compel the individual to obedience, without escaping itself from obedience to collectivity," humanity is trying now to free itself from the bonds of any government whatever, and to respond to its needs of organization by the free understanding between individuals pursuing the same common aims.

Home Rule, even for the smallest territorial unit or group, becomes a growing need. Free agreement is becoming a substitute for law. And free co-operation a substitute for governmental guardianship. One after the other, those activities which were considered as the functions of government during the last two centuries are disputed; society moves better the less it is governed. and the more we study the advance made in this direction, as well as the inadequacy of governments to fulfil the expectations placed in them, the more we are bound to conclude that humanity, by steadily limiting the functions of government, is marching towards reducing them finally to *nil*. We already foresee a state of society where the liberty of the individual will be limited by no laws, no bonds—by nothing else but his own social habits and the necessity, which everyone feels, of finding co-operation, support and sympathy among his neighbours.

Of course, the no-government ethics will meet with at least as many objections as the no-capital economics. Our minds have been so nurtured in prejudices as to the providential functions of government that anarchist ideas *must* be received with distrust. Our whole education, from childhood to the grave, nurtures the belief in the necessity of a government and its beneficial effects. Systems of philosophy have been elaborated to support this view; history has been written from this standpoint; theories of law have been circulated and taught for the same purpose. All politics are based on the same principle, each politician saying to people he wants to support him: "Give me the governmental power; I will, I can relieve you from the hardships of your present life." All our education is permeated with the same teachings. We may open any book of sociology, history, law, or ethics: everywhere we find government, its organization, its deeds, playing so prominent a part that we grow accustomed to suppose that the State and the political men are everything; that there is nothing behind the big Statesmen. The same teachings are daily repeated in the Press. Whole columns are filled up with minutest records of parliamentary debates, of movements of political persons. And while reading these columns, we too often forget that besides those few men whose importance has been so swollen up as to overshadow humanity, there is an immense body of men—mankind, in fact—growing and dying, living in happiness or sorrow, labouring and consuming, thinking and creating.

And yet, if we revert from the printed matter to our real life, and cast a broad glance on society as it is, we are struck with the infinitesimal part played by government in our life. Millions of human beings live and die without having had anything to do with government. Ever day millions of transactions are made without the slightest interference of government; and those who enter into agreements have not the slightest intention of breaking bargains. Nay, those agreements which are not protected by government (those of the exchange, or card debts) are perhaps better kept than any others. The simple habit of keeping one's word, the desire of not losing confidence, are quite sufficient in an overwhelming majority of cases to enforce the keeping of agreements. Of course, it may be said that there is still the government which might enforce them if necessary. But without speaking of the numberless cases which could not even be brought before a court, everyone who has the slightest acquaintance with trade will undoubtedly confirm the assertion that, if there were not so strong a feeling of honour in keeping agreements, trade itself would become utterly impossible. Even those merchants and manufacturers who feel not the slightest remorse when poisoning their customers with all kinds of abominable drugs, duly labelled, even they also keep their commercial agreements. But if such a relative morality as commercial honesty exists now under the present conditions, when enrichment is the chief motive, the same feeling will further develop very quickly as soon as robbing someone of the fruits of his labour is no longer the economic basis of our life.

Another striking feature of our century tells in favour of the same no-government tendency. It is the steady enlargement of the field covered by private initiative, and the recent growth of large organizations resulting merely and simply from free agreement. The railway net of Europe—a confederation of so many scores of separate societies— and the direct transport of passengers and merchandise over so many lines which were built independently and federated together, without even so much as a Central Board of European Railways, is a most striking instance of what is already done by mere agreement. If fifty years ago somebody had predicted that railways built by so many separate companies finally would constitute so perfect a net as they do today, he surely would have been treated as a fool. It would have been urged that so many companies, prosecuting their own interests, would never agree without an International Board of Railways, supported by an International Convention of the European States, and endowed with governmental powers. But no such board was resorted to, and the agreement came nevertheless. The Dutch associations of ship and boat owners are now extending their organizations over the rivers of Germany and even to the shipping trade of the Baltic. The numberless amalgamated manufacturers' associations, and the *syndicates* of France, are so many instances in point. If it be argued that many of these organizations are organizations for exploitation, that proves nothing, because, if men pursuing their own egotistic, often very narrow, interests can agree together, better inspired men, compelled to be more closely connected with other groups, will necessarily agree still more easily and still better.

But there also is no lack of free organizations for nobler pursuits. One of the noblest achievements of our century is undoubtedly the Lifeboat Association. Since its first humble start, it has saved no less than thirty-two thousand human lives. It makes appeal to the noblest instincts of man; its activity is entirely dependent upon devotion to the common cause, while its internal organization is entirely based upon the independence of the local committees. The Hospitals Association and hundreds of like organizations, operating on a large scale and covering each a wide field, may also be mentioned under this head. But, while we know everything about governments and their deeds, what do we know about the results achieved by free co-operation? Thousands of volumes have been written to record the acts of governments; the most trifling amelioration due to law has been recorded; its good effects have been exaggerated, its bad effects passed by in silence. But where is the book recording what has been achieved by free co-operation of well-inspired men? At the same time, hundreds of societies are constituted every day for the satisfaction of some of the infinitely varied needs of civilized man. We have societies for all possible kinds of studies—some of them embracing the whole field of natural science, others limited to a small special branch, societies for gymnastics, for shorthand-writing, for the study of a separate author, for games and all kinds of sports, for forwarding the science of maintaining life, and for favouring the art of destroying it; philosophical and industrial, artistic and anti-artistic; for serious work and for mere amusement—in short, there is not a single direction in which men exercise their faculties without combining together for the accomplishment of some common aim. Every day, new societies are formed, while every year the old ones aggregate together into larger units, federate across the national frontiers, and co-operate in some common work.

The most striking feature of these numberless free growths is that they continually encroach on what was formerly the domain of the State or the Municipality. A householder in a Swiss village on the banks of Lake Leman belongs now to at least a dozen different societies which supply him with what is considered elsewhere as a function of the municipal government. Free federation of independent communes for temporary or permanent purposes lies at the very bottom of Swiss life, and to these federations many a part of Switzerland is indebted for its roads and fountains, its rich vineyards, well-kept forests, and meadows which the foreigner admires. And besides these small societies, substituting themselves for the State within some limited sphere, do we not see other societies doing the same on a much wider scale?

One of the most remarkable societies which has recently arisen is undoubtedly the Red Cross Society. To slaughter men on the battlefields, that remains the duty of the State; but these very States recognize their inability to take care of their own wounded: they abandon the task, to a great extent, to private initiative. What a deluge of mockeries would not have been cast over the poor "Utopist" who should have dared to say twenty-five years ago that the care of the wounded might be left to private societies? "Nobody would go into the dangerous places! Hospitals would all gather where there was no need of them! National rivalries would result in the poor soldiers dying without any help, and so on,"—such would have been the outcry. The war of 1871 has shown how perspicacious those prophets are who never believe in human intelligence, devotion, and good sense.

These facts—so numerous and so customary that we pass by without even noticing them—are in our opinion one of the most prominent features of the second half of the nineteenth century. The just-mentioned organisms grew up so naturally, they so rapidly extended and so easily aggregated together, they are such unavoidable outgrowths of the multiplication of needs of the civilized man, and they so well replace State-interference, that we must recognize in them a growing factor of our life. Modern progress is really towards the free aggregation of free individuals so as to supplant government in all those functions which formerly were entrusted to it, and which it mostly performed so badly.

As to parliamentary rule and representative government altogether, they are rapidly falling into decay. The few philosophers who already have shown their defects have only timidly summed up the growing public discontent. It is becoming evident that it is merely stupid to elect a few men and to entrust them with the task of making laws on all possible subjects, of which subjects most of them are utterly ignorant. It is becoming understood that majority rule is as defective as any other kind of rule; and humanity searches and finds new channels for resolving the pending questions. The Postal Union did not elect an international postal parliament in order to make laws for all postal organizations adherent to the Union. The railways of Europe did not elect an international railway parliament in order to regulate the running of the trains and the partition of the income of international traffic. And the Meteorological and Geological Societies of Europe did not elect either meteorological or geological parliaments to plan polar stations, or to establish a uniform subdivision of geological formations and a uniform colouration of geological maps. They proceeded by means of agreement. To agree together they resorted to congresses; but, while sending delegates to their congresses they did not say to them, "Vote about everything you like—we shall obey." They put forward questions and discussed them first themselves; then they sent delegates returned from the congress with no *laws* in their pockets, but with *proposals of agreements*. Such is the way assumed now (the very old way too) for dealing with questions of public interest—not the way of lawmaking by means of a representative government.

Representative government has accomplished its historical mission; it has given a mortal blow to court-rule; and by its debates it has awakened public interest in public questions. But to see in it the government of the future socialist society is to commit a gross error. Each economic phase of life implies its own political phase; and it is impossible to touch the very basis of the present economic life—private property—without a corresponding change in the very basis of the political organization. Life already shows in which direction the change will be made. Not in increasing the powers of the State, but in resorting to free organization and free federation in all those branches which are now considered as attributes of the State.

The objections to the above may be easily foreseen. It will be said of course: "But what is to be done with those who do not keep their agreements? What with those who are not inclined to work? What with those who would prefer breaking the written laws of society, or—on the anarchist hypothesis—its unwritten customs? Anarchism may be good for a higher humanity—not for the men of our own times."

First of all, there are two kinds of agreements: there is the free one which is entered upon by free consent, as a free choice between different courses equally open to each of the agreeing parties. And there is the enforced agreement, imposed by one party upon the other, and accepted by the latter from sheer necessity; in fact, it is no agreement at all; it is a mere submission to necessity. Unhappily, the great bulk of what are now described as agreements belong to the latter category. When a workman sells his labour to an employer and knows perfectly well that some part of the value of his produce will be unjustly taken by the employer; when he sells it without even the slightest guarantee of being employed so much as six consecutive months, it is a sad mockery to call that a free contract. Modern economists may call it free, but the father of political economy—Adam Smith—was never guilty of such a misrepresentation. As long as three-quarters of humanity are compelled to enter into agreements of that description, force is of course necessary, both to enforce the supposed agreements and to maintain such a state of things. Force—and a great deal of force—is necessary to prevent the labourers from taking possession of what they consider unjustly appropriated by the few; and force is necessary to continually bring new "uncivilized nations" under the same conditions.

But we do not see the necessity of force for enforcing agreements freely entered upon. We never heard of a penalty imposed on a man who belonged to the crew of a lifeboat and at a given moment preferred to abandon the association. All that his comrades would do with him, if he were guilty of a gross neglect, would probably be to refuse to have anything further to do with him. Nor did we hear of fines imposed on a contributor to the dictionary for a delay in his work, or of *gendarmes* driving the volunteers of Garibaldi to the battlefield. Free agreements need not be enforced.

As to the so-often repeated objection that no one would labour if he were not compelled to do so by sheer necessity, we heard enough of it before the emancipation of slaves in America, as well as before the emancipation of serfs in Russia. And we have had the opportunity of appreciating it at its just value. So we shall not try to convince those who can be convinced only by accomplished facts. As to those who reason, they ought to know that, if it really was so with some parts of humanity at its lowest stages, or if it is so with some small communities, or separate individuals, brought to sheer despair by ill success in their struggle against unfavourable conditions, it is not so with the bulk of the civilized nations. With us, work is a habit, and idleness an artificial growth. Of course, when to be a manual worker means to be compelled to work all one's life long for ten hours a day, and often more, at producing some part of something—a pin's head, for instance; when it means to be paid wages on which a family can live only on the condition of the strictest limitation of all its needs; when it means to be always under the menace of being thrown tomorrow out of employment—and we know how frequent are the industrial crises, and what misery they imply; when it means, in a very great number of cases, premature death in a paupers' infirmary, if not in the workhouse; when to be a manual worker signifies to wear a life-long stamp of inferiority in the eyes of those very people who live on the work of these "hands;" when it always means the renunciation of all those higher enjoyments that science and art give to man—oh, then there is no wonder that everybody—the manual workers as well—has but one dream: that of rising to a condition where others would work for him.

Overwork is repulsive to human nature—not work. Overwork for supplying the few with luxury—not work for the well-being of all. Work is a physiological necessity, a necessity of spending accumulated bodily energy, a necessity which is health and life itself. If so many branches of useful work are so reluctantly done now, it is merely because they mean overwork, or they are improperly organized. But we know—old Franklin knew it—that four hours of useful work every day would be more than sufficient for supplying everybody with the comfort of a moderately well-to-do middle-class house, if we all gave ourselves to productive work, and if we did not waste our productive powers as we do waste them now.

As to the childish question, repeated for fifty years: "Who would do the disagreeable work?" frankly, I regret that none of our *savants* has ever been brought to do it, be it for only one day in his life. If there is still work which is really disagreeable in itself, it is only because our scientific men have never cared to consider the means of rendering it less so. They have always known that there were plenty of starving men who would do it for a few pence a day.

As to the third—the chief—objection, which maintains the necessity of a government for punishing those who break the law of society, there is so much to say about it that it hardly can be touched incidentally. The more we study the question, the more we are brought to the conclusion that society itself is responsible for the anti-social deeds perpetrated in its midst, and that no punishment, no prisons, and no hangmen can diminish the numbers of such deeds; nothing short of a reorganization of society itself.

Three quarters of all the acts which are brought before our courts every year have their origin, either directly or indirectly, in the present disorganized state of society with regard to the production and distribution of wealth—not in perversity of human nature. As to the relatively few anti-social deeds which result from anti-social inclinations of separate individuals, it is not by prisons, nor even by resorting to the hangmen, that we can diminish their numbers. By our prisons, we merely multiply them and render them worse. By our detectives, our "price of blood," our executions, and our jails, we spread in society such a terrible flow of basest passions and habits, that he who should realize the effects of these institutions to their full extent would be frightened by what society is doing under the pretext of maintaining morality. *We must* search for other remedies, and the remedies have been indicated long since.

Of course now, when a mother in search of food and shelter for her children must pass by shops filled with the most refined delicacies of refined gluttony; when gorgeous and insolent luxury is displayed side by side with the most execrable misery; when the dog and the horse of a rich man are far better cared for than millions of children whose mothers can earn a pitiful salary in the pit or the manufactory; when each "modest" evening dress of a lady represents eight months, or one year of human labour; when enrichment at somebody else's expense is the avowed aim of the "upper classes," and no distinct boundary can be traced between honest and dishonest means of making money—then force is the only means of maintaining such a state of things. Then an army of policemen, judges, and hangmen becomes a necessary institution.

But if all our children—all children are *our* children—received a sound instruction and education—and we have the means of giving it; if every family lived in a decent home—and they *could* at the present high pitch of our production; if every boy and girl were taught a handicraft at the same time as he or she receives scientific instruction, and *not* to be a manual producer of wealth were considered as a token of inferiority; if men lived in closer contact with one another, and had continually to come into contact on those public affairs which now are vested in the few; and if, in consequence of a closer contact, we were brought to take as lively an interest in our neighbours' difficulties and pains as we formerly took in those of our kinsfolk—then we should not resort to policemen and judges, to prisons and executions. Anti-social deeds would be nipped in the bud, not punished. The few contests which would arise would be easily settled by arbitrators; and no more force would be necessary to impose their decisions than is required now for enforcing the decisions of the family tribunals of China.

And here we are brought to consider a great question: what would become of morality in a society which recognized no laws and proclaimed the full freedom of the individual? Our answer is plain.

Public morality is independent from, and anterior to, law and religion. Until now, the teachings of morality have been associated with religious teachings. But the influence which religious teachings formerly exercised on the mind has faded of late, and the sanction which morality derived from religion has no longer the power it formerly had. Millions and millions grow in our cities who have lost the old faith. Is it a reason for throwing morality overboard, and for treating it with the same sarcasm as primitive cosmogony?

Obviously not. No society is possible without certain principles of morality generally recognized. If everyone grew accustomed to deceiving his fellow-men; if we never could rely on each other's promise and words; if everyone treated his fellow as an enemy, against whom every means of warfare is justifiable—no society could exist. And we see, in fact, that notwithstanding the decay of religious beliefs, the principles of morality remain unshaken. We even see irreligious people trying to raise the current standard of morality. The fact is that moral principles are independent of religious beliefs: they are anterior to them. The primitive Tchuktchis have no religion: they have only superstitions and fear of the hostile forces of nature; and nevertheless we find with them the very same principles of morality which are taught by Christians and Buddhists, Mussulmans and Hebrews. Nay, some of their practices imply a much higher standard of tribal morality than that which appears in our civilized society.

In fact, each new religion takes its moral principles from the only real stock of morality—the moral habits which grow with men as soon as they unite to live together in tribes, cities, or nations. No animal society is possible without resulting in a growth of certain moral habits of mutual support and even self-sacrifice for the common well-being. These habits are a necessary condition for the welfare of the species in its struggle between individuals for the means of existence. The "fittest" in the organic world are those who grow accustomed to life in society; and life in society necessarily implies moral habits. As to mankind, it has during its long existence developed in its midst a nucleus of social habits, of moral habits, which cannot disappear as long as human societies exist. And therefore, notwithstanding the influences to the contrary which are now at work in consequence of our present economic relations, the nucleus of our moral habits continues to exist. Law and religion only formulate them and endeavour to enforce them by their sanction.

Whatever the variety of theories of morality, all can be brought under three chief categories: the morality of religion; the utilitarian morality; and the theory of moral habits resulting from the very needs of life in society. Each religious morality sanctifies its prescriptions by making them originate from revelation; and it tries to impress its teachings on the mind by a promise of reward, or punishment, either in this or in a future life. The utilitarian morality maintains the idea of reward, but it finds it in man himself. It invites men to analyze their pleasures, to classify them, and to give preference to those which are most intense and must durable. We must recognize, however, that although it has exercised some influence, this system has been judged too artificial by the great mass of human beings. And finally—whatever its varieties—there is the third system of morality which sees in moral actions—in those actions which are most powerful in rendering men best fitted for life in society—a mere necessity of the individual to enjoy the joys of his brethren, to suffer when some of his brethren are suffering; a habit and a second nature, slowly elaborated and perfected by life in society. That is the morality of mankind; and that is also the morality of anarchism.

Such are, in a very brief summary, the leading principles of anarchism. Each of them hurts many a prejudice, and yet each of them results from an analysis of the very tendencies displayed by human society. Each of them is rich in consequences and implies a thorough revision of many a current opinion. And anarchism is not a mere insight into a remote future. Already now, whatever the sphere of action of the individual, he can act, either in accordance with anarchist principles or on an opposite line. And all that may be done in that direction will be done in the direction to which further development goes. All that may be done in the opposite way will be an attempt to force humanity to go where it will *not* go.

Anarchism:

Its Philosophy and Ideal

Preface

KROPOTKIN was an arduous and, in the memories of many hearers, and excellent lecturer, putting his points with the clarity of a good nineteenth-century scientist, and delivering them with an enthusiasm that was at once inspiring and disarming. Yet despite the air of spontaneity which his lectures often projected, they were works of exposition as serious as anything he prepared for print, particularly during his long British exile when he had to use the English language, in which acquired some fluidity as he went along, though he never spoke it so well as his native Russian or even his Russian aristocrat's French. Once, in 1889, he prepared a group of lecturers for delivery in Kensington Town Hall, and wrote to May Morris who was helping to arrange them:

> It will take me two months, I suppose, before I could write down these lectures, and I must write them in full, because I cannot trust my speaking in English before having couched the lecture on paper almost entirely, and I cannot reckon to do much work between the lectures, as each lecture fatigues me so much.

Kropotkin served his speaker's apprenticeship as Borodin exhorting the inmates of the Moscow workers' artels and as brilliant young Prince Kropotkin describing his discoveries to his fellow geographers. In Switzerland and France he combined his editing of anarchist papers with addresses to groups of internationalist workers. And when he was imprisoned from 1873 to 1876 in St. Bernard's secularized abbey at Clairvaux, he spent much of his time lecturing on various scientific and political subjects to his fellow convicts.

Almost as soon as he reached England and settled in his first home at Harrow, Kropotkin began the custom of making lecture tours in Britain (supplementing them with later tours in the United States, where his *Memoirs of a Revolutionist* was originally delivered as a series of reminiscent lectures.) He spoke under many auspices, from the British Association and the Royal Geographical Society through groups of teachers and other intelligentsia, to gatherings of political radicals largely organized by the Socialist League which then, under the leadership of William Morris, was veering towards anarchism. Outside London, his most successful lectures were probably in north-east England and in Scotland, where he addressed audiences of two thousand and more people and began cordial associations with leading intellectuals, notably Patrick Geddes, John Stuart Blackie, the translator of Aeschylus, and above all James Mavor, a close and lasting friend who later became a distinguished Canadian economist. Apart from their service to the cause, Kropotkin's lecture tours gave him a fine introduction to British society in all its variations of locality and class. Of these busy days, which continued until the 1990s and were only ended by his increasingly serious attacks of bronchitis and heart trouble, he remembered in his *Memoirs:*

> As I had, as a rule, accepted the first invitation I received to stay the night after the lecture, it consequently happened that I stayed one night in a rich man's mansion, and the next night in the narrow abode of a working-class family. Every night I saw considerable numbers of people of all classes; and whether it was in the worker's small parlour or in the reception-rooms of the wealthy, the most-animated discussions went on about socialism and anarchism till a very late hour of the night—with hope in the workman's home, with apprehension in the mansion, but everywhere with the same earnestness.

"Anarchism: Its Philosophy and Ideal," which was eventually published by Freedom Press as a pamphlet in 1897, followed a theme that dominated many of Kropotkin's lectures, for though he talked often enough on science and education and to an extent allowed the nature of his audience to determine his approach, his main aim was to communicate the great central theme of his life and thought, freedom and how to make a society that would sustain it. It is a clear and balanced account, and it is interesting to read in the same context as "Must We Occupy Ourselves..." since it shows how much more assured Kropotkin had become in his anarchist attitudes. There are no longer any of the points of hesitation which in the earlier piece show how conscious he still was of the need to convince a group of critical comrades. Now he is the man who has thought out his ideas and shed his doubts, and stands before an audience, mainly of the unconverted, seeking to convince them of what to him are self-evident truths. It is, in my view, the best short exposition of anarchism yet written.

Or rather, shall we say, of anarchist communism, which most of the followers of Bakunin had adopted since Kropotkin began expounding it in *La Révolte* during the late 1870s. For there were anarchists of other types, notably in England at that time, the individualists led by Henry Seymour and associated with *The Anarchist*. But even they, while rejecting Kropotkin's economic solution of the free distribution of goods and services through communal systems as offering too many curbs on the individual, would have accepted his general picture of the libertarian as distinct from the authoritarian view of social organization.

Interesting also are the remarks on human and animal societies and the discussion of a balance between manual and intellectual education, which later will figure so greatly in his larger books like *Mutual Aid* and *Fields, Factories and Workshops*, and which show how consistent his ideas were during the greater part of his period as an advocate of anarchism.

G.W.

Anarchism: Its Philosophy and Ideal

THOSE who are persuaded that anarchism is a collection of visions relating to the future, and an unconscious striving towards the destruction of all present civilization, are still very numerous. To clear the ground of such prejudices as maintain this view we should have to enter into many details which it would be difficult to cover briefly.

Anarchists have been spoken of so much lately that part of the public has at last taken to reading and discussing our doctrines. Sometimes men have even given themselves the trouble to reflect, and at the present time we have at least gained the admission that anarchists have an ideal. Their ideal is even found too beautiful, too lofty, for a society not composed of superior beings.

But is it not pretentious on my part to speak of a philosophy, when according to our critics our ideas are but dim visions of a distant future? Can anarchism pretend to possess a philosophy when it is denied that socialism has one?

This is what I am about to answer with all possible precision and clearness. I begin by taking a few elementary illustrations borrowed from natural sciences. Not for the purpose of deducing our social ideas from them—far from it; but simply the better to set certain relations which are easier grasped in phenomena verified by the exact sciences than in examples taken only from the complex facts of human societies.

What especially strikes us at present in exact sciences is the profound modification which they are undergoing in the whole of their conceptions and interpretations of the facts of the universe.

There was a time when man imagined the earth placed in the centre of the universe. Sun, moon, planets and stars seemed to roll round our globe; and this globe inhabited by man represented for him the centre of creation. He himself—the superior being on his planet—was the elected of his Creator. The sun, the moon, the stars were made for him—towards him was directed all the attention of a God who watched the least of his actions, arrested the sun's course for him, launched his showers or his thunderbolts on fields and cities to recompense the virtue or punish the crimes of mankind. For thousands of years man thus conceived the universe.

An immense change in all conceptions of the civilized part of mankind was produced in the sixteenth century when it was demonstrated that far from being the centre of the universe, the earth was only a grain of sand in the solar system—a ball much smaller even than the other planets—that the sun itself, though immense in comparison to our little earth, was but a star among many other countless stars which we see shining in the skies and swarming in the milky way. How small man appeared in comparison to this immensity without limits, how ridiculous his pretensions! All the philosophy of that epoch, all social and religious conceptions, felt the effects of this transformation in cosmogony. Natural science, whose present development we are so proud of, only dates from that time.

But a change much more profound and with far wider-reaching results is being effected at the present time in the whole of the sciences, and anarchism is but one of the many manifestations of this evolution.

Take any work on astronomy of the last century. You will no longer find in it our tiny planet placed in the centre of the universe. But you will meet at every step the idea of a central luminary—the sun—which by its powerful attraction governs our planetary world. From this central body radiates a force guiding the course of the planets, and maintaining the harmony of the system. Issued from a central agglomeration, planets have, so to say, budded from it. They owe their birth to this agglomeration; they owe everything to the radiant star that represents it still: the rhythm of their movements, their orbits set at wisely regulated distances, the life that animates them and adorns their surfaces. And when any perturbation disturbs their course and makes them deviate from their orbits, the central body re-establishes order in the system; it assures and perpetuates its existence.

This conception, however, is also disappearing as the other one did. After having fixed all their attention on the sun and the large planets, astronomers are beginning to study now the infinitely small ones that people the universe. And they discover that the interplanetary and interstellar spaces are peopled and crossed in all imaginable directions by little swarms of matter, invisible, infinitely small when taken separately, but all-powerful in their numbers.

It is to these infinitely tiny bodies that dash through space in all directions with giddy swiftness, that clash with one another, agglomerate, disintegrate everywhere and always, it is to them that today astronomers look for an explanation of the origin of our solar system, the movements that animate its parts, and the harmony of their whole. Yet another step, and soon universal gravitation itself will be but the result of all the disordered and incoherent movements of these infinitely small bodies—of oscillations of atoms that manifest themselves in all

possible directions. Thus the centre, the origin of force formerly trans-
ferred from the earth to the sun, now turns out to be scattered and dis-
seminated. It is everywhere and nowhere. With the astronomer, we
perceive that solar systems are the work of infinitely small bodies; that
the power which was supposed to govern the system is itself but the
result of the collision among those infinitely tiny clusters of matter, that
the harmony of stellar systems is harmony only because it is an adaptation, a resultant of all these numberless movements uniting, complet-
ing, equilibrating one another.

The whole aspect of the universe changes with this new conception. The idea of force governing the world, pre-established law,
preconceived harmony, disappears to make room for the harmony that
Fourier had caught a glimpse of: the one which results from the disor-
derly and incoherent movements of numberless hosts of matter, each of
which goes its own way and all of which hold each in equilibrium.

It if were only astronomy that were undergoing this change! But
no; the same modification takes place in the philosophy of all sciences
without exception; those which study nature as well as those which
study human relations.

In physical sciences, the entities of heat, magnetism, and electricity
disappear. When a physicist speaks today of a heated or electrified
body, he no longer sees an inanimate mass, to which an unknown force
should be added. He strives to recognize in this body and in the surrounding space, the course, the vibrations of infinitely small atoms
which dash in all directions, vibrate, move, live, and by their vibrations,
their shocks, their life, produce the phenomena of heat, light, magnetism or electricity.

In sciences that treat organic life, the notion of species and its variations is being substituted by a notion of the variations of the individual—his life, his adaptations to his surroundings. Changes
produced in him by the action of drought or damp, heat or cold, abundance or poverty of nourishment, of his more or less sensitiveness to
the action of exterior surroundings will originate species; and the variations of species are now for the biologist but resultants—a given sum of
variations that have been produced in each individual separately. A
species will be what the individuals are, each undergoing numberless
influences from the surroundings in which they live, and to which they
correspond each in his own way.

And when a physiologist speaks now of the life of a plant or of an
animal, he sees an agglomeration, a colony of millions of separate individuals rather than a personality, one and invisible. He speaks of a

federation of digestive, sensual, nervous organs, all very intimately connected with one another, each feeling the consequence of the well-being or indisposition of each, but each living its own life. Each organ, each part of an organ in its turn is composed of independent cellules which associate to struggle against conditions unfavourable to their existence. The individual is quite a world of federations, a whole universe in himself.

And in this world of aggregated beings the physiologist sees the autonomous cells of blood, of the tissues, of the nerve-centres; he recognizes the millions of white corpuscles who wend their way to the parts of the body infected by microbes in order to give battle to the invaders. More than that: in each microscopic cell he discovers today a world of autonomous organisms, each of which lives its own life, looks for well-being for itself and attains it by grouping and associating itself with others. In short, each individual is a cosmos of organs, each organ is a cosmos of cells, each cell is a cosmos of infinitely small ones. And in this complex world, the well-being of the whole depends entirely on the sum of well-being enjoyed by each of the least microscopic particles or organized matter. A whole revolution is thus produced in the philosophy of life.

But it is especially in psychology that this revolution leads to consequences of great importance.

Quite recently the psychologist spoke of man as an entire being, one and indivisible. Remaining faithful to religious tradition, he used to class men as good and bad, intelligent and stupid, egotists and altruists. Even with materialists of the eighteenth century, the idea of a soul, of an indivisible entity, was still upheld.

But what would we think today of a psychologist who would still speak like this? The modern psychologist sees in a man a multitude of separate faculties, autonomous tendencies, equal among themselves, performing their functions independently, balancing, opposing one another continually. Taken as a whole, man is nothing but a resultant, always changeable, of all his divers faculties, of all his autonomous tendencies, of brain cells and nerve-centres. All are related so closely to one another that they each react on all the others, but they lead their own life without being subordinated to a central organ—the soul.

Without entering into further details you thus see that a profound modification is being produced at this moment in the whole of natural sciences. Not that this analysis is extended to details formerly neglected. No! the facts are not new, but the way of looking at them is in course of evolution. And if we had to characterize this tendency in a few words, we might say that if formerly science strove to study the results and the great sums (integrals, as mathematicians say), today it strives to study the infinitely small ones—the individuals of which those sums are composed and in which it now recognizes independence and individuality at the same time as this intimate aggregation.

As to the harmony that the human mind discovers in nature, and which harmony is on the whole but the verification of a certain stability of phenomena, the modern man of science no longer tries to explain it by the action of laws conceived according to a certain plan pre-established by an intelligent will.

What used to be called "natural law" is nothing but a certain relation among phenomena which we dimly see, and each 'law' takes a temporary character of causality; that is to say: *If* such a phenomena is produced under such conditions, such another phenomena will follow. No law placed outside the phenomena: each phenomenon governs that which follows it—not law.

Nothing is preconceived in what we call harmony in Nature. The chance of collisions and encounters has sufficed to establish it. Such a phenomenon will last for centuries because the adaptation, the equilibrium it represents has taken centuries to be established; while such another will last but an instant if that form of momentary equilibrium was born in an instant. If the planets of our solar system do not collide with one another and do not destroy one another every day, if they last millions of years, it is because they represent an equilibrium that has taken millions of centuries to establish as a resultant of millions of blind forces. If continents are not continually destroyed by volcanic shocks it is because they have taken thousands and thousands of centuries to build up, molecule by molecule, and to take their present shape. But lightning will only last an instant; because it represents a momentary rupture of the equilibrium, a sudden redistribution of force.

Harmony thus appears as a temporary adjustment established among all forces acting upon a given spot—a provisory adaptation. And that adjustment will only last under one condition: that of being continually modified; of representing every moment the resultant of all conflicting actions. Let but one of those forces be hampered in its action for some time and harmony disappears. Force will accumulate its effect, it *must* come to light, it must exercise its action, and if other forces hinder its manifestation it will not be annihilated by that, but will end by upsetting the present adjustment, by destroying harmony, in order to find a new form of equilibrium and to work to form a new adaptation. Such is the eruption of a volcano, whose imprisoned force ends by breaking the petrified lavas which hindered them to pour forth the gases, the molten lavas, and the incandescent ashes. Such also, are the revolutions of mankind.

An analogous transformation is being produced at the same time in the sciences that treat of man. Thus we see that history, after having been the history of kingdoms, tends to become the history of nations and then the study of individuals. The historian wants to know how the members, of which such a nation was composed, lived at such a time, what their beliefs were, their means of existence, what ideal of society was visible to them, and what means they possessed to march towards this ideal. And by the action of all those forces, formerly neglected, he interprets the great historical phenomena.

So the man of science who studies jurisprudence is no longer content with such or such a code. Like the ethnologist he wants to know the genesis of the institutions that succeed one another; he follows their evolution through ages, and in this study he applies himself far less to written law than to local customs—to the "customary law" in which the constructive genius of the unknown masses has found expression in all times. A wholly new science is being elaborated in this direction and promises to upset established conceptions we learned at school, succeeding in interpreting history in the same manner as natural sciences interpret the phenomena of nature.

And, finally, political economy, which was at the beginning a study of the wealth of *nations,* becomes today a study of the wealth of *individuals.* It cares less to know if such a nation has or has not a large foreign trade; it wants to be assured that bread is not wanting in the peasant's or worker's cottage. It knocks at all doors—at that of the palace as well as that of the hovel—and asks the rich as well as the poor: Up to what point are your needs satisfied both for necessities and luxuries?

And as it discovers that the most pressing needs of nine-tenths of each nation are not satisfied, it asks itself the question that a physiologist would ask himself about a plant or an animal:—"Which are the means to satisfy the needs of all with the least loss of power? How can a society guarantee to each, and consequently to all, the greatest sum of satisfaction?" It is in this direction that economic science is being transformed; and after having been so long a simple statement of phenomena interpreted in the interest of a rich minority, it tends to become a science in the true sense of the word—a physiology of human societies.

While a new philosophy—a new view of knowledge taken as a whole—is thus being worked out, we may observe that a different conception of society, very different from that which now prevails, is in process of formation. Under the name of anarchism, a new interpretation of the past and present life of society arises, giving at the same time a forecast as regards its future, both conceived in the same spirit as the above mentioned interpretation in natural sciences. Anarchism, therefore, appears as a constituent part of the new philosophy, and that is why anarchists come in contact on so many points with the greatest thinkers and poets of the present day.

In fact, it is certain that in proportion as the human mind frees itself from ideas inculcated by minorities of priests, military chiefs and judges, all striving to establish their domination, and of scientists paid to perpetuate it, a conception of society arises in which there is no longer room for those dominating minorities. A society entering into possession of the social capital accumulated by the labour of preceding generations, organizing itself so as to make use of this capital in the interests of all, and constituting itself without reconstituting the power of the ruling minorities. It comprises in its midst an infinite variety of capacities, temperaments and individual energies: it excludes none. It even calls for struggles and contentions; because we know that periods of contests, so long as they were freely fought out without the weight of constituted authority being thrown on one side of the balance, were periods when human genius took its mightiest flights and achieved the greatest aims. Acknowledging, as a fact, the equal rights of its members to the treasures accumulated in the past, it no longer recognizes a division between exploited and exploiters, governed and governor, dominated and dominators, and it seeks to establish a certain harmonious compatibility in its midst—not by subjecting all its members to an authority that is fictitiously supposed to represent society, not by trying to establish uniformity, but by urging all men to develop free initiative, free action, free association.

It seeks the most complete development of individuality combined with the highest development of voluntary association in all its aspects, in all possible degrees, for all imaginable aims; ever changing, ever modified associations which carry in themselves the elements of their durability and constantly assume new forms which answer best to the multiple aspirations of all.

A society to which pre-established forms, crystallized by law, are repugnant; which looks for harmony in an ever-changing and fugitive equilibrium between a multitude of varied forces and influences of every kind, following their own course—these forces themselves promoting the energies which are favourable to their march towards progress, towards the liberty of developing in broad daylight and counterbalancing one another.

This conception and ideal of society is certainly not new. On the contrary, when we analyze the history of popular institutions—the clan, the village community, the guild and even the urban commune of the middle ages in their first stages—we find the same popular tendency to constitute a society according to this idea; a tendency, however, always trammelled by domineering minorities. All popular movements bore this stamp more or less, and with the Anabaptists and their forerunners in the ninth century we already find the same ideas clearly expressed in the religious language which was in use at that time. Unfortunately, till the end of the last century, this ideal was always tainted by a theocratic spirit. It is only nowadays that the conception of society deduced from the observation of social phenomena is rid of its swaddling-clothes.

It is only today that the ideal of a society where each governs himself according to his own will (which is evidently a result of the social influences borne by each) is affirmed in its economic, political and moral aspects at one and the same time, and that this ideal presents itself based on the necessity of communism, imposed on our modern societies by the eminently social character of our present production.

In fact, we know full well today that it is futile to speak of liberty as long as economic slavery exists.

"Speak not of liberty—poverty is slavery!" is not a vain formula; it has penetrated into the ideas of the great working-class masses; it filters through all the present literature; it even carries those along who live on the poverty of others, and takes from them the arrogance with which they formerly asserted their rights to exploitation.

Millions of socialists of both hemispheres already agree that the present form of capitalistic social appropriation cannot last much longer. Capitalists themselves feel that it must go and dare not defend it with their former assurance. Their only argument is reduced to saying to us: "You have invented nothing better!" But as to denying the fatal consequences of the present forms of poverty, as to justifying their rights to property, they cannot do it. They will practice this right as long as freedom of action is left to them, but without trying to base it on an idea. This is easily understood.

For instance, take the town of Paris—a creation of so many centuries, a product of the genius of a whole nation, a result of the labour of twenty or thirty generations. How could one maintain to an inhabitant of that town who works every day to embellish it, to purify it, to nourish it, to make it a centre of thought and art—how could one assert before one who produces this wealth that the palaces adorning the streets of Paris belong in all justice to those who are the legal proprietors today, when we are all creating their value, which would be *nil* without us?

Such a fiction can be kept up for some time by the skill of the people's educators. The great battalions of workers may not even reflect about it; but from the moment a minority of thinking men agitate the question and submit it to all, there can be doubt of the result. Popular opinion answers: "It is by spoliation that they hold these riches!"

Likewise, how can the peasant be made to believe that the bourgeois or manorial land belongs to the proprietor who has a legal claim, when a peasant can tell us the history of each bit of land for ten leagues around? Above all, how make him believe that it is useful for the nation that Mr. So-and-so keeps a piece of land for his park when so many neighbouring peasants would be only too glad to cultivate it?

And, lastly how make the worker in a factory, or the miner in a mine, believe that factory and mine equitably belong to their present masters, when worker and even miner are beginning to see clearly through scandal, bribery, pillage of the State and the legal theft, from which great commercial and industrial property are derived?

It fact, the masters have never believed in sophisms taught by economists, uttered more to confirm exploiters in their rights than to convert the exploited; peasants and workers, crushed by misery and finding no support in the well-to-do classes, have let things go, save from time to time, when they have affirmed their rights by insurrection. And if workers ever thought that the day would come when personal appropriation of capital would profit all by turning it into a stock of wealth to be shared by all, this illusion is vanishing like so many others. The worker perceives that he has been disinherited, and that disinherited he will remain, unless he has recourse to strikes or revolts to tear from his masters the smallest part of riches built up by his own efforts—that is to say, in order to get that little, he already must impose on himself the pangs of hunger and face imprisonment, if not exposure to imperial, royal, or republican fusillades.

But a greater evil of the present system becomes more and more marked; namely, that in a system based on private appropriation, all that is necessary to life and to production—land, housing, food and tools—having once passed into the hands of a few, the production of necessities that would give well-being to all is continually hampered. The worker feels vaguely that our present technical power could give abundance to all, but he also perceives how the capitalist system and the State hinder the conquest of this well-being in every way.

Far from producing more than is needed to assure material riches, we do not produce enough. When a peasant covets the parks and gardens of industrial filibusters, round which judges and police mount guard—when he dreams of covering them with crops which, he knows, would carry abundance to the villages whose inhabitants feed on bread hardly washed down with sloe wine—he understands this.

The miner, forced to be idle three days a week, thinks of the tons of coal he might extract and which are sorely needed in poor households.

The worker whose factory is closed, and who tramps the streets in search of work, sees bricklayers out of work like himself, while one-fifth of the population of Paris live in insanitary hovels; he hears shoemakers complain of want of work, while so many people need shoes—and so on.

In short, if certain economists delight in writing treatises on over-production, and in explaining each industrial crisis by this cause, they would be much at a loss if called upon to name a single article produced by France in greater quantities than are necessary to satisfy the needs of the whole population. It is certainly not corn: the country is obliged to import it. It is not wine either: peasants drink but little wine, and substitute sloe wine in its stead, and the inhabitants of towns have to be content with adulterated stuff. It is evidently not houses: millions still live in cottages of the most wretched description, with one or two apertures.

It is not even good or bad books, for they are still objects of luxury in the villages. Only one thing is produced in quantities greater than needed—it is the budget-devouring individual. But such merchandise is not mentioned in lectures by political economists, although those individuals possess all the attributes of merchandise, being ever ready to sell themselves to the highest bidder.

What economists call over-production is but a production that is above the purchasing power of the worker, who is reduced to poverty by capital and State. Now, this sort of over-production remains fatally characteristic of the present capitalist production, because workers cannot buy with their salaries what they have produced and at the same time copiously nourish the swarm of idlers who live upon their work.

The very essence of the present economic system is that the worker can never enjoy the well-being he has produced, and that the number of those who live at his expense will always augment. The more a country is advanced in industry, the more this number grows. Inevitably, industry is directed, and will have to be directed, not towards what is needed to satisfy the needs of all, but towards that which, at a given moment, brings in the greatest temporary profit to a few. Of necessity, the abundance of some will be based on the poverty of others, and the straitened circumstances of the greater number will have to be maintained at all costs, that there may be hands to sell themselves for a part only of that which they are capable of producing; without which private accumulation of capital is impossible!

These characteristics of our economic system are its very essence. Without them, it cannot exist, for who would sell his labour power for less than it is capable of bringing in if he were not forced thereto by the threat of hunger?

And those essential traits of the system are also its most crushing condemnation.

As long as England and France were pioneers of industry in the midst of nations backward in their technical development, and as long as neighbours purchased their wools, their cotton goods, their silks, their iron and machines, as well as a whole range of articles of luxury, at a price that allowed them to enrich themselves at the expense of their clients—the worker could be buoyed up by hope that he too, would be called upon to appropriate an ever and ever larger share of the booty to himself. But these conditions are disappearing. In their turn, the backward nations have become great producers of cotton goods, wools, silks and machines and articles of luxury. In certain branches of industry they have even taken the lead, and not only do they struggle with the pioneers of industry and commerce in distant lands, but they even compete with those pioneers in their own countries. In a few years Germany, Switzerland, Italy, the United States, Russia and Japan have become great industrial countries. Mexico, the Indies, even Serbia, are on the march—and what will it be when China begins to imitate Japan in manufacturing for the world's market?

The result is that industrial crises, the frequency and duration of which are always augmenting, have passed into a chronic state in many industries.

All is linked, all holds together under the present economic system, and all tends to make the fall of the industrial and mercantile system under which we live inevitable. Its duration is but a question of time that may already be counted by years and no longer by centuries. A question of time—and energetic attack on our part! Idlers do not make history: they suffer it!

That is why such powerful minorities constitute themselves in the midst of civilized nations, and loudly ask for the return to the community of all riches accumulated by the work of preceding generations. The holding in common of lands, mines, factories, inhabited houses, and means of transport is already the watch-word of these imposing factions, and repression—the favourite weapon of the rich and powerful—can no longer do anything to arrest the triumphal march of the spirit of revolt. And if millions of workers do not rise to seize the land and factories from the monopolists by force, be sure it is not for want of desire. They but wait for a favourable opportunity—a chance, such as presented itself in 1848, when they will be able to start the destruction of the present economic system, with the hope of being supported by an international movement.

We have already obtained the unanimous assent of those who have studied the subject, that a society, having recovered the possession of all riches accumulated in its midst, can liberally assure abundance to all in return for four or five hours effective and manual work a day, as far as regards production. If everyone, from childhood, learned whence came the bread he eats, the house he dwells in, the book he studies, and so on; and if each one accustomed himself to complete mental work by manual labour in some branch of manufacture—society could easily perform this task, to say nothing of the further simplification of production which a more or less near future has in store for us.

In fact, it suffices to recall for a moment the present terrible waste to conceive what a civilized society can produce with but a small quantity of labour if all share in it, and what grand works might be undertaken that are out of the question today. Unfortunately, the metaphysics called political economy has never troubled about that which should have been its essence—economy of labour.

There is no longer any doubt as regards the possibility of wealth in a communist society, armed with our present machinery and tools. Doubts only arise when the question at issue is whether a society can exist in which man's actions are not subject to State control; whether, to reach well-being, it is not necessary for European communities to sacrifice the little personal liberty they have reconquered at the cost of so many sacrifices during this century. A section of socialists believe that it is impossible to attain such a result without sacrificing personal liberty on the altar of State. Another section, to which we belong, believes, on the contrary, that it is only by the abolition of the State, by the conquest of perfect liberty by the individual, by free agreement, association, and absolute free federation that we can reach communism—the possession in common of our social inheritance, and the production in common of all riches.

That is the question outweighing all others at present, and socialism *must* solve it, on pain of seeing all its efforts endangered and all its ulterior development paralyzed.

Let us, therefore, analyze it with all the attention it deserves.

If every socialist will carry his thoughts back to an earlier date, he will no doubt remember the host of prejudices aroused in him when, for the first time, he came to the idea that abolishing the capitalist system and private appropriation of land and capital had become an historical necessity.

The same feelings are today produced in the man who for the first time hears that the abolition of the State, its laws, its entire system of management, governmentalism and centralization, also becomes an historical necessity: that the abolition of the one without the abolition of the other is materially impossible. Our whole education—made, be it noted, by church and State, in the interests of both—revolts at this conception.

It is less true for that? And shall we allow our belief in the State to survive the host of prejudices we have already sacrificed for our emancipation?

To begin with, if man, since his origin, has always lived in societies, the State is but one of the forms of social life, quite recent as far as regards European societies. Men lived thousands of years before the first States were constituted; Greece and Rome existed for centuries before the Macedonian and Roman Empires were built up, and for us modern Europeans the centralized States date but from the sixteenth century. It was only then, after the defeat of the free medieval communes had been completed that the mutual insurance company between military, judicial, landlord, and capitalist authority which we call "State," could be fully established.

It was only in the sixteenth century that a mortal blow was dealt to the ideas of local independence, to free union and organization, to federation of all degrees among sovereign groups, possessing all functions now seized upon by the State. It was only then that the alliance between church and the nascent power of royalty put an end to an organization, based on the principle of federation, which had existed from the ninth to the fifteenth century, and which had produced in Europe the great period of free cities of the middle ages.

We know well the means by which this association of lord, priest, merchant, judge, soldier, and king founded its domination. It was by the annihilation of all free unions: of village communities, guilds, trade unions, fraternities, and medieval cities. It was by confiscating the land of the communes and the riches of the guilds. It was by the absolute and ferocious prohibition of all kinds of free agreement between men. It was by massacre, the wheel, the gibbet, the sword, and the fire that church and State established their domination, and that they succeeded henceforth to reign over an incoherent agglomeration of "subjects" who had no more direct union among themselves.

It is only recently that we began to reconquer, by struggle, by revolt, the first steps of the right of association that was freely practised by the artisans and the tillers of the soil through the whole of the middle ages.

And, already, now, Europe is covered by thousands of voluntary associations for study and teaching, for industry, commerce, science, art, literature, exploitation, resistance to exploitation, amusement, serious work, gratification and self-denial, for all that makes up the life of an active and thinking being. We see these societies rising in all nooks and corners of all domains: political, economic, artistic, intellectual. Some are as short-lived as roses, some hold their own for several decades, and all strive—while maintaining the independence of each group, circle, branch, or section—to federate, to unite, across frontiers as well as among each nation; to cover all the life of civilized men with a net, meshes of which are intersected and interwoven. Their numbers can already be reckoned by tens of thousands, they comprise millions of adherents—although less than fifty years have elapsed since church and State began to tolerate a few of them—very few, indeed.

These societies already begin to encroach everywhere on the functions of the State, and strive to substitute free action of volunteers for that of a centralized State. In England we see insurance companies arise against theft; societies for coast defense, volunteer societies for land defense, which the State endeavours to get under its thumb, thereby making them instruments of domination, although their original aim was to do without the State. Were it not for church and State, free societies would have already conquered the whole of the immense domain of education. And, in spite of all difficulties, they begin to invade this domain as well, and make their influence already felt.

And when we mark the progress already accomplished in that direction, in spite of and against the State, which tries by all means to maintain its supremacy of recent origin; when we see how voluntary societies invade everything and are only impeded in their development by the State, we are forced to recognize a powerful *tendency*, a latent force in modern society. And we ask ourselves this question: If five, ten, or twenty years hence—it matters little—the workers succeed by revolt in destroying the said mutual insurance societies of landlords, bankers, priests, judges, and soldiers; if the people become masters of their destiny for a few months, and lay hands on the riches they have created, and which belong to them by right—will they really begin to reconstitute that blood-sucker, the State? Or will they not rather try to organize from the simple to the complex according to mutual agreement and to the infinitely varied, ever-changing needs of each locality, in order to secure the possession of those riches for themselves, to mutually guarantee one another's life, and to produce what will be found necessary for life?

Will they follow the dominant tendency of the century, towards decentralization, home rule and free agreement; or will they march contrary to this tendency and strive to reconstitute demolished authority?

Educated men tremble at the idea that society might someday be without judges, police, or jailers.

But frankly, do you need them as much as you have been told in musty books? Books written, be it noted, by scientists who generally know well what has been written before them, but, for the most part, absolutely ignore the people and their everyday life.

If we can wander, without fear, not only in the streets of Paris, which bristle with police, but especially in rustic walks where you rarely meet passers-by, is it to the police that we owe this security? Or rather to the absence of people who care to rob or murder us? I am evidently not speaking of the one who carries millions about him. That one—a recent trial tells us—is soon robbed, by preference in places where there are as many policemen as lamp-posts. No, I speak of the man who fears for his life and not for his purse filled with ill-gotten sovereigns. Are his fears real?

Besides, has not experience demonstrated quite recently that Jack the Ripper performed his exploits under the eye of the London police—a most active force—and that he only left off killing when the population of Whitechapel itself began to give chase to him?

And in our everyday relations with our fellow-citizens, do you think that it is really judges, jailers, and police that hinder anti-social acts from multiplying? The judge, ever ferocious, because he is a maniac of law, the accuser, the informer, the police spy, all those interlopers that live from hand to mouth around the law courts, do they not scatter demoralization far and wide into society? Read the trials, glance behind the scenes, push your analysis further than the exterior façade of law courts, and you will come out sickened.

Have not prisons—which kill all will and force of character in man, which enclose within their walls more vices than are met with on any other spot of the globe—always been universities of crime? Is not the court of a tribunal a school of ferocity? And so on.

When we ask for the abolition of the State and its organs we are always told that we dream of a society composed of men better than they are in reality. But no; a thousand times, no. All we ask is that men should not be made worse than they are, by such institutions!

If by following the very old advice given by Bentham you begin to think of the fatal consequences—direct, and especially indirect—of legal coercion, then, like Tolstoy, like us, you will begin to hate the use of coercion, and you will begin to say that society possesses a thousand other means for preventing anti-social acts. If it neglects those means today, it is because, being educated by church and State, our cowardice and apathy of spirit hinder our seeing clearly on this point. When a child has committed a fault, it is so easy to punish it: that puts an end to all discussions! It is so easy to hang a man—especially when there is an executioner who is paid so much for each execution—and it relieves us of thinking of the cause of crimes.

It is often said that anarchists live in a world of dreams to come, and do not see things which happen today. We see them only too well, and in their true colours, and that is what makes us carry the hatchet into the forest of prejudices that besets us.

Far from living in a world of visions and imagining men better than they are, we see them as they are; and that is why we affirm that the best of men is made essentially bad by the exercise of authority, and that the theory of the "balancing of powers" and "control of authorities" is a hypocritical formula, invented by those who have seized power, to make the "sovereign people," whom they despise, believe that the people themselves are governing. It is because we know men that we say to those who imagine that men would devour another without those governors: "You reason like the king, who, being sent across the frontier, called out, 'What will become of my poor subjects without me?'"

Ah, if men were those superior beings that the utopians of authority like to speak to us of, if we could close our eyes to reality and live like them in a world of dreams and illusions as to the superiority of those who think themselves called to power, perhaps we also should do like them; perhaps we also should believe in the virtues of those who govern.

If the gentlemen in power were really so intelligent and so devoted to the public cause, as panegyrists of authority love to represent, what a pretty government and paternal utopia we should be able to construct! The employer would never be the tyrant of the worker; he would be the father! The factory would be a palace of delight, and never would masses of workers be doomed to physical deterioration. A judge would not have the ferocity to condemn the wife and children of the one whom he sends to prison to suffer years of hunger and misery and to die some day of anaemia; never would a public prosecutor ask for the head of the accused for the unique pleasure of showing off his oratorical talent; and nowhere would we find a jailer or an executioner to do the bidding of judges who have not the courage to carry out their sentences themselves.

Oh, the beautiful utopia, the lovely Christmas dream we can make as soon as we admit that those who govern represent a superior caste, and have hardly any or no knowledge of simple mortals' weaknesses! It would then suffice to make them control one another in hierarchical fashion, to let them exchange fifty papers, at most, among different administrators, when the wind blows down a tree on the national road. Or, if need be, they would have only to be valued at their proper worth, during elections by those same masses of mortals which are supposed to be endowed with all stupidity in their mutual relations but become wisdom itself when they have to elect their masters.

All the science of government, imagined by those who govern, is imbibed with these utopias. But we know men too well to dream such dreams. We have not two measures for the virtues of the governed and those of the governors; we know that we ourselves are not without faults and that the best of us would soon be corrupted by the exercise of power. We take men for what they are worth—and that is why we hate the government of man by man, and why we work with all our might—perhaps not strong enough—to put an end to it.

But it is not enough to destroy. We must also know how to build, and it is owing to not having thought about it that the masses have always been led astray in all their revolutions. After having demolished they abandoned the care of reconstruction to the middle-class people who possessed a more or less precise conception of what they wished to realize, and who consequently reconstituted authority to their own advantage.

That is why anarchism, when it works to destroy authority in all its aspects, when it demands the abrogation of laws and the abolition of

the mechanism that serves to impose them, when it refuses all hierarchical organization and preaches free agreement, at the same time
strives to maintain and enlarge the precious kernel of social customs
without which no human or animal society can exist. Only instead of
demanding that those social customs should be maintained through
the authority of a few, it demands it from the continued action of all.

Communist customs and institutions are of absolute necessity for
society, not only to solve economic difficulties, but also to maintain and
develop social customs that bring men in contact with one another.
They must be looked to for establishing such relations between men
that the interest of each should be the interest of all; and this alone can
unite men instead of dividing them.

In fact, when we ask ourselves by what means a certain moral level
can be maintained in a human or animal society, we find only three
such means: the repression of anti-social acts; moral teaching; and the
practice of mutual help itself. And as all three have already been put to
the test of practice, we can judge them by their effects.

As to the impotence of repression—it is sufficiently demonstrated
by the disorder of present society and by the necessity of a revolution
that we all desire or feel inevitable. In the domain of economy, coercion
has led us to industrial servitude; in the domain of politics to the State;
that is to say, to the destruction of all ties that formerly existed among
citizens, and to the nation, which becomes nothing but an incoherent
mass of obedient *subjects* of central authority.

Not only has a coercive system contributed and powerfully aided
to create all the present economic, political, and social evils, but it has
given proof of its absolute impotence to raise the moral level of
societies; it has not even been able to maintain it at the level it had already reached. If a benevolent fairy could only reveal to our eyes all the
crimes that are committed every day, every minute, in a civilized
society, under the cover of the unknown, or the protection of law itself,
society would shudder at that terrible state of affairs. The authors of the
greatest political crimes, like Napoleon III's *coup d'état*, or the bloody
week in May after the fall of the Commune of 1871, never are arraigned.

Practised for centuries, repression has so badly succeeded that it
has but led us into a blind alley from which we can only issue by carrying torch and hatchet into the institutions of our authoritarian past.

Far be it from us not to recognize the importance of the second factor, moral teaching—especially that which is unconsciously transmitted in society and results from the whole of the ideas and comments

emitted by each of us on facts and events of everyday life. But this force can only act on society under one condition, that of not being crossed by a mass of contradictory immoral teachings resulting from the practice of institutions.

In that case, its influence is *nil* or baneful. Take Christian morality: what other teaching could have had more hold on minds than that spoken in the name of a crucified God, and could have acted with all its mystical force, all its poetry of martyrdom, its grandeur in forgiving executioners? And yet the institution was more powerful than the religion. Soon Christianity—a revolt against imperial Rome—was conquered by that same Rome; it accepted the Roman law as its own, and as such—allied to the State—it became in history the most furious enemy of all semi-communist institutions, to which Christianity appealed at its origin.

Can we for a moment believe that moral teaching, patronized by circulars from ministers of public instruction, would have the creative force that Christianity has not had? And what could the verbal teaching of truly social men do, if it were counteracted by the whole teaching derived from institutions based, as our present institutions of property and State are, upon unsocial principles?

The third element alone remains—*the institution itself,* acting in such a way as to make social acts a state of habit and instinct. This element—history proves it—has never missed its aim, never has it acted as a double-bladed sword; and its influence has only been weakened when custom strove to become immovable, crystallized to become in its turn a religion not to be questioned when it endeavoured to absorb the individual, taking all freedom of action from him and compelling him to revolt against that which had become, through its crystallization, an enemy to progress.

In fact, all that was an element of progress in the past or an instrument of moral and intellectual improvement of the human race is due *to the practice of mutual aid,* to the customs that recognized the equality of men and brought them to ally, to unite, to associate for the purposes of defense, to federate and to recognize no other judges in fighting out their differences than the arbitrators they took from their own midst.

Each time these institutions, issued from popular genius, when it had reconquered its liberty for a moment—each time these institutions developed in a new direction, the moral level of society, its material well-being, its liberty, its intellectual progress, and the affirmation of individual originality made a step in advance. And, on the contrary, each time that in the course of history, whether following upon a foreign conquest, or whether by developing authoritarian prejudices, men become more and more divided into governors and governed, exploiters and exploited, the moral level fell, the well-being of the masses decreased in order to insure riches to a few, and the spirit of the age declined.

History teaches us this, and from this lesson we have learned to have confidence in free communist institutions to raise the moral level of societies, debased by the practice of authority.

Today we live side by side without knowing one another. We come together at meetings on an election day: we listen to the lying or fanciful professions of faith of a candidate, and we return home. The State has the care of all questions of public interest; the State alone has the function of seeing that we do not harm the interests of our neighbour, and, if it fails in this, of punishing us in order to repair the evil.

Our neighbour may die of hunger or murder his children—is it no business of ours; it is the business of the policeman. You hardly know one another, nothing unites you, everything tends to alienate you from one another, and finding no better way, you ask the Almighty (formerly it was a God, now it is the State) to do all that lies within his power to stop anti-social passions from reaching their highest climax.

In a communist society such estrangement, such confidence in an outside force, could not exist. Communist organizations cannot be left to be constructed by legislative bodies called parliaments, municipal or communal councils. It must be the work of all, a natural growth, a product of the constructive genius of the great mass. Communism cannot be imposed from above; it could not live even for a few months if the constant and daily co-operation of all did not uphold it. It must be free.

It cannot exist without creating a continual contact between all for the thousands and thousands of common transactions; it cannot exist without creating local life, independent in the smallest unities—the block of houses, the street, the district, the commune. It would not answer its purpose if it did not cover society with a network of thousands of associations to satisfy its thousand needs: the necessaries of life, articles of luxury, of study, enjoyment, amusements. And such associations cannot remain narrow and local; they must necessarily tend (as is already the case with learned societies, cyclist clubs, humanitarian societies and the like) to become international.

And the sociable customs that communism—were it only partial at its origin—must inevitably engender in life, would already be a force incomparably more powerful to maintain and develop the kernel of sociable customs than all repressive machinery.

This, then, is the form—sociable institution—of which we ask the development of the spirit of harmony that church and State had undertaken to impose on us—with the sad result we know only too well. And these remarks contain our answer to those who affirm that communism and anarchism cannot go together. They are, you see, a necessary complement to one another. The most powerful development of individuality, of individual originality—as one of our comrades has so well said—can only be produced when the first needs of food and shelter are satisfied; when the struggle for existence against the forces of nature has been simplified; when man's time is no longer taken up entirely by the meaner side of daily subsistence, then only, his intelligence, his artistic taste, his inventive spirit, his genius, can develop freely and ever strive to greater achievements.

Communism is the best basis for individual development and freedom; not that individualism which drives man to the war of each against all—this is the only one known up till now, but that which represents the full expansion of man's faculties, the superior development of what is original in him, the greatest fruitfulness of intelligence, feeling and will.

Such being our ideal, what does it matter to us that it cannot be realized at once!

Our first duty is to find out by analysis of society, its characteristic *tendencies* at a given moment of evolution and to state them clearly. Then, to act according to those tendencies in our relations with all those who think as we do. And, finally, from today and especially during a revolutionary period, work for the destruction of the institutions, as well as the prejudices that impede the development of such tendencies.

That is all we can do by peaceable or revolutionary methods, and we know that by favouring those tendencies we contribute to progress, while those who resist them impede the march of progress.

Nevertheless men often speak of stages to be travelled through, and they propose to work to reach what they consider to the nearest station and only *then* take the highroad leading to what they recognize to be a still higher ideal.

But reasoning like this seems to me to misunderstand the true character of human progress and to make use of a badly chosen military comparison. Humanity is not a rolling ball, nor even a marching column. It is a whole that evolves simultaneously in the multitude of millions of which it is composed. And if you wish for a comparison you must rather take it in the laws of organic evolution than in those of an inorganic moving body.

The fact is that each phase of development of a society is a resultant of all the activities of the intellects which compose that society; it bears the imprint of all those millions of wills. Consequently whatever may be the stage of development that the twentieth century is preparing for us, this future state of society will show the effects of the awakening of libertarian ideas which is now taking place. And the depth with which this movement will be impressed upon twentieth-century institutions will depend on the number of men who will have broken today with authoritarian prejudices, on the energy they will have used in attacking old institutions, on the impression they will make on the masses, on the clearness with which the ideal of a free society will have been impressed on the minds of the masses.

Now it is the workers' and peasants' initiative that all parties—the socialist authoritarian party included—have always stifled, wittingly or not, by party discipline. Committees, centres, ordering everything; local organs having but to obey, "so as not to put the unity of the organization in danger." A whole teaching, in a word; a whole false history, written to serve that purpose, a whole incomprehensible pseudo-science of economics, elaborated to this end.

Well, then, those who will work to break up these super-annulated tactics, those who will know how to rouse the spirit of initiative in individuals and in groups, those who will be able to create in their mutual relations a movement and a life based on the principles of free understanding—those that will understand that *variety, conflict even, is life and that uniformity is death,*—they will work, not for future centuries, but in good earnest for the next revolution, for our own times.

We need not fear the dangers and "abuses" of liberty. It is only those who do nothing who make no mistakes. As to those who only know how to obey, they make just as many, and more mistakes than those who strike out their own path in trying to act in the direction their intelligence and their social education suggest to them. The ideal of liberty of the individual—if it is incorrectly understood owing to surroundings where the notion of solidarity is insufficiently accentuated by institutions—can certainly lead isolated men to acts that are repugnant to the social sentiments of humanity. Let us admit that it does happen: is it, however, a reason for throwing the principle of those masters who, in order to prevent "digressions," re-establish the censure of an enfranchised press and guillotine advanced parties to maintain uniformity and discipline—that which, when all is said, was in 1793 the best means of insuring the triumph of reaction?

The only thing to be done when we see anti-social acts committed in the name of liberty of the individual, is to repudiate the principle of "each for himself and God for all," and to have the courage to say aloud in anyone's presence what we think of such acts. This can perhaps bring about conflict but conflict is life itself. And from the conflict will arise an appreciation of those acts far more just than all those appreciations which could have been produced under the influence of old-established ideas.

It is evident that so profound a revolution producing itself in people's minds cannot be confined to the domain of ideas without expanding to the sphere of action.

Consequently, the new ideas have provoked a multitude of acts of revolt in all countries, under all possible conditions: first, individual revolt against capital and State; then collective revolt—strikes and working-class insurrections—both preparing, in men's minds as in actions, a revolt of the masses, a revolution. In this, socialism and anarchism have only followed the course of evolution, which is always accomplished by force-ideas at the approach of great popular risings.

That is why it would be wrong to attribute the monopoly of acts of revolt to anarchism. And, in fact, when we pass in review the acts of revolt of the last quarter of a century, we see them proceeding from all parties.

In all Europe we see a multitude of risings of working masses and peasants. Strikes, which were once "a war of folded arms," today easily turning to revolt, and sometimes taking the proportions of vast insurrections. In the new and old worlds it is by the dozen that we count the risings of strikers having turned to revolts.

If you wish, like us, that the entire liberty of the individual and, consequently, his life be respected, you are necessarily brought to repudiate the government of man by man, whatever shape it assumes; you are forced to accept the principles of anarchism that you have spurned so long. You must then search with us the forms of society that can best realize that ideal and put an end to all the violence that rouses your indignation.

Anarchist Morality

Preface

THE most important difference between anarchists and Marxist-Leninists has lain in the fact that Marx's determinist teachings and Lenin's attempt to develop them in practice, removed their activities and their attitudes from the realm of the moral. What eventually emerged during the worst periods of Communist tyranny, whether in Russia or China or Cambodia or in Peru during the recent terror organized by the Maoist "Shining Path" guerillas, was in fact an anti-morality derived ultimately from the arguments of the extreme nihilist, Sergei Nechaev, who taught that there was no morality other than the will to sacrifice and destroy everything in the cause of the revolution. In grafting such an anti-morality on to the eschatological concept of a determined course towards their own kind of Heaven, the Marxists and especially Lenin and his followers, shed even the shallow systems of ethics that the old religions pretended to foster.

The anarchists, however, from Godwin onward, strove to develop an ethical structure within their political concepts. Even Bakunin, who reacted with horror when he realized the full amoral implications of Nechaev's proposals, had been an example of this tendency, and with Kropotkin it perhaps achieved its peak of self-consciousness. The morality that held together human as well as animal societies, the great natural urge towards mutual aid, lay always at the heart of his teachings.

As he develops the idea in *Anarchist Morality* (1892) Kropotkin is clearly seeing the matter from two standpoints. First, he is an evolutionist detecting and describing a process that balanced the struggle for existence theories that would form the basis of social Darwinism. But he was also replacing a group of ethical laws, that were held to exist by divine sanction, with a natural moral process, an evolutionary tendency throughout the natural world that produces beneficial results whether it operates among animals or men, and offers the model of a society that can function by the momentum of its natural moral urges, by natural human and animal sociality rather than by the commands of State or church.

His arguments represent, of course, the modest beginning of the stream of thought that would give added substance to his anarchist teachings, rooting them in the very heart of collective life patterns, and lead both to his most widely read book, *Mutual Aid,* and to his last, virtually testamentary work, *Ethics.*

What Kropotkin in fact does in *Anarchist Morality*, as in his two later and more substantial works in the field of ethics, is to give the support of the science of his time and of the anarchist faith to an old philosophical insight. For one of the most striking aspects of his teachings here is the way in which they parallel those of that greatly maligned and misrepresented ancient philosopher, Epicurus.

Each in his own austere way, Kropotkin and Epicurus are saying that everything in life must be judged by the pleasure it gives; what gives only pain—mental or physical—must be rejected. But at the same time the successful pursuit of pleasure lies in balancing restraints. Libertarianism is not libertinism. Carried to thoughtless excess, it is self-defeating, since it turns into pain, even for the enjoyer. No socialist thinker, except perhaps Charles Fourier, has come nearer to Epicurus in the recognition that the asceticism of political authoritarians is no less spurious than that of most religious teachers.

Kropotkin's concern for co-operation among animals and the lessons for human beings which are implied in the survival of species inclined to live collectively, has often been linked with contemporary ecological interests. Yet it would be a mistake to assume that, like the modern ecologically concerned libertarian, Kropotkin identifies human fate with that of other species and of the earth itself. He never really faced up, any more than other radical or socialist thinkers of his time did, to the limitations of our earth, to the boundaries of its power to endure continuous exploitation, to the ultimate limitation of human expansion by the dimensions and the nature of the planet. In all his works one becomes aware of the underlying assumption, projected with a kind of uncritical optimism, that the earth's resources are unlimited, that we can continue to exploit them for ever. Malthus, whose insights are being uneasily recognized today, was rejected as merely an enemy of progress rather than a voice genuinely warning of disaster if we did not observe restraint in our consumption and above all—that necessary condition for abundance and even sufficiency—restraint of our population. The horizons for mankind seemed infinite; all he had to do was arrange the just distribution of a production whose possibilities were boundless.

At the same time, though Kropotkin identifies humanity with the other species in finding among them the same tendencies towards mutual aid as among ourselves, he does not show the awareness, so widespread among modern anarchist-ecologists, that we and other animals are in fact parts of the same natural pattern, of the same series of ecosystems in which animals and plants and habitat are all interdependent. He showed surprisingly little concern for species that were being threatened or destroyed in his lifetime; where does one hear an elegiac note sounding for the great bison herds that were being killed off at the same time as he himself suffered in the gaol of Clairvaux? Where does he write at any length or in any depth of the pollution of environments, of the rendering of animal and even human habitats uninhabitable? Rarely indeed, yet the vast problems that face the anarchist-ecologist today were already emerging by the time he died, as animal as well as human societies were being destroyed with steady ruthlessness in the cause of profit.

What Kropotkin would in fact create in his three works from *Anarchist Morality* through *Ethics* was essentially a human morality, secular but limited in its conception of man's place in nature. What we are creating today as we think of anarchism in the modern world, is the concept of an extra-human morality, embracing all forms of life, and the earth itself, though the universe will always be beyond our power and our ken.

G.W.

Anarchist Morality

THE history of human thought recalls the swinging of a pendulum which takes centuries to swing. After a long period of slumber comes a moment of awakening. Then thought frees herself from the chains with which those interested—rulers, lawyers, clerics—have carefully enwound her.

She shatters the chains. She subjects to severe criticism all that has been taught her and lays bare the emptiness of the religious, political, legal, and social prejudices amid which she has vegetated. She starts research in new paths, enriches our knowledge with new discoveries, creates new sciences.

But the inveterate enemies of thought—the government, the lawgiver, and the priest—soon recover from their defeat. By degrees they gather together their scattered forces, and remodel their faith and their code of laws to adapt them to the new needs.Then, profiting by the servility of thought and of character, which they themselves have so effectually cultivated; profiting too, by the momentary disorganization of society, taking advantage of the laziness of some, the greed of others, the best hopes of many, they softly creep back to their work by first of all taking possession of childhood through education.

A child's spirit is weak. It is so easy to coerce it by fear. This they do. They make the child timid, and then they talk to him of the torments of hell. They conjure up before him the sufferings of the condemned, the vengeance of an implacable god. The next minute they will be chattering of the horrors of revolution, and using some excess of the revolutionists to make the child "a friend of order." The priest accustoms the child to the idea of law, to make it obey better what he calls the "divine law," and the lawyer prates of divine law, that the civil law may be the better obeyed.

And by that habit of submission, with which we are only too familiar, the thought of the next generation retains this religious twist, which is at once servile and authoritative; for authority and servility walk ever hand in hand.

During these slumberous interludes, morals are rarely discussed. Religious practices and judicial hypocrisy take their place. People do not criticize, they let themselves be drawn by habit, or indifference.

They do not put themselves out for or against the established morality. They do their best to make their actions appear to accord with their *professions*.

All that was good, great, generous or independent in man, little by little becomes moss-grown; rusts like a disused knife. A lie becomes a virtue, a platitude, a duty. To enrich oneself, to seize one's opportunities, to exhaust one's intelligence, zeal and energy, no matter how, become the watchwords of the comfortable classes, as well as of the crowd of poor folk whose ideal is to appear bourgeois. Then the degradation of the ruler and of the judge, of the clergy and of the more or less comfortable classes becomes so revolting that the pendulum begins to swing the other way.

Little by little, youth frees itself. It flings overhead its prejudices, and it begins to criticize. Thought reawakens, at first among the few: but insensibly the awakening reaches the majority. The impulse is given, the revolution follows.

And each time the question of morality comes up again. "Why should I follow the principles of this hypocritical morality?" asks the brain, released from religious terrors. "Why should any morality be obligatory?"

Then people try to account for the moral sentiment that they meet at every turn without having explained it to themselves. And they will never explain it so long as they believe it a privilege of human nature, so long as they do not descend to animals, plans and rocks to understand it. They seek the answer, however, in the science of the hour.

And, if we may venture to say so, the more the basis of conventional morality, or rather of the hypocrisy that fills its place is sapped, the more the moral plane of society is raised. It is above all at such times, precisely when folks are criticizing and denying it, that moral sentiment makes the most progress. It is then that it grows, that it is raised and refined.

Years ago the youth of Russia were passionately agitated by this very question. " I will be immoral!" a young nihilist came and said to his friend, thus translating into action the thoughts that gave him no rest. "I will be immoral, and why should I not? Because the Bible wills it? But the Bible is only a collection of Babylonian and Hebrew traditions, traditions collected and put together like the Homeric poems, or as is being done still with Basque poems and Mongolian legends. Must I then go back to the state of mind of the half civilized people of the East?

"Must I be moral because Kant tells me of a categoric imperative, of a mysterious command which comes to me from the depths of my own being and bids me be moral? But why should this 'categoric imperative' exercise a greater authority over my actions than that other imperative, which at times may command me to get drunk. A word, nothing but a word, like the words 'Providence,' or 'Destiny,' invented to conceal our ignorance.

"Or perhaps I am to be moral to oblige Bentham, who wants me to believe that I shall be happier if I drown to save a passerby who has fallen into the river than if I watched him drown?

"Or perhaps because such has been my education? Because my mother taught me morality? Shall I then go and kneel down in a church, honour the Queen, bow before the judge I know for a scoundrel, simply because our mothers, our good ignorant mothers, have taught us such a pack of nonsense?

"I am prejudiced—like everyone else. I will try to rid myself of prejudice? Even though immorality be distasteful, I will yet force myself to be immoral, as when I was a boy I forced myself to give up fearing the dark, the churchyard, ghosts and dead people—all of which I had been taught to fear.

"It will be immoral to snap a weapon abused by religion; I will do it, were it only to protect against the hypocrisy imposed on us in the name of a word to which the name morality has been given!"

Such was the way in which the youth of Russia reasoned when they broke with old-world prejudices, and unfurled this banner of nihilist or rather of anarchist philosophy: to bend the knee to no authority whatsoever, however respected; to accept no principle so long as it is unestablished by reason.

Need we add, that after pitching into the waste-paper basket the teachings of their fathers, and burning all systems of morality, the nihilist youth developed in their midst a nucleus of moral customs, infinitely superior to anything that their fathers had practised under the control of the "Gospel," of the "Conscience," of the "Categoric Imperative," or of the "Recognized Advantage" of the utilitarian. But before answering the question, "Why am I to be moral?" let us see if the question is well put; let us analyze the motives of human action.

II

When our ancestors wished to account for what led men to act in one way or another, they did so in a very simple fashion. Down to the present day, certain catholic images may be seen that represent this explanation. A man is going on his way, and without being in the least aware of it, carries a devil on his left shoulder and an angel on his right. The devil prompts him to do evil, the angel tries to keep him back. And if the angel gets the best of it and the man remains virtuous, three other angels catch him up and carry him to heaven. In this way everything is explained wondrously well.

Old Russian nurses full of such lore will tell you never to put a child to bed without unbuttoning the collar of its shirt. A warm spot at the bottom of the neck should be left bare, where the guardian angel may nestle. Otherwise the devil will worry the child even in its sleep.

These artless conceptions are passing away. But though the old words disappear, the essential idea remains the same.

Well brought up folks no longer believe in the devil, but as their ideas are no more rational than those of our nurses, they do but disguise devil and angel under a pedantic wordiness honoured with the name of philosophy. They do not say "devil" now-a-days, but "the flesh," of "the passions." The "angel" is replaced by the words "conscience" or "soul," by "reflection of the thought of a divine creator" or "the Great Architect," as the Free Masons say. But man's action is still represented as the result of a struggle between two hostile elements. And a man is always considered virtuous just in the degree to which one of these two elements—the soul or conscience—is victorious over the other—the flesh or passions.

It is easy to understand the astonishment of our great-grandfathers when the English philosophers, and later the Encyclopedists, began to affirm in opposition to these primitive ideas that the devil and the angel had nothing to do with human action, but that all acts of man, good or bad, useful or baneful, arise from a single motive: the lust for pleasure.

The whole religious confraternity, and, above all, the numerous sects of the pharisees shouted "immorality." They covered the thinkers with insult, they excommunicated them. And when later on in the course of the century the same ideas were again taken up by Bentham, John Stuart Mill, Tchernischevsky, and a host of others, and when these thinkers begin to affirm and prove that egoism, or the lust for pleasure, is the true motive of all our actions, the maledictions redoubled. The books were banned by a conspiracy of silence; the authors were treated as dunces.

And yet what can be more true than the assertion they made?

Here is a man who snatches its last mouthful of bread from a child. Every one agrees in saying that he is a horrible egoist, that he is guided solely by self-love.

But now here is another man, whom every one agrees to recognize as virtuous. He shares his last bit of bread with the hungry, and strips off his coat to clothe the naked. And the moralists, sticking to their religious jargon, hasten to say that this man carries the love of his neighbour to the point of self-abnegation, that he obeys a wholly different passion from that of the egoist. And yet with a little reflection we soon discover that however great the difference between the two actions in their result for humanity, the motive has still been the same. It is the quest for pleasure.

If the man who gives away his last shirt found no pleasure in doing so, he would do it. If he found pleasure in taking bread from a child, he would also do that, but this is distasteful to him. He finds pleasure in giving, and so he gives. If it were not inconvenient to cause confusion by employing in a new sense words that have a recognized meaning, it might be said that in both cases the men acted under the impulse of their egoism. Some have actually said this, to give prominence to the thought and precision to the idea by presenting it in a form that strikes the imagination, and at the same time to destroy the myth which asserts that these two acts have two different motives. They have the same motive, the quest of pleasure, or the avoidance of pain, which comes to the same thing.

Take for example the worst of scoundrels: a Thiers, who massacres thirty-five thousand Parisians, or an assassin who butchers a whole family in order that he may wallow in debauchery. They do it because for the moment the desire of glory or of money gains in their minds the upper hand of every other desire. Even pity and compassion are extinguished for the moment by this other desire, this other thirst. They act almost automatically to satisfy a craving or their nature. Or again, putting aside the stronger passions, take the petty man who deceives his friends, who lies at every step to get out of somebody the price of a pot of beer, or from sheer love of brag, or from cunning. Take the employer who cheats his workmen to buy jewels for his wife or his mistress. Take any petty scoundrel you like. He again only obeys on impulse. He seeks satisfaction of a craving, or he seeks to escape what would give him trouble.

We are almost ashamed to compare such petty scoundrels with one who sacrifices his whole existence to free the oppressed, and like a Russian nihilist mounts the scaffold. So vastly different for humanity are the results of these two lives; so much do we feel ourselves drawn towards the one and repelled by the other.

And yet were you to talk to such a martyr, to the woman who is about to be hanged, even just as she nears the gallows, she would tell you that she would not exchange either her life or her death for the life of the petty scoundrel who lives on the money stolen from his work-people. In her life, in the struggle against the monstrous might, she finds her highest joys. Everything else outside the struggle, all the little joys of the bourgeois and his little troubles seem to her so contemptible, so tiresome, so pitiable! "You do not live, you vegetate," she would reply; "I have lived."

We are speaking of course of the deliberate, conscious acts of men, reserving for the present what we have to say about that immense series of unconscious, all but mechanical acts, which occupy so large a portion of our life. In his deliberate, conscious acts man always seeks what will give him pleasure.

One man gets drunk, and every day lowers himself to the condition of a brute because he seeks in liquor the nervous excitement he cannot get from his own nervous system. Another does not get drunk; he takes no liquor, even though he finds it pleasant, because he wants to keep the freshness of his thoughts and the plentitude of his powers, that he may be able to taste other pleasures which he prefers to drink. But how does he act if not like the judge of good living who, after glancing at the menu of an elaborate dinner, rejects one dish that he likes very well to eat his fill of another that he likes better?

When a woman deprives herself of her last piece of bread to give it to the first comer, when she takes off her own scanty rags to cover another woman who is cold, while she herself shivers on the deck of a vessel, she does so because she would suffer infinitely more in seeing a hungry man, or a woman starved with cold, than in shivering or feeling hungry herself. She escapes a pain of which only those who have felt it know the intensity.

When the Australian, quoted by Guyau, wasted away beneath the idea that he has not yet revenged his kinsman's death; when he grows thin and pale, a prey to the consciousness of his cowardice, and does not return to life till he has done the deed of vengeance, he performs this action, a heroic one sometimes, to free himself of a feeling which possesses him, to regain that inward peace which is the highest of pleasures.

When a troupe of monkeys has seen one of its members fall in consequence of a hunters's shot, and comes to besiege his tent and claim the body despite the threatening gun; when at length the Elder of the band goes right in, first threatens the hunter, then implores him, and finally by his lamentations induces him to give up the corpse, which the groaning troupe carry off into the forest, these monkeys obey a feeling of compassion stronger than all considerations of personal security. This feeling in them exceeds all others. Life itself loses its attraction for them while they are not sure whether they can restore life to their comrade or not. This feeling becomes so oppressive that the poor brutes do everything to get rid of it.

When the ants rush by thousands into the flames of the burning ant-hill, which that evil beast, man, has set on fire, and perish by hundreds to rescue their larvae, they again obey a craving to save their offspring. They risk everything for the sake of bringing away the larvae that they have brought up with more care than many women bestow on their children.

To seek pleasure, to avoid pain, is the general line of action (some would say law) of the organic world.

Without this quest of the agreeable, life itself would be impossible. Organisms would disintegrate, life cease.

Thus, whatever a man's actions and line of conduct may be, he does what he does in obedience to a craving of his nature. The most repulsive actions, no less than actions which are indifferent or most attractive, are all equally dictated by a need of the individual who performs them. Let him act as he may, the individual acts as he does because he finds a pleasure in it, or avoids, or thinks he avoids, a pain.

Here we have a well-established fact. Here we have the essence of what has been called the egoistic theory.

Very well, are we any better off for having reached this general conclusion?

Yes, certainly we are. We have conquered a truth and destroyed a prejudice which lies at the root of all prejudices. All materialist philosophy in its relation to man is implied in this conclusion. But does it follow that all the actions of the individual are indifferent, as some have hastened to conclude? This is what we have now to see.

III

We have seen that men's actions (their deliberate and conscious actions, for we will speak afterwards of unconscious habits) all have the same origin. Those that are called virtuous and those that are designated as vicious, great devotions and petty knaveries, acts that attract and acts that repel, all spring from a common source. All are performed in answer to some need of the individual's nature. All have for their end the quest of pleasure, the desire to avoid pain.

We have seen this in the last section, which is but a very succinct summary of a mass of facts that might be brought forward in support of this view.

It is easy to understand how this explanation makes those still im-
bued with religious principles cry out. It leaves no room for the super-
natural. It throws over the idea of an immortal soul. If man only acts in
obedience to the needs of his nature, if he is, so to say, but a "conscious
automaton," what becomes of the immortal soul? What of immortality,
that last refuge of those who have known too few pleasures and too
many sufferings, and who dream of finding some compensation in
another world?

It is easy to understand how people who have grown up in
prejudice and with but little confidence in science, which has so often
deceived them, people who are led by feeling rather than thought,
reject an explanation which takes from them their last hope.

IV

Mosaic, Buddhist, Christian and Mussulman theologians have had
recourse to divine inspiration to distinguish between good and evil.
They have seen that man, be he savage or civilized, ignorant or learned,
perverse or kindly and honest, always knows if he is acting well or ill,
especially always knows if he is acting ill. And as they have found no
explanation of this general fact, they have put it down to divine inspiration. Metaphysical philosophers, on their side, have told us of conscience, of a mystic "imperative," and, after all, have changed nothing
but the phrases.

But neither have known how to estimate the very simple and very
striking fact that animals living in societies are also able to distinguish
between good and evil, just as man does. Moreover, their conceptions
of good and evil are of the same nature as those of man. Among the best
developed representatives of each separate class—fish, insects, birds,
mammals—they are even identical.

Forel, that inimitable observer of ants, has shown by a mass of observations and facts that when an ant who has her crop well willed
with honey meets other ants with empty stomachs, the latter immediately ask her for food. And amongst these little insects it is the duty of
the satisfied ant to disgorge the honey that her hungry friends may
also be satisfied. Ask the ants if it would be right to refuse food to
other ants of the same ant-hill when one has had one's share. They
will answer, by actions impossible to mistake, that it would be extremely wrong. So selfish an ant would be more harshly treated than
enemies of another species. If such a thing happens during a battle between two different species, the ants would stop fighting to fall upon

their selfish comrade. This fact has been proved by experiments which exclude all doubt.

Or again, ask the sparrows living in your garden if it is right not to give notice to all the little society when some crumbs are thrown out, so that all may come and share in the meal. Ask them if that hedge sparrow has done right in stealing from his neighbour's nest those straws he had picked up, straws which the thief was too lazy to go and collect himself. The sparrows will answer that he is very wrong, by flying at the robber and pecking him.

Or ask the marmots if it is right for one to refuse access to his underground storehouse to other marmots of the same colony. They will answer that it is very wrong, by quarrelling in all sorts of ways with the miser.

Finally, ask primitive man if it is right to take food in the tent of a member of the tribe during his absence. He will answer that, if the man could get his food for himself, it was very wrong. On the other hand, if he was weary or in want, he ought to take food where he finds it; but in such a case, he will do well to leave his cap or his knife, or even a bit of knotted string, so that the absent hunter may know on his return that a friend has been there, not a robber. Such a precaution will save him the anxiety caused by the possible presence of a marauder near his tent.

Thousands of similar facts might be quoted, whole books might be written, to show how identical are the conceptions of good and evil amongst men and other animals.

The ant, the bird, the marmot, the savage have read neither Kant nor the Fathers of the Church nor even Moses. And yet all have the same idea of good and evil. And if you reflect for a moment on what lies at the bottom of this idea, you will see directly that what is considered as *good* among ants, marmots, and Christian or atheist moralists is that which is *useful* for the preservation of the race; and that which is considered *evil* is that which is *hurtful* for race preservation. Not for the individual, as Bentham and Mill put it, but fair and good for the whole race.

The idea of good and evil has thus nothing to do with religion or a mystic conscience. It is a natural need of animal races. And when founders of religions, philosophers, and moralists tell us of divine or metaphysical entities, they are only recasting what each ant, each sparrow practices in its little society.

Is this useful to society? Then it is good. Is this hurtful? Then it is bad.

This idea may be extremely restricted among inferior animals, it may be enlarged among the more advanced animals; but its essence always remains the same.

Among ants it does not extend beyond the ant-hill. All sociable customs, all rules of good behaviour are applicable only to the individuals in that one ant-hill, not to any others. One ant-hill will not consider another as belonging to the same family, unless under some exceptional circumstances, such as a common distress falling upon both. In the same way the sparrows in the Luxembourg Gardens in Paris, though they will mutually aid one another in a striking manner, will fight to the death with another sparrow from the Monge Square who may dare to venture into the Luxembourg. And the savage will look upon a savage of another tribe as a person to whom the usages of his own tribe do not apply. It is even allowable to sell to him, and to sell is always to rob the buyer more or less; buyer or seller, one or other is always "sold." A Tchoutche would think it a crime to sell to the members of his tribe: to them he gives without any reckoning. And civilized man, when at last he understands the relations between himself and the simplest Papuan, close relations, though imperceptible at the first glance, will extend his principles of solidarity to the whole human race, and even to the animals. The idea enlarges, but its foundation remains the same.

On the other hand, the conception of good or evil varies according to the degree of intelligence or of knowledge acquired. There is nothing unchangeable about it.

Primitive man may have thought it very right—that is, useful to the race—to eat his aged parents when they became a charge upon the community—a very heavy charge in the main. He may have also thought it useful to the community to kill his new-born children, and only keep two or three in each family, so that the mother could suckle them until they were three years old and lavish more of her tenderness upon them.

In our days ideas have changed, but the means of subsistence are no longer what they were in the Stone Age. Civilized man is not in the position of the savage family who have to choose between two evils: either to eat the aged parents or else all to get insufficient nourishment and soon find themselves unable to feed both the aged parents and the young children. We must transport ourselves into those ages, which we can scarcely call up in our mind, before we can understand that in the circumstances then existing, half-savage man may have reasoned rightly enough.

Ways of thinking may change. The estimate of what is useful or hurtful to the race changes, but the foundation remains the same. And if we wished to sum up the whole philosophy of the animal kingdom in a single phrase, we should see that ants, birds, marmots and men are agreed on one point.

The morality which emerges from the observation of the whole animal kingdom may be summed up in the words: "Do to others what you would have them do to you in the same circumstances."

And it adds: "Take note that this is merely a piece of *advice;* but this advice is the fruit of the long experience of animals in society. And among the great mass of social animals, man included, it has become *habitual* to act on this principle. Indeed, without this no society could exist, no race could have vanquished the natural obstacles against which it must struggle."

Is it really this very simple principle which emerges from the observation of social animals and human societies? Is it applicable? And how does this principle pass into a habit and continually develop? This is what we are now going to see.

V

The idea of good and evil exists within humanity itself. Man, whatever degree of intellectual development he may have attained, however his ideas may be obscured by prejudices and personal interest in general, considers as good that which is useful to the society wherein he lives, and as evil that which is hurtful to it.

But whence comes this conception, often so vague that it can scarcely be distinguished from a feeling? There are millions and millions of human beings who have never reflected about the human race. They know for the most part only the clan or family, rarely the nation, still more rarely mankind. How can it be that they should consider what is useful for the human race as good, or even attain a feeling of solidarity with their clan, in spite of all their narrow, selfish interests?

This fact has greatly occupied thinkers at all times, and it continues to occupy them still. We are going in our turn to give our view of the matter. But let us remark in passing that though the *explanations* of the fact may vary, the fact itself remains none the less incontestable. And should our explanation not be the true one, or should it be incomplete, the fact with its consequences to humanity will still remain. We may not be able fully to explain the origin of the planets revolving around the sun, but the planets revolve none the less, and one of them carries us with it in space.

We have already spoken of the religious explanation. If man distinguishes between good and evil, say theologians, it is God who has inspired him with this idea. Useful or hurtful is not for him to inquire; he must merely obey the fiat of his creator. We will not stop at

this explanation, fruit of the ignorance and terrors of the savage. We
pass on.

Others have tried to explain the fact by *law*. It must have been law
that developed in man the sense of just and unjust, right and wrong.
Our readers may judge of this explanation for themselves. They know
that law has merely utilized the social feelings of man, to slip in, among
the moral precepts he accepts, various mandates useful to an exploiting
minority, to which his nature refuses obedience. Law has perverted the
feeling of justice instead of developing it. Again let us pass on.

Neither let us pause at the explanation of the Utilitarians. They will
have it that man acts morally from self-interest, and they forget his feelings of solidarity with the whole race, which exist, whatever be their
origin. There is some truth in the Utilitarian explanation. But it is not
the whole truth. Therefore, let us go further.

It is again to the thinkers of the eighteenth century that we are indebted for having guessed, in part at all events, the origin of the moral
sentiment.

In a fine work, *The Theory of Moral Sentiment*, left to slumber in
silence by religious prejudice, and indeed but little known even among
anti-religious thinkers, Adam Smith has laid his finger on the true
origin of the moral sentiment. He does not seek it in mystic religious
feelings; he finds it simply in the feeling of sympathy.

You see a man beat a child. You know that the beaten child suffers.
Your imagination causes you yourself to suffer the pain inflicted upon
the child; or perhaps its tears, its little suffering face tell you. And if you
are not a coward, you rush at the brute who is beating it and rescue it
from him.

This example by itself explains almost all the moral sentiments. The
more powerful your imagination, the better you can picture to yourself
what any being feels when it is made to suffer, and the more intense
and delicate will your moral sense be. The more you are drawn to put
yourself in the place of the other person, the more you feel the pain inflicted upon him, the insult offered him, the injustice of which he is a
victim, the more will you be urged to act so that you may prevent the
pain, insult, or injustice. And the more you are accustomed by circumstances, by those surrounding you, or by the intensity of your own
thought and your own imagination, to *act* as your thought and imagination urge, the more will the moral sentiment grow in you, the
more will it become habitual.

This is what Adam Smith develops with a wealth of examples. He
was young when he wrote this book which is far superior to the work

of his old age upon political economy. Free from religious prejudice, he sought the explanation of morality in a physical fact of human nature, and this is why official and non-official theological prejudice has put the treatise on the Black List for a century.

Adam Smith's only mistake was not to have understood that this same feeling of sympathy in its habitual stage exists among animals as well as among men.

The feeling of solidarity is the leading characteristic of all animals living in society. The eagle devours the sparrow, the wolf devours the marmot. But the eagles and the wolves respectively aid each other in hunting, the sparrow and the marmot unite among themselves against the beasts and birds of prey so effectually that only the very clumsy ones are caught. In all animal societies solidarity is a natural law of far greater importance than that struggle for existence, the virtue of which is sung by the ruling classes in every strain that may best serve to stultify us.

When we study the animal world and try to explain to ourselves that struggle for existence maintained by each living being against adverse circumstances and against its enemies, we realize that the more the principles of solidarity and equality are developed in an animal society and have become habitual to it, the more chance has it of surviving and coming triumphantly out of the struggle against hardships and foes. The more thoroughly each member of the society feels his solidarity with each other member of the society, the more completely are developed in all of them those two qualities which are the main factors of all progress: courage on the one hand, and on the other, free individual initiative. And on the contrary, the more any animal society or little group of animals loses this feeling of solidarity—which may change as the result of exceptional scarcity or else of exceptional plenty—the more do the two other factors of progress, courage and individual initiative, diminish. In the end they disappear, and the society falls into decay and sinks before its foes. Without mutual confidence no struggle is possible; there is no courage, no initiative, no solidarity—and no victory! Defeat is certain.

We can prove with a wealth of examples how in the animal and human worlds the law of mutual aid is the law of progress, and how mutual aid with the courage and individual initiative which follow from it secures victory to the species most capable of practising it.

Now let us imagine this feeling of solidarity acting during the millions of ages which have succeeded one another since the first beginnings of animal life appeared upon the globe. Let us imagine how this feeling little by little became a habit, and was transmitted by heredity from the simplest microscopic organism to its descendants—insects, birds, reptiles, mammals, man—and we shall comprehend the origin of the moral sentiment, which is a necessity to the animal, like food or the organ for digesting it.

Without going further back and speaking of complex animals springing from colonies of extremely simple little beings, here is the origin of the moral sentiment. We have been obliged to be extremely brief in order to compress this great question within the limits of a few pages, but enough has already been said to show that there is nothing mysterious or sentimental about it. Without this solidarity of the individual with the species, the animal kingdom would never have developed or reached its present perfection. The most advanced being upon the earth would still be one of these tiny specks swimming in the water and scarcely perceptible under a microscope. Would even this exist? For are not the earliest aggregations of cellules themselves an instance of association in the struggle?

VI

Thus by an unprejudiced observation of the animal kingdom, we reach the conclusion that wherever society exists at all, this principle may be found: *Treat others as you would like them to treat you under similar circumstances.*

And when we study closely the evolution of the animal world, we discover that the aforesaid principle, translated by the one word, *Solidarity,* has played an infinitely larger part in the development of the animal kingdom than all the adaptations that have resulted from a struggle between individuals to acquire personal advantages.

It is evident that in human societies a still greater degree of solidarity is to be met with. Even the societies of monkeys highest in the animal scale offer a striking example of practical solidarity, and man has taken a step further in the same direction. This and this alone has enabled him to preserve his puny race amid the obstacles cast by nature in his way, and to develop his intelligence.

A careful observation of those primitive societies still remaining at the level of the Stone Age shows to what a great extent the members of the same community practise solidarity among themselves.

This is the reason why practical solidarity never ceases; not even during the worst periods of history. Even when temporary circumstances of domination, servitude, exploitation cause the principle to be disowned, it still lives deep in the thoughts of the many, ready to bring about a strong recoil against evil institutions, a revolution. If it were otherwise society would perish.

For the vast majority of animals and men this feeling remains, and must remain an acquired habit, a principle always present to the mind even when it is continually ignored in action.

It is the whole evolution of the animal kingdom speaking in us. And this evolution has lasted long, very long. It counts by hundreds of millions of years.

Even if we wished to get rid of it we could not. It would be easier for a man to accustom himself to walk on all fours than to get rid of the moral sentiment. It is anterior in animal evolution to the upright posture of man.

The moral sense is a natural faculty in us like the sense of smell or of touch.

As for law and religion, which also have preached this principle, they have simply filched it to cloak their own wares, their injunctions for the benefit of the conqueror, the exploiter, the priest. Without this principle of solidarity, the justice of which is so generally recognized, how could they have laid hold on men's minds?

Each of them covered themselves with it as with a garment; like authority which made good its position by posing as the protector of the weak against the strong.

By flinging overboard law, religion and authority, mankind can regain possession of the moral principle which has been taken from them. Regain that they may criticize it, and purge it from the adulterations wherewith priest, judge and ruler have poisoned it and are poisoning it yet.

Besides, this principle of treating others as one wishes to be treated oneself, what is it but the very same principle as equality, the fundamental principle of anarchism? And how can any one manage to believe himself an anarchist unless he practices it?

We do not wish to be ruled. And by this very fact, do we not declare that we ourselves wish to rule nobody? We do not wish to be deceived, we wish always to be told nothing but the truth. And by this very fact, do we not declare that we ourselves do not wish to deceive anybody, that we promise to always tell the truth, nothing by the truth, the whole truth? We do not wish to have the fruits of our labour stolen from us. And by that very fact, do we not declare that we respect the fruits of others' labour?

By what right indeed can we demand that we should be treated in one fashion, reserving it to ourselves to treat others in a fashion entirely different? Our sense of equality revolts at such an idea.

Equality in mutual relations with the solidarity arising from it, this is the most powerful weapon of the animal world in the struggle for existence. And equality is equity.

By proclaiming ourselves anarchists, we proclaim beforehand that we disavow any way of treating others in which we should not like them to treat us; that we will no longer tolerate the inequality that has allowed some among us to use their strength, their cunning or their ability after a fashion in which it would annoy us to have such qualities used against ourselves. Equality in all things, the synonym of equity, this is anarchism in very deed. It is not only against the abstract trinity of law, religion, and authority that we declare war. By becoming anarchists we declare war against all this wave of deceit, cunning, exploitation, depravity, vice—in a word, inequality—which they have poured into all our hearts. We declare war against their way of acting, against their way of thinking. The governed, the deceived, the exploited, the prostitute, wound above all else our sense of equality. It is in the name of equality that we are determined to have no more prostituted, exploited, deceived and governed men and women.

Perhaps it may be said—it has been said sometimes—"But if you think that you must always treat others as you would be treated yourself, what right have you to use force under any circumstances whatever? What right have you to level a cannon at any barbarous or civilized invaders of your country? What right have you to dispossess the exploiter? What right to kill not only a tyrant but a mere viper?"

What right? What do you mean by that singular word, borrowed from the law? Do you wish to know if I shall feel conscious of having acted well in doing this? If those I esteem will think I have done well? Is this what you ask? If so, the answer is simple.

Yes, certainly! Because we ourselves should ask to be killed like venomous beasts if we went to invade Burmese or Zulus who have done us no harm. We should say to our son or our friend: "Kill me, if I ever take part in the invasion!"

Yes, certainly! Because we ourselves should ask to be dispossessed, if giving the lie to our principles, we seized upon an inheritance, did it fall from on high, to use it for the exploitation of others.

Yes, certainly! Because any man with a heart asks beforehand that he may be slain if ever he becomes venomous; that a dagger may be plunged into his heart if ever he should take the place of a dethroned tyrant.

Ninety-nine men out of a hundred who have a wife and children would try to commit suicide for fear they should do harm to those they love, if they felt themselves going mad. Whenever a good-hearted man feels himself becoming dangerous to those he loves, he wishes to die before he is so.

Perovskaya and her comrades killed the Russian Czar. And all mankind, despite the repugnance to the spilling of blood, despite the sympathy for one who had allowed the serfs to be liberated, recognized their right to do as they did. Why? Not because the act was generally recognized as *useful;* two out three still doubt if it were so. But because it was felt that not for all the gold in the world would Perovskaya and her comrades have consented to become tyrants themselves. Even those who know nothing of the drama are certain that it was no youthful bravado, no palace conspiracy, no attempt to gain power. It was hatred of tyranny, even to the scorn of self, even to the death.

"These men and women," it was said, "had conquered the right to kill;" as it was said of Louise Michel, *"She* had the right to rob." Or again, *"They* have the right to steal," in speaking of those terrorists who lived on dry bread, and stole a million or two of the Kishineff treasure. Mankind has never refused the right to use force on those who have conquered that right, be it exercised upon the barricades or in the shadow of a cross-way. But if such an act is to produce a deep impression upon men's minds, *the right must be conquered.* Without this, such an act whether useful or not will remain merely a brutal fact, of no importance in the progress of ideas. People will see in it nothing but a displacement of force, simply the substitution of the one exploiter for another.

VII

We have hitherto been speaking of the conscious, deliberate actions of man, those performed intentionally. But side by side with our conscious life we have an unconscious life which is very much wider. Yet we have only to notice how we dress in the morning, trying to fasten a button that we know we lost last night, or stretching out our hand to take something that we ourselves have moved away, to obtain an idea of this unconscious life and realize the enormous part it plays in our existence.

It makes up three-fourths of our relations with others. Our ways of speaking, smiling, frowning, getting heated or keeping cool in a discussion, are unintentional, the result of habits, inherited from our human or pre-human ancestors (only notice the likeness in expression between an angry man and an angry beast), or else consciously or unconsciously acquired.

Our manner of acting towards others thus tends to become habitual. To treat others as he would wish to be treated himself becomes with man and all sociable animals, simply a habit. So much so that a person does not generally even ask himself how he must act under such and such circumstances. It is only when the circumstances are exceptional, in some complex case or under the impulse of strong passion that he hesitates, and a struggle takes place between the various portions of his brain—for the brain is a very complex organ, the various portions of which act to a certain degree independently. When this happens, the man substitutes himself in imagination for the person opposed to him; he asks himself if he would like to be treated in such a way, and the better he has identified himself with the person whose dignity or interests he has been on the point of injuring, the more moral will his decision be. Or maybe a friend steps in and says to him: "Fancy yourself in his place; should you have suffered from being treated by him as he has been treated by you?" And this is enough.

Thus we only appeal to the principle of equality in moments of hesitation, and in ninety-nine cases out of a hundred act morally from habit.

It must have been obvious that in all we have hitherto said, we have not attempted to enjoin anything. We have simply set forth the manner in which things happen in the animal world and amongst mankind.

Formerly the church threatened men with hell to moralize them, and she succeeded in demoralizing them instead. The judge threatens with imprisonment, flogging, the gallows, in the name of those social principles he has filched from society; and he demoralizes them. And yet the very idea that the judge may disappear from the earth at the same time as the priest causes authoritarians of every shade to cry out about peril to society.

But we are not afraid to forego judges and their sentences. We forego sanctions of all kinds, even obligations to morality. We are not afraid to say: "Do what you will; act as you will"; because we are persuaded that the great majority of mankind, in proportion to their degree of enlightenment and the completeness with which they free themselves from existing fetters will behave and act always in a direction useful to society just as we are persuaded beforehand that a child will one day walk on its two feet and not on all fours, simply because it is born of parents belonging to the genus *homo*.

All we can do is to give advice. And again while giving it we add: "This advice will be valueless if your own experience and observation do not lead you to recognize that it is worth following."

When we see a youth stooping and so contracting his chest and lungs, we advise him to straighten himself, hold up his head and open his chest. We advise him to fill his lungs and take long breaths, because this will be his best safeguard against consumption. But at the same time we teach him physiology that he may understand the functions of the lungs, and himself choose the posture he knows to be the best.

And this is all we can do in the case of morals. We have only a right to give advice, to which we add: "Follow it *if* it seems good to you."

But while leaving to each the right to act as he thinks best; while utterly denying the right of society to punish anyone in any way for any anti-social act he may have committed, we do not forego our own capacity to love what seems to us good and to hate what seems to us bad. Love and hate; for only those who know how to hate know how to love. We keep this capacity; and as this alone serves to maintain and develop the moral sentiments in every animal society, so much the more will it be enough for the human race.

We only ask one thing, to eliminate all that impedes the free development of these two feelings in the present society, all that perverts our judgment—the State, the church, exploitation; judges, priests, governments, exploiters.

Today when we see a Jack the Ripper murder one after another some of the poorest and most miserable of women, our first feeling is one of hatred.

If we had met him the day when he murdered that woman who asked him to pay her for her slum lodging, we should have put a bullet through his head, without reflecting that the bullet might have been better bestowed in the brain of the owner of that wretched den.

But when we recall to mind all the infamies which have brought him to this; when we think of the darkness in which he prowls, haunted by images drawn from indecent books or thoughts suggested by stupid books, our feeling is divided. And if some day we hear that Jack is in the hands of some judge who has slain in cold blood a far greater number of men, women and children than all the Jacks together; if we see him in the hands of one of those deliberate maniacs, then all our hatred of Jack the Ripper will vanish. It will be transformed into hatred of a cowardly and hypocritical society and its recognized representatives. All the infamies of a Ripper disappear before that long series of infamies committed in the name of law. It is these we hate.

At the present day our feelings are continually thus divided. We feel that all of us are more or less, voluntarily or involuntarily, abettors of this society. We do not dare to hate. Do we even dare to love? In a society based on exploitation and servitude human nature is degraded.

But as servitude disappears we shall regain our rights. We shall feel within ourselves strength to hate and to love, even in such complicated cases as that we have just cited.

In our daily life, we do already give free scope to our feelings of sympathy or antipathy; we are doing so every moment. We all love moral strength, we all despise moral weakness and cowardice. Every moment our words, looks, smiles express our joy in seeing actions useful to the human race, those which we think good. Every moment our words, looks, smiles express our joy in seeing actions useful to the human race, those which we think good. Every moment our looks and words show the repugnance we feel towards cowardice, deceit, intrigue, want of moral courage. We betray our disgust, even when under the influence of a worldly education we try to hide our contempt beneath those lying appearances which will vanish as equal relations are established among us.

This alone is enough to keep the conception of good and ill at a certain level and to communicate it one to another. It will be still more efficient when there is no longer judge or priest in society, when moral principles have lost their obligatory character and are considered merely as relations between equals.

Moreover in proportion to the establishment of these relations, a loftier moral conception will arise in society. It is this conception which we are about to analyze.

VIII

Thus far our analysis has only set forth the simple principle of equality. We have revolted and invited others to revolt against those who assume the right to treat their fellows otherwise than they would be treated themselves; against those who, not themselves wishing to be deceived, exploited, prostituted or ill-used, yet behave thus to others. Lying, and brutality are repulsive we have said, not because they are disapproved by codes of morality, but because such conduct revolts the sense of equality in everyone to whom equality is not an empty word.

And above all does it revolt him who is a true anarchist in his way of thinking and acting.

If nothing but this simple, natural, obvious principle were generally applied in life, a very lofty morality would be the result; a morality comprising all that moralists have taught.

The principle of equality sums up the teachings of moralists. But it also contains something more. This something more is respect for the individual. By proclaiming our morality of equality, or anarchism, we refuse to assume a right which moralists have always taken upon themselves to claim, that of mutilating the individual in the name of some ideal. We do not recognize this right at all, for ourselves or anyone else.

We recognize the full and complete liberty of the individual; we desire for him plentitude of existence, the free development of all his faculties. We wish to impose nothing upon him; thus returning to the principle which Fourier placed in opposition to religious morality when he said: "Leave men absolutely free. Do not mutilate them as religions have done enough and to spare. Do not fear even their passions. In a *free* society these are not dangerous."

Provided that you yourself do not abdicate your freedom; provided that you yourself do not allow others to enslave you; and provided that to the violent and anti-social passions of this or that person you oppose your equally vigorous social passions, then you have nothing to fear from liberty.

We renounce the idea of mutilating the individual in the name of any ideal whatsoever. All we reserve to ourselves is the frank expression of our sympathies and antipathies towards what seems to us good or bad. A man deceives his friends. It is his bent, his character to do so. Very well, it is our character, our bent to despise liars. And as this is our character, let us be frank. Do not let us rush and press him to our bosom or cordially shake hands with him, as is sometimes done today. Let us vigorously oppose our active passion to his.

This is all we have the right to do, this is all the duty we have to perform to keep up the principle of equality in society. It is the principle of equality in practice.

But what of the murderer, the man who debauches children? The murderer who kills from sheer thirst for blood is excessively rare. He is a madman to be cured or avoided. As for the debauchee, let us first of all look to it that society does not pervert our children's feelings, then we shall have little to fear from rakes.

All this it must be understood is not *completely* applicable until the great sources of moral depravity—capitalism, religion, justice, government—shall have ceased to exist. But the greater part of it may be put in practice from this day forth. It is in practice already.

And yet if societies knew only this principle of equality; if each man practised merely the equity of a trader, taking care all day long not to give others anything more than he was receiving from them, society would die of it. The very principle of equality itself would die of it. The very principle of equality itself would disappear from our relations. For, if it is to be maintained, something grander, more lovely, more vigorous than mere equity must perpetually find a place in life.

And this greater than justice is here.

Until now humanity has never been without large natures overflowing with tenderness, with intelligence, with goodwill, and using their feeling, their intellect, their active force in the service of the human race without asking anything in return.

This fertility of mind, of feeling or of good-will takes all possible forms. It is in the passionate seeker after truth, who renounces all other pleasures to throw his energy into the search for what he believes true and right contrary to the affirmations of the ignoramuses around him. It is in the inventor who lives from day to day forgetting even his food, scarcely touching the bread with which perhaps one woman devoted to him feeds him like a child, while he follows out the invention he thinks is destined to change the face of the world. It is in the ardent revolutionist to whom the joys of art, of science, even of family life, seem bitter, so long as they cannot be shared by all, and who works despite misery and persecution for the regeneration of the world. It is in the youth who, hearing of the atrocities of invasion, and taking literally the heroic legends of patriotism, inscribes himself in a volunteer corps and marches bravely through snow and hunger until he falls beneath the bullets. It was in the Paris street Arab, with his quick intelligence and bright choice of aversions and sympathies, who ran to the ramparts with his little brother, stood steady amid the rain of shells, and died murmuring: "Long live the Commune!" It is in the man who is revolted at the sight of a wrong without waiting to ask what will be its result to himself, and when all backs are bent stands up to unmask the iniquity and brand the exploiter, the petty despot of a factory or great tyrant of an empire. Finally it is in all those numberless acts of devotion, less striking and therefore unknown and almost misprized, which may be continually observed, especially among women, if we will take the trouble to open our eyes and notice what lies at the very foundation of human life, and enables it to enfold itself one way or another in spite of the exploitation and oppression it undergoes.

Such men and women as these, some in obscurity, some within a larger arena, create the progress of mankind. And mankind is aware of it. This is why it encompasses such lives with reverence, with myths. It adorns them, makes them the subject of its stories, songs, romances. It adores in them the courage, goodness, love and devotion which are lacking in most of us. It transmits their memory to the young. It recalls even those who have acted only in the narrow circle of home and friends, and reveres their memory in family tradition.

Such men and women as these make true morality, the only morality worthy the name. All the rest is merely equality in relations. Without their courage, their devotion, humanity would remain besotted in the mire of petty calculations. It is such men and women as these who prepare the morality of the future, that which will come when our children have ceased to *reckon,* and have grown up to the idea that the best use for all energy, courage and love is to expend it where the need of such devotion has existed in every age. It is to be met with among sociable animals. It is to be found among men, even during the most degraded epochs.

And religions have always sought to appropriate it, to turn it into current coin for their own benefit. In fact, if religions are still alive, it is because—ignorance apart—they have always appealed to this very devotion and courage. And it is to this that revolutionists appeal.

The moral sentiment of duty which each man has felt in his life, and which it has been attempted to explain by every sort of mysticism, the unconsciously anarchist Guyau says, "is nothing but a superabundance of life, which demands to be exercised, to give itself; at the same time, it is the consciousness of a power."

All accumulated force creates a pressure upon the obstacles placed before it. *Power* to act is *duty* to act. And all this moral "obligation" of which so much has been said or written is reduced to the conception: *the condition of the maintenance of life is its expansion.*

"The plant cannot prevent itself from flowering. Sometimes to flower means to die. Never mind, the sap mounts all the same" concludes the young anarchist philosopher.

It is the same with the human being when he is full of force and energy. Force accumulates in him. He expands his life. He gives without calculation, otherwise he could not live. If he must die like the flower when it blooms, never mind. The sap rises, if sap there be.

Be strong. Overflow with emotional and intellectual energy, and you will spread your intelligence, your love, your energy of action broadcast among others! This is what all moral teaching comes to.

IX

That which mankind admires in a truly moral man is his energy, the exuberance of life which urges him to give his intelligence, his feeling, his action, asking nothing in return.

The strong thinker, the man overflowing with intellectual life, naturally seeks to diffuse his ideas. There is no pleasure in thinking unless the thought is communicated to others. It is only the mentally poverty-stricken man, who after he has painfully hunted up some idea, carefully hides it that later on he may label it with his own name. The man of powerful intellect runs over with ideas; he scatters them by the handful. He is wretched if he cannot share them with others, cannot scatter them to the four winds, for in this is his *life*.

The same with regard to feeling. "We are not enough for ourselves: we have more tears than our own sufferings claim, more capacity for joy than our own existence can justify," says Guyau, thus summing up the whole question of morality in a few admirable lines, caught from nature. The solitary being is wretched, restless, because he cannot share his thoughts and feelings with others. When we feel some great pleasure, we wish to let others know that we exist, we feel, we love, we live, we struggle, we fight.

At the same time, we feel the need to exercise our will, our active energy. To act, to work has become a need for the vast majority of mankind. So much so that when absurd conditions divorce a man or woman from useful work, they invent something to do, some futile and senseless obligations whereby to open out a field for their active energy. They invent a theory, a religion, a "social duty"—to persuade themselves that they are doing something useful. When they dance, it is for a charity. When they ruin themselves with expensive dresses, it is to keep up the position of the aristocracy. When they do nothing, it is on principle.

"We *need* to help our fellows, to lend a hand to the coach laboriously dragged along by humanity; in any case, we buzz round it," says Guyau. This need of lending a hand is so low in the scale. What is all the enormous amount of activity spent uselessly in politics every day but an expression of the need to lend a hand to the coach of humanity, or at least to buzz around it.

Of course this "fecundity of will," this thirst for action, when accompanied by poverty of feeling and an intellect incapable of *creation*, will produce nothing but a Napoleon I or a Bismarck, wiseacres who try to force the world to progress backwards. While on the other hand, mental fertility destitute of well-developed sensibility will bring forth such barren fruits as literary and scientific pendants who only hinder the advance of knowledge. Finally, sensibility unguided by large intelligence will produce such persons as the woman ready to sacrifice everything for some brute of a man, upon whom she pours forth all her love.

If life is to be really fruitful, it must be so at once in intelligence, in feeling and in will. This fertility in every direction is *life;* the only thing worthy the name. For one moment of this life, those who have obtained a glimpse of it give years of vegetative existence. Without this overflowing life, a man is old before his time, an impotent being, a plant that withers before it has ever flowered.

"Let us leave to latter-day corruption this life that is no life," cries youth, the true youth full of sap that longs to live and scatter life around. Every time a society falls into decay, a thrust from such youth as this shatters ancient economic and political and moral forms to make room for the up-springing of a new life. What matter if one or another fall in the struggle! Still the sap rises. For youth to live is to blossom whatever the consequences! It does not regret them.

But without speaking of the heroic periods of mankind, taking everyday existence, is it life to live in disagreement with one's ideal?

Nowadays it is often said that men scoff at the ideal. And it is easy to understand why. The word has so often been used to cheat the simple-hearted that a reaction is inevitable and healthy. We too should like to replace the word "ideal," so often blotted and stained, by a new word more in conformity with new ideas.

But whatever the word, the fact remains; every human being has his ideal. Bismarck had his—however strange—a government of blood and iron. Even every philistine has his ideal however low.

But besides these, there is the human being who has conceived a loftier ideal. The life of a beast cannot satisfy him. Servility, lying, bad faith, intrigue, inequality in human relations fill him with loathing. How can he in his turn become servile, be a liar, and intriguer, lord it over others? He catches a glimpse of how lovely life might be if better relations existed among men; he feels in himself the power to succeed in establishing these better relations with those he may meet on his way. He conceives what is called an ideal.

Whence come this ideal? How is it fashioned by heredity on one side and the impressions of life on the other? We know not. At most we could tell the story of it more or less truly in our own biographies. But it is an actual fact—variable, progressive, open to outside influences but always give the greatest amount of vitality, of the joy of life.

Life is vigorous, fertile, rich in sensation only on condition of answering to this feeling of the ideal. Act *against* this feeling, and you feel your life bent back on itself. It is no longer at one, it loses its vigour. Be untrue often to your ideal and you will end by paralyzing your will, your active energy. Soon you will no longer regain the vigour, the spontaneity of decision you formerly knew. You are a broken man.

Nothing mysterious in all this, once you look upon a human being as a compound of nervous and cerebral centres acting independently. Waver between the various feelings striving within you, and you will soon end by breaking the harmony of the organism; you will be a sick person without will. The intensity of your life will decrease. In vain will you seek for compromises. Never more will you be the complete, strong, vigourous being you were when your acts were in accordance with the ideal conceptions of your brain.

There are epochs in which the moral conception changes entirely. A man perceives that what he had considered moral in the deepest immorality. In some instances it is a custom, a venerated tradition, that is fundamentally immoral. In others we find a moral system framed in the interests of a single class. We cast them over-board and raise the cry "Down with morality!" It becomes a duty to act "immorally."

Let us welcome such epochs for they are epochs of criticism. They are an infallible sign that thought is working in society. A higher morality has begun to be wrought out.

What this morality will be we have sought to formulate, taking as our basis the study of man and animal.

We have seen the kind of morality which is even now shaping itself in the ideas of the masses and of the thinkers.

This morality will issue no commands. It will refuse once and for all to model individuals according to an abstract idea, as it will refuse to mutilate them by religion, law or government. It will leave to the individual man full and perfect liberty. It will be but a simple record of facts, a science. And this science will say to man: "If you are not conscious of strength within you, if your energies are only just sufficient to maintain a colourless, monotonous life, without strong impressions, without deep joys, but also without deep sorrows, well then, keep to the simple principles of a just equality. In relations of equality you will find probably the maximum of happiness possible to your feeble energies.

"But if you feel within you the strength of youth, if you wish to live, if you wish to enjoy a perfect, full and overflowing life—that is, know the highest pleasure which a living being can desire—be strong, be great, be vigorous in all you do.

"Sow life around you. Take heed that if you deceive, lie, intrigue, cheat, you thereby demean yourself, belittle yourself, confess your own weakness beforehand, play the part of the slave of the harem who feels himself the inferior of his master. Do this if it so pleases you, but know that humanity will regard you as petty, contemptible and feeble, and will treat you as such. Having no evidence of your strength, it will act towards you as one worthy of pity—and pity only. Do not blame humanity if of your own accord you thus paralyze your energies. Be strong on the other hand, and once you have seen unrighteousness and recognized it as such—inequity in life, a lie in science, or suffering inflicted by another—rise in revolt against the iniquity, the lie or the injustice.

"Struggle! To struggle is to live, and the fiercer the struggle, the intenser the life. Then you will have lived; and a few hours of such life are worth years spent vegetating.

"Struggle so that all may live this rich, overflowing life. And be sure that in this struggle you will find a joy greater than anything else can give."

This is all that the science of morality can tell you. Yours is the choice.

The State:

Its Historic Role

Preface

KROPOTKIN boldly states his theme in "The State: Its Historic Role"—and the leading theme of most anarchist argument since his day—when he says in the first sentence of the essay: "It is above all over the question of the State that socialists are divided."

Indeed, the division has become so profound and so unbridgeable that today the anarchists no longer call themselves "socialist" as they did for most of the nineteenth century. They have long taken to heart the dramatic exclusions of their representatives from Socialist (Second) International conferences around the turn of the century, and now rarely associate themselves with socialism, which seems irrevocably committed to the transformation of society not through co-operative agreement but by decree, through the State.

The world's most absolute States since the fall of the fascist powers have been called "socialist," even though they have been operated by Communist parties, just as the word "socialist" was embedded in the full form of Nazism (Naztionalsocialismus), for a time the strongest and most active of all totalitarian movements. In fact, it is the socialist with doubts about the competence of the all powerful State to achieve a free and decent society, as Orwell had, who has the greatest problems in reconciling ideals and practice, and the true anti-State libertarian socialist like Orwell, or William Morris before him, has become increasingly a figure of the past. On the left at least, anarchists hold an undesired monopoly in this direction.

It is because "The State: Its Historic Role" argues so well and so historically the case against the nation-State that it has become the most important of Kropotkin's shorter works and is often the first of his pieces that the neophyte reads. That it broadens and deepens a theme already sketched out in early books like *The Conquest of Bread* and *Words of a Rebel* makes it an important transitional work in the direction of his major and mainly historical studies like *Mutual Aid* and *The Great French Revolution*.

An account of the writing and publication of "The State: Its Historic Role" reflects some recurrent elements in the history of anarchism and its enemies. During the 1890s the terrorist activities of some individual French anarchists led to a general attack on the movement by the republican authorities, culminating in August 1894 in the Trial of the Thirty, who were mainly anarchist intellectuals.

Among them was Jean Grave who had taken over *La Révolte* when Kropotkin was imprisoned in 1893 and had edited it from Paris. *La Révolte* was suppressed in 1894, one of a number of libertarian papers that were victims of the great persecution, but when Grave and his comrades were acquitted, he decided to initiate a new magazine. Carrying the work of many of the distinguished writers and artists of the period, it was to be called *Les Temps Nouveaux,* and Grave asked the help of leading anarchist intellectuals like Kropotkin and Elisée Reclus. Among the other promotional activities that he devised was a series of lectures by authorities on libertarian questions. Kropotkin was scheduled to appear on March 7, at the Milles Colonnes Hall in Paris, one of the larger meeting places in the capital, and he prepared his lecture, "The State: Its Historic Role," for delivery then.

However, the French State would have its say about that. Though the French government had been forced by domestic and foreign public opinion to release Kropotkin in 1886, he remained on the black list maintained at the frontiers. However, the police would probably not have tried to keep him out had his lecture not coincided with a State visit to Nice of the crown prince of Russia, the future and ill-fated Nicholas II, in celebration of the new entente between the countries. And Kropotkin was duly stopped at Dieppe by a police officer who sent him back to Newhaven. His undelivered lecture was published in *Les Temps Nouveaux* on December 19, 1896.

"The State" appeared in an English translation in 1903. It was an execrable rendering whose perpetrator I have never been able to identify. I do remember how, when Freedom Press—with which I was then associated—decided to reprint the pamphlet in the mid-1940s, I failed to find a copy of the French original in wartime England, and so had to be content with editing out its worst solecisms, an action some of my comrades who had a reverence for the integrity of texts—even bad ones— did not entirely approve. The present excellent translation was prepared by Vernon Richards in the 1960s and is reproduced with his permission.

"The State: Its Historic Role" can perhaps be described as a concise anarchist history of civilization, its birth in free communities, its corruption under the weight of authority. One thinks of a great rival study of the development of authoritarian forms, Freud's *Totem and Taboo,* and recognizes that Kropotkin's vision of primitive co-operation, like that of social animals, first dominating human society, is more feasible than Freud's dark vision of an original patriarchal tyranny and an ever-repeated conflict between fathers and sons. Man, in fact, in moving towards "civilization" may have shed his primal virtues rather than rejecting his primal vices.

Still, there are areas, as later in *Mutual Aid*, when he sees the stages through which we have passed as perhaps more idyllic than they were, largely through an optimistic misinterpretation of primitive practices and social forms. Violence was not quite as completely absent from Inuit society as he would have us believe, and if there were no petty kings among the wandering bands of Arctic hunters, the shaman was already powerful. Similarly, in finding a lack of organized law among tribal groups, he tends to ignore the full power of taboo, that system of moral restraints supported by an accepted psychological terror. The power wielded by the "big man" chief in a Melanesian village is far less than that of the understood rather than codified system of restraints to which his fellows resign themselves for fear of the world of spirits.

Kropotkin indeed shared with most of his socialist contemporaries, of whatever faction, a kind of Janus position that has been lost to the contemporary political left. He looked with undue nostalgia to the primitive past, and with undue optimism to the liberated future. But, like some of his fellow anarchists, he also saw the basic elements of a free co-operative society surviving around him, still incompletely destroyed by authority, or even springing up anew, and he knew we had only to recognize them for the real social revolution to begin.

Man, for him, was naturally social; the attempt to make him so through institutions was unnecessary and harmful. And thus the historic role of the State is, ultimately, to vanish.

G.W.

The State: Its Historic Role

I

IN taking the State and its historic role as the subject for this study, I think I am satisfying a need much felt at the present time: to examine in depth the very concept of the State; to study its essence, its past role, and the part it may be called upon to play in the future.

It is above all over the question of the State that socialists are divided. Two main currents can be discerned in the factions that exist among us, which correspond to differences in temperament as well as in ways of thinking, but above all to the extent that one believes in the coming revolution.

There are those, on the one hand, who hope to achieve the social revolution through the State by preserving and even extending most of its powers to be used for the revolution. And there are those like ourselves who see in the State, both in its present form, in its very essence, and in whatever guise it might appear, an obstacle to the social revolution, the greatest hindrance to the birth of society based on equality and liberty, as well as the historic means designed to prevent this blossoming. The latter work to abolish the State and not to reform it.

It is clear that the division is a deep one. It corresponds with two divergent currents which in our time are manifest in all philosophical thought, in literature as well as in action. And if the prevailing views on the State remain as obscure as they are today, there is no doubt whatsoever that when—and we hope soon—communist ideas are subjected to practical application in the daily life of communities, it will be on the question of the State that the most stubborn struggles will be waged.

Having so often criticized the State as it is today it becomes necessary to seek the reason for its emergence, to study in depth its past role, and to compare it with the institutions that is has replaced.

First of all let us be agreed as to what we wish to include in the term the State.

There is, of course, the German school which enjoys confusing State with society. The best German thinkers and many among the French are guilty of this confusion because they cannot conceive of society without a concentration of the State; and because of this anarchists are usually accused of wanting to "destroy society" and of advocating a return to "the permanent war of each against all."

Yet to argue thus is to overlook altogether the advances made in the domain of history during the last thirty-odd years; it is to overlook the fact that man lived in societies for thousands of years before the State had been heard of; it is to forget that so far as Europe is concerned the State is of recent origin— it barely goes back to the sixteenth century; finally, it is to ignore that the most glorious periods in man's history are those in which civil liberties and communal life had not yet been destroyed by the State, and in which large numbers of people lived in communes and free federations.

The State is only one of the forms adopted by society in the course of history. Why then make no distinction between what is permanent and what is accidental?

Then again the State has also been confused with government. Since there can be no State without government, it has sometimes been said that what one must aim at is the absence of government and not the abolition of the State.

However, it seems to me that in State and government we have two concepts of a different order. The State idea means something quite different from the idea of government. It not only includes the existence of a power situated above society, but also of a territorial concentration as well as the concentration of many functions of the life of societies in the hands of a few. It carries with it some new relationships between members of society which did not exist before the establishment of the State. A whole mechanism of legislation and of policing has to be developed in order to subject some classes to the domination of others.

This distinction, which at first sight might not be obvious, emerges especially when one studies the origins of the State. Indeed, there is only one way of really understanding the State, and that is to study its historic development, and this is what we will try to do.

The Roman Empire was a State in the real sense of the word. It remains to this day the legist's ideal. Its organs covered a vast domain with a tight network. Everything flowed toward Rome: economic and military life, wealth, education, even religion. From Rome came the laws, the magistrates, the legions to defend the territory, the prefects, and the gods. The whole life of the empire went back to the senate— later to the Caesar, the all-powerful, omniscient god of the empire. Every province, every district had its capital in miniature, its small portion of Roman sovereignty to govern every aspect of daily life. A single law, imposed by Rome, dominated the empire which did not represent a confederation of fellow citizens but was simply a herd of subjects.

Even now, the legist and the authoritarian still admire the unity of that empire, the unitarian spirit of its laws and, as they put it, the beauty and harmony of that organization.

But the disintegration from within, hastened by the barbarian invasion; the extinction of local life, which could no longer resist the attacks from outside on the one hand nor the cancer spreading from the centre on the other; the domination by the rich who had appropriated the land to themselves and the misery of those who cultivated it—all these causes reduced the empire to a shambles, and on these ruins a new civilization was developed which is ours.

So, if we ignore the civilizations of antiquity, and concentrate our attention on the origins and developments of this young barbarian civilization, right up to the times when, in its turn, it gave birth to our modern States, we will be able to capture the essence of the State. This is better than if we had directed our studies to the Roman Empire or to that of Alexander of Macedonia, or to the despotic monarchies of the East.

In taking these powerful barbarian overthrowers of the Roman Empire as our point of departure, we will be able to retrace the evolution of our whole civilization from its beginnings up to the stage of the State.

II

Most eighteenth-century philosophers had very elementary ideas on the origin of societies.

According to them, in the beginning men lived in small isolated families, and perpetual welfare between them was the normal state of affairs. But one fine day, realizing at last the disadvantages that resulted from their endless struggles, men decided to join forces. A social contract was concluded among the scattered families who willingly submitted themselves to an authority which—need I say?—became the starting point as well as the initiator of all progress. And does one have to add what we have all been told at school, that our present governments have so far kept within the limits of this fine role of being the salt of the earth, the pacifiers and civilizers of the human race?

The idea dominated the eighteenth century, a period in which very little was known about the origins of man; and one must add that in the hands of the encyclopedists and of Rousseau, the idea of the "social contract" became a weapon with which to fight against the divine right of kings. Nevertheless, in spite of the services it may have rendered in the past, this theory must be seen to be false.

The fact is that all animals, with the exception of some carnivores and birds of prey and some species which are becoming extinct, live in societies. In the struggle for life, the gregarious species have an advantage over those that are not. In every animal classification they are at the top of the ladder, and there cannot be the slightest doubt that the first beings with human attributes were already living in societies. Man did not create society; society existed before man.

We now also know—and it has been convincingly demonstrated by anthropology—that the point of departure for mankind was not the family but the clan, the tribe. The patriarchal family as we know it or as it is portrayed in Hebrew traditions did not appear until very much later. Man spent tens of thousands of years in the clan or tribal phase— let us call it the primitive or, if you will, savage tribe—during which he developed all kinds of institutions, habits and customs all much earlier than the institutions of the patriarchal family.

In these tribes, the separate family existed no more than it exists among so many other sociable mammals. Any division within the tribe was rather between generations; and from a far distant age, going right back to the dawn of the human race, limitations had been imposed to prevent sexual relations between the different generations, which however were allowed between those of the same generation. One can still find traces of that period in some contemporary tribes as well as in the language, customs, and superstitions of peoples of a much higher culture.

Hunting and food gathering were engaged in by the whole tribe in common, and once their hunger was satisfied, they gave themselves up with passion to their dramatized dances. To this day one still finds tribes who are very close to this primitive phase living on the periphery of the large continents or in the vicinity of mountainous regions in the least accessible parts of the world.

The accumulation of private property could not then take place, since anything that had been the personal possession of a member of the tribe was destroyed or burned where his body was buried. This is still done, in England too, by the gypsies, and funeral rites of "civilized" people still bear the imprint of this custom; thus the Chinese burn paper models of the dead person's possessions, and at the military leader's funeral his horse, his sword, and decorations accompany him as far as his grave. The meaning of the institution has been lost though the form has survived.

Far from expressing contempt for human life, those primitive people hated murder and blood. To spill blood was considered such a grave matter that every drop spilled—not only human blood but also that of some animals—required that the aggressor should lose an equal amount of his own blood.

Furthermore, murder within the tribe is something quite un-known. For instance among the Inuit or Eskimo—those survivors of the Stone Age who inhabit the Arctic regions—or among the Aleuts and others one definitely knows that there has not been a single murder within the tribe for fifty, sixty or more years.

But when tribes of different origin, colour and language met in the course of their migrations, it often ended in war. It is true that even then men were seeking to make these encounters more pacific. Tradition, as Main, Post and Ernest Nys have so well demonstrated, was already developing the germs of what in due course became international law. For instance, a village could not be attacked without warning the in-habitants. Never would anyone dare to kill on the path used by women to reach the spring. And often to make peace it was necessary to balance the numbers of men killed on both sides.

However, all these precautions and many others beside were not enough: solidarity did not extend beyond the confines of the clan or tribe; quarrels arose between people of different clans and tribes, which could end in violence and even murder.

From that period a general law began to be developed between the clans and tribes. "Your members have wounded or killed one of ours; we have a right therefore to kill one of you or to inflict a similar wound on one of you." And it did not matter who, since the tribe was always responsible for the individual acts of its members. The well-known biblical verse: "Blood for blood, an eye for an eye, a tooth for a tooth, a wound for a wound, a life for a life"—but no more! as Koenigswarter so well put it—owe their origin to them. It was their concept of justice; and we have no reason to feel superior since the principle of a life which prevails in our codes is only one of its many survivals.

Clearly, a whole series of institutions (and many others I have not mentioned) as well as a whole code of tribal morality were already developed during this primitive phase. And this nucleus of sociable customs was kept alive by usage, custom, and tradition only. There was no authority with which to impose it.

There is no doubt that primitive society had temporary leaders. The sorcerer, the rainmaker—the learned men of that age—sought to profit from what they knew about nature in order to dominate their fellow beings. Similarly, he who could more easily memorize the proverbs and songs in which all traditions was embodied became influential. At popular festivities he would recite these proverbs and songs in which were incorporated the decisions that had been taken on such and such an occasion by the people's assembly in such a connection. In many small tribes this is still done. And dating from that age, these "edu-cated" members sought to ensure a dominant role for themselves by communicating their knowledge only to the chosen few, to the in-itiates. All religions, and even the arts and all trades have begun with "mysteries," and modern research demonstrates the important role that secret societies of the initiates play to maintain some traditional prac-tices in primitive clans. Already the germs of authority are present here.

It goes without saying that the courageous, the daring, and above all the prudent also became the temporary leaders in the struggles with other tribes or during migrations. But there was no alliance between the bearer of the "law" (the one who knew by heart the tradition and past decisions), the military chief, and the sorcerer; and the State was no more part of these tribes than it is of the society of bees or ants, or of our contemporaries the Patagonians and the Eskimos.

Nevertheless that phase lasted for many thousands of years, and the barbarians who overran the Roman Empire had also gone through this phase and were only just emerging from it.

In the early centuries of our era there were widespread migrations of the tribes and confederations of tribes that inhabited central and northern Asia. Whole waves of small tribes were driven by more or less civilized peoples who had come down from the high tablelands of Asia—they themselves had probably been driven away by the rapid desiccation of these plateaus[1]—and spread all over Europe, each driv-ing the other and being assimilated in their push toward the west.

In the course of these migrations, in which so many tribes of dif-ferent origins became assimilated, the primitive tribe which still existed among most of the savage inhabitants of Europe could not avoid disin-tegration. The tribe was based on a common origin and the cult of com-mon ancestors; but to which common origin could these agglo-merations of people appeal when they emerged from the confusion of migrations, drives, intertribal wars, during which here and there one could already observe the emergence of the paternal family the nucleus formed by the exclusive possession by some of women won over or car-ried off from neighbouring tribes?

The old ties were broken, and to avoid disruption (which, in fact, did occur for many tribes, which disappeared forever) new links had to be established. And they were established through the communal pos-session of the land—of the territory on which each agglomeration had finally settled.[2]

The possession in common of a particular area—of this small valley or those hills—became the basis for a new understanding. The ancestral gods lost all meaning; so then local gods, of that small valley or this river or that forest, gave their religious sanction to the new agglomerations by replacing the gods of the original tribe. Later Christianity, always willing to adjust to pagan survivals, made them into local saints.

Henceforth, the village community, consisting entirely or partly of individual families—all united, however, by the possession in common of the land—became the essential link for centuries to come.

Over vast areas of eastern Europe, Asia and Africa it still survives. The barbarians—Scandinavians, Germans, Slavs and others—who destroyed the Roman Empire lived under such an organization. And by studying the codes of the barbarians of that period, as well as the confederations of village communities that exist today among the Kabyles, the Mongols, the Hindus, the Africans, and others, it has been possible to reconstruct in its entirety that form of society which was the starting point of our civilization as it is today.

Let us therefore have a look at this institution.

III

The village community consisted then, as it does now, of individual families. But all the families of the same village owned the land in common. They considered it as their common heritage and shared it out among themselves on the basis of the size of each family—their needs and their potential. Hundreds of millions of human beings still live in this way in eastern Europe, India, Java, etc. It is the same kind of system that has been established in our time by Russian peasants, freely in Siberia, as soon as the State gave them a chance to occupy the vast Siberian territory in their own way.

Today, the cultivation of the land in a village community is carried out by each household independently. Since all the arable land is shared out between the families (and further shared out when necessary) each cultivates its fields as best it can. But originally, the land was also worked in common, and this custom is still carried on in many places—at least on a part of the land. As to the clearing of woodland and the thinning of forests, the construction of bridges, the building of small forts and turrets for use as places of safety in the event of invasion—all these activities were carried out on a communal basis, just as hundreds of millions of peasants still do where the village commune was held out against the encroachments of the State. But "consumption"—to use a modern term—was already operating on a family basis, each family having its cattle, its kitchen garden, and stores. The means both for hoarding and for handing down goods and chattels accumulated through inheritance had already been introduced.

In all its affairs the village commune was sovereign. Local custom was the law, and the plenary assembly of all the heads of family, men and women, was the judge, the only judge, in civil and criminal matters. When an inhabitant had lodged a complaint against another and stuck his knife in the ground in the place where the commune normally assembled, the commune had to "find the sentence" according to local custom once the fact of an offence had been established by the juries of the two parties in litigation.

Were I to recount all the interesting aspects of this phase, I would not have the space in which to do so. I must therefore refer the reader to *Mutual Aid*. It will suffice to mention here that all the institutions which States were to seize later for the benefit of minorities, that all notions of law that exist in our codes (which have been mutilated in favour of minorities) and all forms of judicial procedure, insofar as they offer guarantees to the individual, had their beginnings in the village commune. So when we imagine that we have made great advances in introducing, for instance, the jury, all we have done is to return to the institution of the so-called "barbarians" after having changed it to the advantage of the ruling classes. Roman law was simply grafted to customary law.

The sense of national unity was developing at the same time through large free federations of village communes. The village commune, being based on the possession in common and very often of the cultivation in common of the land and being sovereign both as judge and legislator of customary law, satisfied most of the needs of the social being.

But not all its needs: there were still others that had to be satisfied. Now, the spirit of the times was not to appeal to a government as soon as a new need was making itself felt. On the contrary the individuals themselves would take the initiative and come together, to join forces, and to federate; to create an entente, large or small, numerous or restricted, which was in keeping with the new need. And society then was literally covered as if by a network of sworn brotherhoods, of guilds for mutual aid, of "con-jurations," in the village as well as outside it, in the federation.

We may observe this phase and spirit at work, even today, among many barbarian federations which have remained outside the modern States copied on the Roman or rather the Byzantine model.

Thus, to take one example among many, the Kabyles have maintained their village community, with the characteristics I have just mentioned: land in common, communal tribunals and so forth. But man feels the need for action beyond the narrow confines of his hamlet. Some rove the world seeking adventure as peddlers. Others take up some kind of trade—or "art." And those peddlers and artisans join together in "fraternities," even when they belong to different villages, tribes, or confederations. Union is needed for mutual succour on voyages to distant lands, for the mutual exchange of the mysteries of one's trade, and so they join forces. They swear brotherhood and practice it in a way that makes a deep impression on Europeans; it is a real brotherhood and not just empty words.

Furthermore, misfortune can overtake anyone. Who knows but that tomorrow in a brawl a normally gentle and quiet man may exceed the established limits of decorum and sociability? Who know whether he might inflict blows and wounds? It may be necessary to pay heavy compensation to the offended or wounded party; it may be necessary to plead one's cause before the village assembly, and to reconstruct the facts on the testimony of six, ten or twelve "sworn brothers." All the more reason to enter a fraternity.

Besides, man feels the need to meddle in politics, to engage in intrigue perhaps, or to propagate a particular moral opinion or a particular custom. Finally, external peace has to be safeguarded; alliances with other tribes to be concluded; federations to be constituted far and wide; elements of intertribal law to be spread abroad. Well then, to gratify all these needs of an emotional or intellectual order, the Kabyles, the Mongols, and the Malays do not appeal to a government; they haven't one. Being men of customary law and individual initiative, they have not been perverted from acting for themselves by the corrupting force of government and church. They unite spontaneously. They form sworn brotherhoods, political and religious associations, craft associations—guilds as they were called in the Middle Ages, and *cofs* as they are called today by the Kabyles. And these *cofs* extend beyond the boundaries of the hamlet; they extend far and wide into the desert and to foreign cities; and brotherhood is practised in these associations. To refuse help to a member of one's *cof*—even at the risk of losing all one's possessions and one's life—is to commit an act of treason to the brotherhood; it is to be treated as one's brother's murder.

What we find today among the Kabyles, Mongols, Malays and others was the very essence of life of the barbarians in Europe from the fifth to the twelfth and even until the fifteenth century. Under the name of guilds, friendships, brotherhoods and so forth, associations abounded for mutual defense, to avenge affronts suffered by some members of the union and to express solidarity, to replace the "eye for an eye" vengeance by compensation, followed by the acceptance of the aggressor in the brotherhood; for the exercise of trades, for aid in care of illness, for defense of the territory; to prevent the encroachments of a nascent authority; for commerce, for the practice of "good neighbourliness"; for propaganda—in a word, for all that Europeans, educated by the Rome of the Caesars and the Popes, nowadays expect from the State. It is even very doubtful whether there was a single man in that period, free man or serf, apart from those who had been banned by their own brotherhoods, who did not belong to a brotherhood or some guild as well as to his commune.

The Scandinavian sagas extol their achievements; the devotion of sworn brothers is the theme of the most beautiful poems. Of course, the church and the nascent kings, representatives of the Byzantine (or Roman) law which reappeared, hurled their excommunications and their rules and regulations at the brotherhood, but fortunately they remained a dead letter.

The whole history of the epoch loses its meaning and is quite incomprehensible if one does not take those brotherhoods into consideration, these unions of brothers and sisters, which sprang up everywhere to deal with the main needs in the economic and personal lives of the people.

In order to appreciate the immense progress achieved by this double institution of village communities and freely sworn brotherhoods outside any Roman, Christian or Statist influence—take for instance Europe as it was at the time of the barbarian invasion, and compare it with what it became in the tenth and eleventh centuries. The untamed forest is conquered and colonized; villages cover the country and are surrounded by fields and hedges and protected by small forts interlinked by paths crossing the forests and the marshes.

In these villages one finds the seeds of industrial arts and one discovers a whole network of institutions for maintaining internal and external peace. In the event of murder or woundings the villagers no longer seek, as in the tribe, to eliminate or to inflict an equivalent wound on the aggressor, or even one of his relatives or some of his fellow villagers. Rather is it the brigand-lords who still adhere to that principle (hence their wars without end), whereas among villagers, *compensation*, fixed by arbiters, becomes the rule after which peace is reestablished, and the aggressor is often, if not always, adopted by the family who has been wronged by his aggression.

Arbitration for all disputes becomes a deeply rooted institution in daily use—in spite of and against the bishops and the nascent kinglets who would wish that every difference should be laid before them or their agents that they might benefit from the *fred*—the fine formerly levied by the villagers on violators of the peace when they brought their dispute before them, and which the kings and bishops now appropriate.

And finally, hundreds of villages are already united in powerful federations sworn to internal peace, who look upon their territory as a common heritage, and are united for mutual protection. This is the seed of European nations. And to this day one can still study these federations in operation among the Mongol, the Turko-Finnish, and Malayan tribes.

Meanwhile black clouds are gathering on the horizon. Other unions—of dominant minorities—are also established, which seek slowly to make these free men into serfs, into subjects. Rome is dead, but its tradition is reborn; and the Christian church, haunted by the visions of Eastern theocracies, gives its powerful support to the new powers that seek to establish themselves.

Far from being the bloodthirsty beast he was made out to be in order to justify a need to dominate, man has always preferred peace and quiet. Quarrelsome rather than fierce, he prefers his cattle, the land, and his hut to soldiering. For this reason, no sooner had the hordes and the tribes fortified themselves more or less in their respective territories than we see that defence of the territory against new waves of migrants is entrusted to someone who engages a small band of adventurers—hardened warriors or brigands who follow him, while the overwhelming majority engages in rearing cattle, in working the land. And that defender soon begins to accumulate riches; he gives horses and iron (then very expensive) to the miserable cultivator who has neither horse nor plough, and reduces him to servitude. He also begins to lay down the bases for military power.

And at the same time, little by little, the tradition that makes the law is being forgotten by the majority. In each village only a few old folk can remember the verses and song containing the "precedents" on which customary law is based, and on festive occasions they repeat these before the community. And slowly, certain families make it their speciality, transmitted from father to son, of remembering these songs and verses, of preserving the purity of the law. Villagers would go to them to adjudicate on complicated disputes, especially when two confederations could not agree to accept the decisions of the arbiters chosen from among themselves.

Princely and royal authority is already germinating in these families, and the more I study the institutions of that period the more I see that customary law did much more to create that authority than did the power of the sword. Man allowed himself to be enslaved much more by his desire to "punish" the aggressor "according to the law" than by direct military conquest.

And gradually the first "concentration of powers," the first mutual assurance for domination—by judge and military leader—is made against the village community. A single man assumes these two functions. He surrounds himself with armed men to carry out the judicial decisions; he fortifies himself in his turret; he accumulates for his family the riches of the time—bread, cattle, iron—and slowly imposes his domination over the peasants in the vicinity.

The learned man of the period, that is, the sorcerer or the priest, soon gives him his support either to share his power or, by adding force and the knowledge of customary law to his powers as a feared magician, the priest takes it over himself. From this stems the temporal authority of the bishops in the ninth, tenth and eleventh centuries.

I would need a whole series of lectures rather than a chapter to deal in-depth with this subject which is so full of new lessons, and to recount how free men gradually became serfs, forced to work for the lord of the manor, temporal or clerical; of how authority was built up over the villages and boroughs in a tentative, groping manner, of how the peasants leagued together, rebelled, struggled to oppose this growing domination; of how they perished in those attacks against the thick walls of the castle and against the men clad in iron defending it.

It will be enough for me to say that about the tenth and eleventh centuries the whole of Europe appeared to be moving toward the constitution of those barbarian kingdoms similar to the ones found today in the heart of Africa or of those theocracies one learns of in Oriental history. This could not happen in a day; but the seeds for those petty royalties and for those petty theocracies were already there and were increasingly manifesting themselves.

Fortunately the "barbarian" spirit—Scandinavian, Saxon, Celtic, German, Slavic—which for seven or eight centuries had incited men to seek the satisfaction of their needs through individual initiative and through free agreement between the brotherhoods and guilds: fortunately that spirit persisted in the villages and boroughs. The barbarians allowed themselves to be enslaved, they worked for the master, but their feeling for free action and free agreement had not yet been broken down. Their brotherhoods were more alive than ever, and the crusades had only succeeded in arousing and developing them in the West.

And so the revolution of the urban communities, resulting from the union of the village community and the sworn brotherhood of the artisan and the merchant—which had been prepared long since by the federal mood of the period—exploded in the eleventh and twelfth centuries with striking effect in Europe. It had already started in the Italian communities in the tenth century.

This revolution, which most university historians prefer to ignore altogether or to underestimate, saved Europe from the disaster with which it was threatened. It arrested the development of theocratic and despotic kingdoms in which our civilization might well have ended by foundering after a few centuries of pompous splendour, just as did the civilizations of Mesopotamia, Assyria and Babylon. It opened the way for a new way of life: that of the free communes.

IV

It is easy to understand why modern historians, trained in the Roman way of thinking and seeking to associate all institutions with Rome, should have such difficulty in appreciating the communalist movement that existed in the eleventh and twelfth centuries. This movement, with its virile affirmation of the individual, and which succeeded in creating a society through the free federation of men, villages and town, was the complete negation of the unitarian, centralizing Roman outlook with which history is explained in our university curriculum. Nor is it linked to any historic personality, or to any central institution.

It is a natural development, belonging, just as did the tribe and the village community, to a certain phase in human evolution, and not to any particular nation or region. This is the reason why academic science cannot be sensitive to its spirit and why the Augustin Thierrys and the Sismondis, historians who really understood the mood of the period, have not had followers in France, where Luchaire is still the only one to take up—more or less—the tradition of the great historians of the Merovingian and communalist periods. It further explains why, in England and Germany, the research into this period as well as an appreciation of its motivating forces are of very recent origin.

The commune of the Middle Ages, the free city, owes its origin on the one hand to the village community, and on the other, to those thousands of brotherhoods and guilds which were coming to life in that period independently of the territorial union. As a federation between those two kinds of unions, it was able to assert itself under the protection of its fortified ramparts and turrets.

In many regions it was a peaceful development. Elsewhere—and this applied in general to western Europe—it was the result of a revolution. As soon as the inhabitants of a particular borough felt themselves to be sufficiently protected by their walls, they made a "conjuration." They mutually swore an oath to drop all pending matters concerning slander, violence or wounding, and undertook, so far as disputes that might arise in the future, never again to have recourse to any judge other than the syndics which they themselves would nominate. In every art, or good neighbourly guild, in every sworn brotherhood, it had been normal practice for a long time. In every village community, such had been the way of life in the past, before the bishop and the petty king had managed to introduce and later to impose on it their judges.

Now, the hamlets and parishes which made up the borough, as well as the guilds and brotherhoods which developed within it, looked upon themselves as a single amitas, nominated their judges and swore permanent union between all those groups.

A charter was soon drawn up and accepted. If need be, someone would be sent off to copy the charter of some neighbouring small community (we know of hundreds of such charters) and the community was set up. The bishop or the prince, who had been until then the judge in the community and often more or less its master, could in such circumstances only recognize the *fait accompli*—or oppose the new conjuration by force of arms. Often the king—that is the prince who sought to be a cut above the other princes and whose coffers were always empty—would "grant" the charter for ready cash. Thus he refrained from imposing his judge on the community, while at the same time gaining prestige in the eyes of the other feudal lords. But this was by no means the rule; hundreds of communes remained active with no other authority than their good will, their ramparts and their lances.

In the course of a hundred years, this movement spread in an impressively harmonious way throughout Europe—by imitation, to be sure—covering Scotland, France, the Low Countries, Scandinavia, Germany, Italy, Poland and Russia. And when we now compare the charters and the internal organization of all these communities we are struck by their virtual uniformity and the organization that grew in the shadow of these "social contracts." What a striking lesson for the Romanists and the Hegelians for whom servitude before the law is the only means of achieving conformity in institutions!

From the Atlantic to the middle course of the Volga, and from Norway to Sicily, Europe was being covered with such communities—some becoming populated cities such as Florence, Venice, Amiens, Nuremberg, or Novgorod, others remaining struggling villages of a hundred or as few as some twenty families treated nevertheless as equals by their more prosperous sisters.

As organisms bubbling with life, communities obviously developed in different ways. Geographical location, the nature of external commerce, and resistance to external interference all gave to each community its own history. But for all of them the basic principle was the same. The same friendship (amitas) of the village communities and the guilds associated within the precincts whether it was Pskov in Russia or Bruges in Flanders, a village of three hundred inhabitants in Scotland or prosperous Venice with its islands, a village in the north of France or one in Poland, or even Florence la Belle. Their constitutions, broadly speaking, were the same.

In general, the town—whose walls grew longer and thicker with the growth of population, and were flanked by towers which grew taller and taller, and were each raised by this and that district, or guild, and consequently displayed individual characteristics—the town was divided into four, five or six sections, or sectors, which radiated from the citadel or the cathedral toward the city ramparts. Each of these sectors was inhabited mainly by an "art" or trade, whereas the new trades—the "young arts"—occupied the suburbs, which in due course were enclosed by a new fortified wall.

The street, or the parish, represented the territorial unit, corresponding to the earlier village community. Each street or parish had its popular assembly, its forum, its popular tribunal, its priest, its militia, its banner, and often its seal, the symbol of its sovereignty. Though federated with other streets it nevertheless maintained its independence.

The professional unit which often was more or less identified with the district or with the sector, was the guild—the trade union. The latter also had its saints, its assembly, its forum, and its judges. It had its fund, its landed property, its militia, and its banner. It also had its seal, symbol of its sovereignty. In the event of war, its militia joined, assuming it was considered expedient, with the other guilds and placed its own banner alongside the large banner of the city.

Thus the city was the union of districts, streets, parishes and guilds, held its plenary assembly in the grand forum, and had its large belfry, its elected judges, and its banner to rally the militias of the guilds and districts. It dealt with other cities as sovereign, federated with whomever it wished, concluded alliances either nationally or outside the national territory. Thus the Cinque Ports around Dover were federated with French and Dutch ports across the Channel; the Russian Novgorod was the ally of the Germanic-Scandinavian Hansa and so on. In its external relations each city possessed all the attributes of the modern State, and from that period onward there was formed, by free contracts, what was to be known later as international law, which was subject to the sanctions of public opinion in all the cities, as later it was to be more often violated than respected by the States.

On how many occasions would a particular city, unable "to find the sentence" in a particularly complicated case, send someone to "seek the sentence" in a neighbouring city! How often was that dominating spirit of the period—arbitration rather than the judge's authority— demonstrated with two communes taking a third one as arbitrator!

The trades also acted in this way. Their commercial and craft relations went beyond the city, and their agreements were made without taking into account nationality. And when in our ignorance we boast of our international workers' congresses, we forget that already by the fifteenth century international congresses of trades and even apprentices were being held.

Lastly, the city either defended itself against aggressors and itself waged fierce war against the feudal lords in the neighbourhood, naming each year one or two military commanders for its militias; or it accepted a "military defender"—a prince or a duke which it selected for one year and dismissed at will. For the maintenance of his soldiers, he would be given the receipts from judicial fines; but he was forbidden to interfere in the affairs of the city.

Or if the city were too weak to free itself from its neighbours the feudal vultures, it kept as its more or less permanent military defender the bishop or the prince of a particular family—Guelph or Ghibelline in Italy, the Riurik family in Russia, or the Olgerds in Lithuania—but was jealously vigilant in preventing the authority of the bishop or the prince extending beyond the men encamped in the castle. They were even forbidden to enter the city without permission. To this day the king of England cannot enter the city of London without the permission of the lord mayor.

The economic life of the cities of the Middle Ages deserves to be recounted in detail. The interested reader is referred to what I have written on the subject in *Mutual Aid* in which I rely on a vast quantity of up-to-date historical research on the subject. Here it must suffice simply to note that internal commerce was dealt with entirely by the guilds—not by the individual artisans—prices being established by mutual agreement. Furthermore, at the beginning of that period external commerce was dealt with exclusively by the city. It was only later that it became the monopoly of the merchants' guild, and later still of individual merchants.

Furthermore, nobody worked on Sundays, nor on Saturday afternoons (bath day). The provisioning of the provincial consumer goods was always handled by the city, and this custom was preserved in some Swiss towns for corn until the middle of the nineteenth century.

In conclusion, it is shown by an immense documentation from many sources, that never, either before or since, has mankind known a period of relative well-being for all as in the cities of the Middle Ages. The poverty, insecurity and physical exploitation of labour that exist in our times were then unknown.

V

With these elements—liberty, organization growing from the simple to the complex, production and exchange by the different trades (guilds), foreign trade handled by the whole city and not by individuals, and the purchase of provisions by the city for resale to the citizens at cost price—with such elements, the towns of the Middle Ages for the first two centuries of their free existences, became centres of well-being for all inhabitants, centres of wealth and culture such as we have not seen since.

One has but to consult the documents which make it possible to compare the rates at which work was remunerated and the cost of provisions—Rogers has done this for England and a great number of German writers have done so for Germany—to see that the labour of an artisan and even of a simple day labourer was paid at a rate not reached in our time, not even by the elite among workers. The account books of colleges of Oxford University (which cover seven centuries beginning at the eleventh) and of some English landed estates, as well as those of a large number of German and Swiss towns, are there to bear witness.

If one considers the artistic finish and amount of decorative work the craftsman of that period put into not only the objects of art he produced, but also into the simplest of household utensils—a railing, a candlestick, a piece of pottery—one realizes that he did not know what it meant to be hurried in his work or overworked as is the case in our time; that he could forge, sculpt, weave, or embroider as only a very small number of worker-artists among us can manage to do nowadays.

And, in addition, one should go through the list of donations made to the churches and the communal houses of the parish, the guild, or the city, both in works of art—decorative panels, sculptures, wrought iron and cast metal—and in money, to realize the degree of well-being attained by those cities; one also has an insight into the spirit of research and invention which manifested itself, and of the breath of freedom which inspired their works, the feeling of brotherly solidarity that grew up in those guilds in which men of the same trade were united not simply for commercial and technical reasons, but by bonds of sociability and brotherhood. Was it not in fact the rule of the guild that two brothers should sit at the bedside of each sick brother—a custom which certainly required devotion in those times of contagious diseases and the plague—and follow him as far as the grave, and then look after his widow and children?

Abject poverty, misery, uncertainty of the morrow for the majority, and the isolation in poverty which are the characteristics of our modern cities were quite unknown in those "free oases which emerged amidst the feudal jungle in the twelfth century."

In those cities, sheltered by their conquered liberties, inspired by the spirit of free agreement and of free initiative, a whole new civilization grew up and flourished in a way unparalleled to this day.

All modern industry comes to us from these cities. In three centuries, industries and the arts attained such perfection that our century has only been able to surpass them in speed of production, but rarely in quality, and very rarely in the intrinsic beauty of the product. All the arts we seek in vain to revive now—the beauty of a Raphael, the strength and boldness of a Michelangelo, the art and science of a Leonardo da Vinci, the poetry and language of a Dante, and not least, the architecture to which we owe the cathedrals of Laon, Rheims, Cologne, Pisa, Florence—as Victor Hugo so well put it *"le peuple en fut le maçon"* ("they were built by the people")—the treasures of sheer beauty of Florence and Venice, the town halls of Bremen and Prague, the towers of Nuremberg and Pisa, and so on *ad infinitum*, all were the product of that age.

Do you wish to measure the progress of that civilization at a glance? Then compare the dome of St. Mark in Venice with the rustic arch of the Normans; the paintings of Raphael with the embroidery of the Bayeux tapestry; instruments of mathematics and physics, and the clocks of Nuremberg with the hourglasses of the preceding centuries; the rich language of a Dante with the uncouth Latin of the tenth century. A new world was born between the two!

With the exception of that other glorious period—once more of free cities—of ancient Greece, never had humanity made such a giant step forward. Never, in the space of two or three centuries, had man undergone such far-reaching changes, nor so extended his power over the forces of nature.

You are perhaps thinking of the civilization and progress of our century which comes in for so much boasting? But in each of its manifestations it is only the child of the civilization that grew up within the free communes. All the great discoveries made by modern science—the compass, the clock, the watch, printing, maritime discoveries, gunpowder, the laws of gravitation, atmospheric pressure of which the steam engine is a development, the rudiments of chemistry, the scientific method already outlined by Roger Bacon and applied in Italian universities— where do all these originate if not in the free cities, in the civilization which was developed under the protection of communal liberties?

It will perhaps be pointed out that I am forgetting the internal conflicts, the domestic struggles, with which the history of these communes is filled, the street riots, the bitter wars waged against the lords, the insurrections of the "young arts" against the "old arts," the blood spilled in those struggles and in the reprisals that followed.

No, in fact I forget nothing. But like Leo and Botta—the two historians of medieval Italy—and Sismondi, Ferrari, Gino Capponi, and so many others, I see that those struggles were the very guarantee of a free life in a free city. I perceive a renewal, a new impulse towards progress after each one of those struggles.

After having recounted in detail these struggles and conflicts, and after having measured also the greatness of the progress achieved while blood was being shed in the streets, well-being assured for all the inhabitants, and civilization renewed—Leo and Botta concluded with this idea which is so just and of which I am frequently reminded. I would wish to see it engraved in the mind of every modern revolutionary. "A commune [they said] does not present the picture of a moral whole, does not appear universal in its manner of being, like the human mind itself, except when it has admitted conflict, opposition."

Yes, conflict freely debated, without an outside force—the State— adding its immense weight to the balance in favour of one of the forces engaged in the struggle.

I believe with these two writers, that often "more harm has been done by imposing peace, because it linked together opposites, in seeking to create a general political order, and sacrificed individualities and small organisms, in order to absorb them in a vast colourless and lifeless whole."

It is for this reason that the communes—so long as they did not themselves seek to become States and to impose around them "submission in a vast colourless and lifeless whole"—for this reason they grew and gained a new lease on life from each struggle, and blossomed to the clatter of swords in the streets; whereas two centuries later that same civilization collapsed in the wake of wars fathered by the States.

In the commune, the struggle was for the conquest and defense of the liberty of the individual, for the federative principle, for the right to unite and to act; whereas the States' wars had as their objective the destruction of these liberties, the submission of the individual, the annihilation of the free contract, and the uniting of men into a universal slavery to king, judge and priest—to the State.

Therein lies all the difference. There are struggles and conflicts which are destructive. And there are those which drive humanity forward.

VI

In the course of the sixteenth century, the modern barbarians were to destroy all that civilization of the cities of the Middle Ages. These barbarians did not succeed in annihilating it, but in halting in progress for at least two or three centuries. They launched it in a different direction, in which humanity is struggling at this moment without knowing quite how to escape.

They subjugated the individual. They deprived him of all his liberties, they expected him to forget all his unions based on free agreement and free initiative. Their aim was to level the whole of society to a common submission to the master. They destroyed all ties between men, declaring that the State and the church alone must henceforth form the union between their subjects; that the church and the State along have the task of watching over the industrial, commercial, judicial, artistic, and emotional interests for which men of the twentieth century were accustomed to meet directly.

And who are these barbarians? It is the State: the triple alliance, finally constituted, of the military chief, the Roman judge, and the priest—the three, united in one power which will command in the name of the interest of society—and will crush that same society.

One naturally asks oneself how these new barbarians were able to overcome the communes, hitherto so powerful? Where did they find the strength to conquer?

They found it in the first place in the village. Just as the communes of ancient Greece proved unable to abolish slavery and for that reason perished—so the communes of the Middle Ages failed to free the peasant from serfdom at the same time as the townsman.

It is as true that almost everywhere, at the time of his emancipation, the townsman—himself a farming craftsman—had sought to carry the country along with him to help it to free itself. For two centuries, the townsmen in Italy, Spain and Germany were engaged in a bitter war against the feudal lords. Feats of heroism and perseverance were displayed by the burghers in that war on the castles. They bled themselves white to become masters of the castles of feudalism and to cut down the feudal forest that surrounded them.

But they only partially succeeded. War-weary, they finally made peace over the heads of the peasants. To buy peace, they handed over the peasants to the lord as long as he lived outside the territory conquered by the commune. In Italy and Germany they ended by accepting the lord as burgher, on condition that he come to live in the commune. Elsewhere they finished by sharing his dominion over the peasant. And the lord took his revenge on the "low rabble" of the towns, whom he hated and despised, making blood flow in the streets in struggles resulting from the practice of retaliation among noble families, which did not bring their differences before the syndics and the communal judges but settled them with the sword, in the street, driving one section of town dwellers against another.

The lord also demoralized the commune with his favours, by intrigues, by his lordly way of life, and by his education received at the court of the bishop or the king. He induced it to share his ambitions. And the burgher ended by imitating the lord. He became in his turn a lord, he too getting rich from distant commerce or from the labour of the serfs penned up in the villages.

After which, the peasant threw in his lot with the kings, the emperors, budding tsars, and the popes when they set about building their kingdoms and subjecting the town. Where the peasant did not march under his order, he did nothing about it.

It was in the country, in a fortified castle situated in the middle of rural communities that monarchy slowly came to be established. In the twelfth century, it existed in name only, and we know today what to think of the rogues, leaders of small bands of brigands, who adorned themselves with that name—a name which in any case (as Augustin Thierry has so well observed) didn't mean very much at the time, when there were "the king (the superior, the senior) of the law courts," the "king of the nets" (among fishermen), the "king of the beggars."

Slowly, gropingly, a baron who was favourably situated in one region, who was more powerful or more cunning than the others, would succeed in raising himself above his confreres. The church hastened to support him. And by force, scheming, money, sword, and poison if need be, one such feudal baron would grow in power at the expense of the others. But royal authority never succeeded in constituting itself in any of the free cities, which had their noisy forum, their Tarpeian Rock, or their river for the tyrants; it succeeded in the towns which had grown in the bosom of the country.

After having sought in vain to constitute this authority in Rheims or in Laon, it was in Paris—an agglomeration of villages and boroughs surrounded by a rich countryside which had not yet known the life of free cities; it was in Westminster, at the gates of the populous city of London; it was in the Kremlin, built in the centre of rich villages on the banks of the Moskva after having failed in Suzdal and in Vladimir—but never in Novgorod, Pskov, Nuremberg, Laon, or Florence—that royal authority was consolidated.

The peasants from the surrounding areas supplied the nascent monarchies with food, horses, and men; commerce—royal and not communal in this case—added to their wealth. The church surrounded them with its attention. It protected them, came to their aid with its wealth, invented for them their local saint and his miracles. It surrounded with its veneration the Notre Dame of Paris, or the Image of the Virgin of Iberia in Moscow. And while the civilization of the free cities, freed from the bishops, gathered its youthful momentum, the church worked relentlessly to reconstitute its authority through the intermediary of the nascent monarchy, surrounding with its attention, incense, and money the royal cradle of the one it had finally chosen, in order to reestablish with and through the monarchy its ecclesiastical authority. In Paris, Moscow, Madrid, and Prague you see her bending over the cradle of royalty, a lighted torch in her hand, the executioner by her side.

Hardworking and tenacious, strengthened by her Statist education, leaning on the man of strong will or cunning whom she would look for in no matter what class of society, made for intrigue and versed in Roman and Byzantine law—you can see her unrelentingly marching toward her ideal; the absolute Judaic king who nevertheless obeys the high priest—the secular arm at the order of the ecclesiastical power.

In the sixteenth century, this slow labour of the two conspirators is already operating at full force. A king already dominates his rival fellow barons, and this power will soon be directed against the free cities to crush them in their turn.

Besides, the towns of the sixteenth century were no longer what they had been in the twelfth, thirteenth, and fourteenth centuries.

Born of the libertarian revolution, they nevertheless lacked the courage or the strength to spread their ideas of equality to the neighbouring countryside, not even to those who had come later to settle in the city precincts, those sanctuaries of freedom, where they created the industrial crafts.

In every town one finds a distinction being drawn between the families who made the revolution of the twelfth century (simply known as "the families") and those who came later and established themselves in the city. The old merchant guild would not hear of accepting newcomers. It refused to absorb the "young arts" into the commercial field. And from the simple steward to the city that it was in former times, when it carried out the external trade for the whole city, it became the middleman who got rich on his own account through foreign trade. It imported oriental ostentation, it became moneylender to the city, and later joined the city lord and the priest against "the lower orders"; or instead it looked to the nascent king for support of its right to enrichment and its commercial monopoly. When commerce became a personal matter, the free city was destroyed.

Moreover, the guilds of the old trades, which at the beginning made up the city and its government, did not wish to recognize the same rights for the young guilds, established later by the new crafts. The latter had to conquer their rights by a revolution. And this is what they did everywhere. But whereas in some cities that revolution was the starting point for a renewal of all aspects of life as well as the arts (this is so clearly seen in Florence), in other cities it ended in the victory of the *popolo grasso* over the *popolo basso*—by a crushing repression with mass deportations and executions, above all when the seigneurs and priests interfered.

And need one add that the king will use as a pretext the defence of the "lower classes" in order to crush the "fat classes" and to subjugate both at once? He had become master of the city!

And again, the cities had to die, since the very ideas of men had changed. The teaching of canonic law and Roman law had modified people's way of thinking.

The twelfth-century European was fundamentally a federalist. As a man of free enterprise and free understanding, of associations which were freely sought and agreed to, he saw in himself the point of departure for the whole of society. He did not seek safety through obedience nor did he ask for a saviour for society. The idea of Christian and Roman discipline was unknown to him.

But under the influence of the Christian church—always in love with authority, always anxious to be the one to impose its dominion over the souls, and above all the work of the faithful and on the other hand, under the influence of Roman law which by the twelfth century had already appeared at the courts of the powerful lords, the kings, and

the popes and soon became the favourite subject at the universities—
under the influence of these two teachings which are so much in accord even though originally they were bitter enemies, minds became
corrupted as the priest and legislator took over.

Man fell in love with authority. If a revolution of the lower trades
took place in a commune, the commune would call for a saviour, thus
saddling itself with a dictator, a municipal Caesar; it would grant him
the full powers to exterminate the opposition party. And he took advantage of the situation, using all the refinements in cruelty suggested
to him by the church or those borrowed from the despotic kingdoms of
the Orient.

He would no doubt have the support of the church. Had she not always dreamed of the biblical king who will kneel before the high priest
and be his docile instrument? Had she not always hated with all her
force those rationalist ideas which breathed in the free towns at the
time of the first renaissance, that of the twelfth century? Did she not lay
her curse on those "pagan" ideas which brought man back to nature
under the influence of the rediscovery of Greek civilization? And later
did she not get the princes to strike these ideas which, in the name of
primitive Christianity, raised up men against the pope, the priest, and
religion in general? Fire, the wheel and the gibbet—those weapons so
dear at all times to the church—were used to crush the heretics. It mat-
tered not what the instrument might be, pope, king or dictator, so long
as fire, the wheel, and the gibbet were in operation against her
enemies.

And in the shadow of this double indoctrination of the Roman
jurist and the priest, the federalist spirit which had created the free
commune, the spirit of initiative and free association, was dying out
and giving place to the spirit of discipline and to pyramidal authoritarian organization. Both the rich and the poor were asking for a
saviour.

And when the saviour appeared—when the king, enriched far
from the turmoil of the forum in some town of his creation, propped up
by the inordinately wealthy church and followed by defeated nobles
and by their peasants, knocked at the gates of the city, promising the
"lower classes" royal protection against the rich and to the submissive
rich his protection against the rebellious poor—the towns, already undermined by the cancer of authority, lacked the strength to resist him.

The great invasions of Europe by waves of people who had come
once more from the East, assisted the rising royalty in the work of the
concentration of powers.

The Mongols had conquered and devastated eastern Europe in the thirteenth century, and soon an empire was founded there, in Moscow, under the protection of the Tartar khans and the Russian Christian church. The Turks had come to impose themselves in Europe and pushed forward as far as Vienna, destroying everything in their way. As a result a number of powerful States were created in Poland, Bohemia, Hungary and in central Europe to resist these two invasions. Meanwhile at the other extremity, the wars of extermination waged against the Moors in Spain allowed another powerful empire to be created in Castille and Aragon, supported by the Roman Church and the Inquisition—by the sword and the stake.

These invasions and wars inevitably led Europe to enter a new phase—that of military States.

Since the communes themselves were becoming minor States, these were bound in due course to be swallowed up by the large ones.

VII

The victory of the State over the communes of the Middle Ages and the federalist institutions of the time was nevertheless not sudden. There was a period when it was sufficiently threatened for the outcome to be in doubt.

A vast popular movement—religious in its form and expressions but eminently equalitarian and communist in its aspirations—emerged in the towns and countryside of central Europe.

Already in the fourteenth century (in 1358 in France and in 1381 in England) two similar movements had come into being. The two powerful uprisings of the Jacqueries and of Wat Tyler had shaken society to its very foundations. Both, however, had been principally directed against the nobility, and though both had been defeated, they had broken feudal power. The uprising of peasants in England had put an end to serfdom and the Jacquerie in France had so severely checked serfdom in its development that from then on the institution simply vegetated without ever reaching the power that it was to achieve later in Germany and throughout eastern Europe.

Now, in the sixteenth century, a similar movement appeared in central Europe. Under the name of the Hussite uprising in Bohemia, Anabaptism in Germany, Switzerland, and in the Low Countries, it was—apart from the revolt against the lords—a complete revolt against the State and church, against Roman and canon law, in the name of primitive Christianity. For a long time misrepresented by Statist and ecclesiastical historians, this movement is only beginning to be understood today.

The absolute freedom of the individual, who must only obey the commands of his conscience, and communism were the watchwords of this uprising. And it was only later, once the State and church had succeeded in exterminating its most ardent defenders and directing it to their own ends, that this movement, reduced in importance and deprived of its revolutionary character, became the Lutheran Reformation.

With Luther the movement was welcomed by the princes; but it had begun as communist anarchism, advocated and put into practice in some places. And if one looks beyond the religious phraseology which was a tribute to the times, one finds in it the very essence of the current of ideas which we represent today: the negation of laws made by the State or said to be divinely inspired, the individual conscience being the one and only law; the commune, absolute master of its destiny, taking back from the lords the communal lands and refusing to pay dues in kind or in money to the State; in other words communism and equality put into practice. Thus when Denck, one of the philosophers of the Anabaptist movement, was asked whether nevertheless he recognized the authority of the Bible, he replied that only the rule of conduct which each individual find for himself in the Bible is obligatory for him. And meanwhile, these very formulas which are so vague—they are derived from ecclesiastical jargon—that authority "of the book," from which one can so easily draw arguments for and against communism, for and against authority, and so indefinite when it is a question of clearly affirming freedom—did not this religious tendency alone contain the germ for the certain defeat of the uprising?

Born in the towns, the movement soon spread to the countryside. The peasants refused to obey anybody, and fixing an old shoe on a pike in the manner of a flag they would go about recovering the land from the lords, breaking the bonds of serfdom, driving away priest and judge, and forming themselves into free communes. And it was only by the stake, the wheel, and the gibbet, by the massacre of a hundred thousand peasants in a few years, that royal or imperial power, allied to the papal or reformed church—Luther encouraging the massacre of the peasants with more virulence than the pope—put an end to those uprisings which had for a period threatened the consolidation of the nascent States.

The Lutheran Reformation, which had sprung from popular Anabaptism, was supported by the State, massacred the people, and crushed the movement from which it had drawn its strength in the beginning. Then, the remnants of the popular wave sought refuge in the communities of the Moravian Brethren, who in their turn were destroyed a century later by the church and the State. Those among them who were not exterminated went to seek sanctuary, some in the southeast of Russian (the Mennonite community has since emigrated to Canada), some to Greenland where they have managed ever since to live in communities, refusing all service to the State.

Henceforth the State was assured of its existence. The jurist, the priest, and the warlord, formed into an alliance around the thrones, were able to pursue their work of annihilation. How many lies have been accumulated by Statist historians, in the pay of the State, on that period!

Indeed have we not all learned at school for instance that the State had performed the great service of creating, out of the ruins of feudal society, national unions which had previously been made impossible by the rivalries between cities? Having learned this at school, almost all of us have gone on believing it to be true in adulthood.

And yet now we learn that in spite of all the rivalries, medieval cities had worked four centuries toward building those unions, through federation, freely consented, and that they had succeeded.

For instance, the union of Lombardy comprised the cities of northern Italy with its federal treasury in Milan. Other federations such as the union of Tuscany, the union of the Rhineland (which comprised sixty towns), the federations of Westphalia, of Bohemia, of Serbia, of Poland and of Russian towns, covered Europe. At the same time, the commercial union of the Hanse included Scandinavian, German, Polish and Russian towns in all the Baltic basin. There were there already all the elements, as well as the fact itself, of large human groupings freely constituted.

Do you require the living proof of these groupings? You have it in Switzerland! There, the union first asserted itself among the village communes (the old cantons), just as at the same time in France it was constituted in the Laonnais. And since in Switzerland the separation between town and village had not been as far-reaching as in the countries where the towns were engaged in large-scale commerce with distant areas, the towns gave assistance to the peasant insurrection of the sixteenth century and thus the union included towns and villages to constitute a federation which continues to this day.

But the State, by its very nature, cannot tolerate a free federation: it represents that nightmare of all jurists, "a State within the State." The

State cannot recognize a freely formed union operating within itself; it only recognizes subjects. The State and its sister the church arrogate to themselves alone the right to serve as the link between men.

Consequently, the State must, perforce, wipe out cities based on the direct union between citizens. It must abolish all unions within the city, as well as the city itself, and wipe out all direct union between the cities. For the federal principle it must substitute the principle of submission and discipline. Such is the stuff of the State, for without this principle it ceases to be State.

And the sixteenth century—a century of carnage and wards—can be summed up quite simply by this struggle of the nascent State against the free towns and their federations. The towns were besieged, stormed and sacked, their inhabitants decimated or deported.

The State in the end wins total victory. And these are the consequences: in the sixteenth century Europe was covered with rich cities, whose artisans, masons, weavers, and engravers produced marvellous works of art; their universities established the foundations of modern empirical science, their caravans covered the continents, their vessels ploughed the seas and the rivers.

What remained two centuries later? Towns with anything from fifty thousand to a hundred thousand inhabitants and which (as was the case of Florence) had had a greater proportion of schools and beds in the communal hospitals, in relation to the population than is the case with the most favoured towns today, became rotten boroughs. Their populations decimated or deported, the State and church took over their wealth, industry died out under the rigorous control of the State's employees. Commerce was dead. Even the roads, which had hitherto linked these cities, became impassable in the seventeenth century.

The State is synonymous with war. Wars devastated Europe, and managed to finish off the towns which the State had not yet directly destroyed.

With the towns crushed, at least did the villages gain something from the concentration of State power? Of course not! One has only to read what the historians tell us of life in the Scottish countryside, or in Tuscany and in Germany in the sixteenth century, and compare these accounts with those of extreme poverty in England in the years around 1648, in France under Louis XIV—the "Roi Soleil"—in Germany, in Italy, everywhere, after a century of State domination.

The historians are unanimous in declaring that extreme poverty existed everywhere. In those places where serfdom had been abolished, it was reconstituted under a thousand new guises; and where it had not yet been destroyed, it emerged under the aegis of the State, as a fierce institution, displaying all the characteristics of ancient slavery or worse. In Russia it was the nascent State of the Romanovs that introduced serfdom and soon gave it the characteristics of slavery.

But could anything else come out of Statist wretchedness since its first concern, once the town had been crushed, was to destroy the village commune and all the ties between the peasants, and then to surrender their lands to sacking by the rich and to bring them all individually into subjection to the official, the priest, or the lord?

VIII

The role of the nascent State in the sixteenth and seventeenth centuries in relation to the urban centres was to destroy the independence of the cities; to pillage the rich guilds of merchants and artisans; to concentrate in its hands the external commerce of the cities and ruin it; to lay hands on the internal administration of the guilds and subject internal commerce as well as all manufacturers totally to the control of a host of officials—and in this way to kill industry and the arts; by taking over the local militias and the whole municipal administration, crushing the weak in the interest of the strong by taxation, and ruining the countries by wars.

Obviously the same tactic was applied to the villages and the peasants. Once the State felt strong enough it eagerly set about destroying the village commune, ruining the peasants in its clutches and plundering the common lands.

Historians and economists in the pay of the State teach us, of course, that the village commune having become an outdated form of land possession—which hampered progress in agriculture—had to disappear under "the action of natural economic forces." The politicians and the bourgeois economists are still saying the same thing now; and there are even some revolutionaries and socialists who claim to be scientific socialists who repeat this stock fable learned at school.

Well, never has such an odious lie been uttered by science. A calculated lie since history abounds with documents to prove for those who want to know—and for France it would virtually suffice to consult Dalloz—that the village commune was in the first place deprived of all its powers by the State; of its independence, its juridical and legislative powers; and that afterwards its lands were either simply stolen by the rich with the connivance of the State or confiscated by the State directly.

In France the pillage was started from the sixteenth century, and followed its course at a greater pace in the following century. From 1659 the State started taking the communes under its wing, and one has only to refer to Louis XIV's edict of 1667 to appreciate on what a scale communal goods were already being pillaged during that period. "Men have taken the land for their own best interests; . . . lands have been divided; . . . to fleece the communes, fictitious debts have been devised 'the Roi Soleil'" said in that edict, and two years later he confiscated all the communes' income to his own advantage. Such is the meaning of "a natural death" in the language which claims to be scientific.

In the following century, at a low estimate half of the communally owned lands were simply taken over by the nobility and the clergy under the aegis of the State. And nevertheless the commune continued in existence until 1787. The village assembly met under the elm tree, apportioned the lands, distributed the tax demands—documentary evidence can be found in Babeau (*Le village sous l'ancien régime*). Turgot, in the province in which he was the administrator, had already found the village assemblies "too noisy," and under his administration they were abolished and replaced by assemblies elected from among the village big wigs. In 1787, on the eve of the revolution, the State generalized that measure. The commune had been abolished, and its affairs thus came into the hands of a few syndics, elected by the richest bourgeois and peasants.

The Constituent Assembly lost no time in confirming this law in December 1789, and the bourgeois took the place of the lords to divest the communes of what communal lands remained to them. It therefore needed one jacquerie after another in 1791 to confirm what the peasants in revolt had just achieved in eastern France. That is to say the Constituent Assembly gave orders for the return of the communal lands to the peasants, which was in fact only done when already achieved by revolutionary action. This is the fate of all revolutionary laws, and it is time that it was understood. They are only enacted after the *fait accompli*.

But while recognizing the right of the communes to the lands that had been taken away from them since 1669, the law had to add some of its bourgeois venom. Its intent was that the communal lands should be shared in equal parts only among the "citizens"—that is among the village bourgeoisie. By a stroke of the pen it wanted to dispossess the "inhabitants" and the bulk of the impoverished peasants, who were most in need of these lands. Whereupon, fortunately, there were new jacqueries and in July 1793, the Convention authorized the distribution of the land among all the inhabitants individually—and again this was carried out only here and there, and served as a pretext for a new pillage of communal lands.

Were these measures not already enough to provoke what those gentlemen call "the natural death" of the commune? Yet for all that the commune went on living. So on August 24, 1794, reaction having seized power, it struck the major blow. The State confiscated all the communal lands and used them as a guarantee fund for the national debt, putting them up for auction and surrendering them to its creatures, the Thermidorians.

This law was happily repealed on 2 Prairial, year V, after three years of rushing after the spoils. But by the same stroke of the pen the communes were abolished and replaced by cantonal councils, in order that the State could the more easily pack them with its creatures. This lasted until 1801 when the village communes were reintroduced; but then the government itself undertook to appoint the mayors and syndics in each of the thirty-six thousand communes! And this absurdity lasted until the revolution of July 1830, after which the law of 1789 was reintroduced. And in the meantime, the communal lands were again confiscated entirely by the State in 1813 and pillaged for the next three years. What remained was not returned to the communes until 1816.

Do you think that was the end? Not at all! Each new regime saw in the communal lands a means of compensation for its henchmen. Thus from 1830, on three different occasions—the first in 1837 and the last under Napoleon III—laws were promulgated to force the peasants to share what remained to them of the communal forests and pastures, and three times was the State obliged to abrogate these laws because of the resistance of the peasants. Nevertheless, Napoleon III took advantage of this situation to seize a few large estates and to make presents of them to his creatures.

Such are the facts. And this is what those gentlemen call in "scientific" language the natural death of communal ownership "under the influence of economic laws." One might as well call the massacre of a hundred thousand soldiers on the battlefield natural death.

Now, what was done in France was also done in Belgium, in England, Germany, and in Austria—everywhere in Europe except in the Slav countries.[3] But then, the periods of outbreaks of the pillaging of the communes are linked throughout Europe. Only the methods vary. Thus, in England they dared not proceed with general measures; they preferred to pass through parliament some thousands of separate enclosure acts by which, in every special case, parliament sanctioned confiscation—it does so to this day—and gave the squire the right to keep the communal lands that he had ring-fenced. And whereas nature had until now respected the narrow furrows by which the communal fields were divided temporarily among the families of a village in England, and though we have in the books of Marshal clear descriptions of this form of possession at the beginning of the nineteenth century, and though communal economy has survived in some communes[4] up to the present time, there is no lack of scholars (such as Seebohm, worthy emulator of Fustel de Coulanges) to maintain and teach that the commune never existed in England except in the form of serfdom!

In Belgium, in Germany, in Italy, and Spain we find the same methods being used. And in one way or another the individual seizure of the lands that were once communal almost completed in western Europe by the 1850s. Of those communal lands the peasants only retain a few scraps.

This is the way the mutual alliance between the lord, the priest, the soldier, and the judge, that we call the "State" acted towards the peasants, in order to strip them of their last guarantee against extreme poverty and economic bondage.

But while the State was condoning and organizing this pillage could it respect the institution of the commune as the organ of local affairs? Obviously, it could not. For to admit that some citizens should constitute a federation which takes over some of the functions of the State would have been a contradiction in principle. The State demands from its subjects a direct, personal submission without intermediaries; it demands equality within slavery; it cannot admit of a "State within a State."

Thus as soon as the State began to be constituted in the sixteenth century, it sought to destroy all the links which existed among the citizens both in the towns and in the villages. Where it tolerated, under the name of municipal institutions, some remnants of autonomy—never of independence—it was only for fiscal reasons, to reduce correspondingly the central budget; or also to give the bigwigs of the province a chance to get rich at the expense of the people, as was the case in England, quite legally until recent years.

This is understandable. Local affairs are a matter of customary law whereas the centralization of powers is a matter of Roman law. The two cannot live side by side; the latter had to destroy the former.

It is for this reason that under the French regime in Algeria, when a *Kabyle djemmah*—a village commune—wants to plead for its lands, each inhabitant of the commune must lodge a personal complaint with the tribunals, who will deal with fifty or two hundred isolated cases rather than accept the commune's collective plea. The Jacobin code developed in the Code Napoleon hardly recognizes customary law, preferring Roman law or rather Byzantine law.

It is for this reason, again in France, that when the wind blows down a tree onto the national highway, or a peasant whose turn it is to repair the communal lane prefers to pay two or three francs to a stone breaker to do it—from twelve to fifteen employees of the ministries of the interior and of finance have to be involved and more than fifty documents passed between these austere functionaries before the tree can be sold, or before the peasant can receive permission to hand over his two or three francs to the communal treasury.

Those who may have doubts as to the veracity of this statement will find these fifty documents listed and duly numbered by Mr. Tricoche in the *Journal des Economistes* (April 1893).

This was of course under the Third Republic, for I am not talking about the barbaric procedure of the ancien régime which was satisfied with five or at the most six documents. But the scholars will tell you that in more barbaric days, the control by the State was fictitious.

And if it were only paper work! It would only mean, after all, twenty thousand officials too many, and another billion added to the budget. A mere trifle for the lovers of "order" and alignment! But at the bottom of all this is something much worse. There is the principle that destroys everything.

Peasants in a village have a large number of interests in common: household interests, neighbourhood, constant relationships. They are inevitably led to come together for a thousand different things. But the State does not want this, nor can it allow them to join together! After all the State gives them the school and the priest, the gendarme and the judge—this should be sufficient. And if other interests arise they can be dealt with through the usual channels of the State church!

Thus until 1883, villagers in France were strictly prohibited from combining be it only for the purpose of bulk buying of chemical fertilizers or the irrigation of their meadows. It was not until 1883-1886 that the republic made up its mind to grant the peasants this right, by voting in the law on the trade unions which however was hedged in provisos and conditions.

And because we are stupefied by State education, we can rejoice in the sudden advances made by agricultural unions, without blushing at the thought that this right which has been denied the peasants until now was one enjoyed without question by every man—free or serf—in the Middle Ages. We have become such slaves that we already look upon it as a "victory for democracy." This is the stage we have reached in brainwashing thanks to our education deformed and vitiated by the State, and our State prejudices!

IX

"If in the town and the village you have common interests, then ask the State or the church to deal with them. But for you to get together and deal with these interests in prohibited." This is the formula that echoes through Europe from the sixteenth century onward.

Already at the end of the sixteenth century an edict by Edward III, king of England, stated that "every alliance, connivance, gatherings, meetings, enactments, and solemn oaths made or to be made between carpenters and masons, are null and void." But it was only after the defeat of the villages and of the popular uprisings, to which we have already referred, that the State dared to interfere with all the institutions—guilds, brotherhoods, and so forth—which bound the artisans together, to disband and destroy them. This is what one sees so clearly in England since the vast documentation available allows one to follow this movement step by step. Little by little the State takes over the guilds and the brotherhoods. It besets them, abolishes their conjurations, their syndics, which they replace by their offices, their tribunals and their banquets; and at the beginning of the sixteenth century under Henry VIII, the State simply confiscates all that the guilds possess without bothering with formalities or procedure. The heir of the great Protestant king completes the job.

It is daylight robbery without apologies, as Thorold Rogers so well put it. And again, it is this theft that the so-called scientific economists describe as the "natural" death of the guilds under the influence of "economic laws"!

Indeed, could the State tolerate the guild, the trade corporation, with its tribunal, its militia, its treasury, its sworn organization? It was "the State within the State"! The real State had to destroy it and this it did everywhere: in England, in France, in Germany, Bohemia, and Russia, maintaining only the pretence for the sake of tax collector and as part of its huge administrative machine. And surely there is no reason to be surprised that the guilds and guild masterships were deprived of all that hitherto had been their lives; were put under the orders of the royal officials and had simply become cogs in the machinery of administration; that by the eighteenth century they were a hindrance, an obstacle to industrial development, in spite of the fact that for four centuries before that they represented life itself. The State had destroyed them.

But the State was not satisfied with putting a spoke in the wheels of life of the sworn brotherhoods of trades which had embarrassed it by placing themselves between it and its subjects. It was not satisfied with confiscating their funds and their properties. The State had to take over their functions as well as their assets.

In a city of the Middle Ages, when there was a conflict of interests within a trade or where two different guilds were in disagreement, the only recourse was to the city. They were obliged to come to an agreement, to any kind of compromise arrangement, since they were all mutually tied up with the city. And the latter never failed to assert itself, either by arbitration or, if necessary, by referring the dispute to another city.

From then on, the State was the only judge. All local conflicts including insignificant disputes in small towns with only a few hundred inhabitants, had to pile up in the form of documents in the offices of the king or of parliament. The English parliament was literally inundated by thousands of minor local squabbles. As a result thousands of officials were required in the capital—most of them were corruptible—to read, classify and form an opinion on all this litigation and adjudicate on the smallest details: for example how to shoe a horse, to bleach linen, to salt herrings, to make a barrel and so on *ad infinitum,* and the wave of questions went on increasing in volume.

But this was not all. In due course the State took over export trade, seeing it as a source of profit. Formerly, when a difference arose between two towns on the value of cloth that had been exported, or of the quality of wool or over the capacity of herring barrels, the towns themselves would remonstrate with each other. If the disagreement dragged on, more often than not they would invite another town to arbitrate. Alternatively a congress of weavers' or coppers' guilds would be summoned to decide on an international level the quality and value of cloth and the capacity of barrels.

But henceforth it was the State in London or in Paris which undertook to deal with these disputes. Through its officials it controlled the capacity of barrels, defined the quality of cloth, allowing for variations as well as establishing the number of threads and their thickness in the warp and the woof, and by its ordinances meddling with the smallest details in every industry. You can guess the result. Under this control, industry in the eighteenth century was dying.

What had in fact come of Benvenuto Cellini's art under State tutelage? It had disappeared! And the architecture of those guilds of masons and carpenters whose works of art we still admire? Just observe the hideous monuments of the Statist period and at one glance you will come to the conclusion that architecture was dead, to such an extent that it has not yet recovered form the blows it received at the hands of the State.

What was happening to the textiles of Bruges and the cloth from Holland? Where were these ironsmiths, so skilled in handling iron and who, in every important European village, knew how to make this ungrateful metal lend itself to transformation into the most exquisite decorations? Where were those turners, those watchmakers, those fitters who had made Nuremberg one of the glories of the Middle Ages for precision instruments? Talk about it to James Watt who two centuries later spent thirty years in vain, looking for a worker who could produce a more or less circular cylinder for his steam engine. Consequently his machine remained at the project stage for thirty years because there were no craftsmen able to construct it. Such was the role of the State in the industrial field. All it was capable of doing was to tighten the screw for the worker, depopulate the countryside, spread misery in the towns, reduce millions of human beings to a state of starvation and impose industrial serfdom.

And it is these pitiful remains of the old guilds, these organisms which have been battered and overtaxed, these useless cogs of the administrative machine, of which the ever "scientific" economists are so ignorant as to confuse the guilds of the Middle Ages. What the Great French Revolution swept away as harmful to industry was not the guild, nor even the trade union, but the useless and harmful cog in the machinery of State.

But what the revolution was at pains to sweep away was the power of the State over industry, over the factory serf.

Do you remember the discussion which took place at the Convention—at the terrible Convention—apropos of a strike? To the complaints of the strikers the Convention replied: "The State alone has the duty to watch over the interests of all citizens. By striking, you are forming a coalition, you are creating a State within the State. So—death!"

In this reply only the bourgeois nature of the revolution has been discerned. But has it not, in fact, a much deeper significance? Does it not sum up the attitude of the State, which found its complete and logical expression with regard to society as a whole in the Jacobinism of

1793? "Have you something to complain about? Then address your complaint to the State! It alone has the mission to redress the wrongs to its subjects. As for a condition to defend yourselves—[that] never." It was in this sense that the republic called itself one and indivisible.

Does not the modern socialist Jacobin think in the same way? Did not the Convention express the gist of Jacobin thought with the cold logic that is typical of it?

In this answer of the Convention was summed up the attitude of all States with regard to all coalitions and all private societies, whatever their aim.

In the case of the strike, it is a fact that in Russia it is still considered a crime of high treason. In most of Germany too where Wilhelm would say to the miners: "Appeal to me; but if ever you presume to act for yourselves you will taste the swords of my soldiers."

Such is still almost always the case in France. And even in England, only after having struggled for a century by means of secret societies, by the dagger for traitors and for the masters, by explosive powders under machines (as late as 1860), by emery powder poured into grease boxes and so on, did British workers begin to win the right to strike, and will soon have it altogether—if they don't fall into the traps already set for them by the State, which seeks to impose compulsory arbitration in exchange for the law of an eight-hour day.

More than a century of bitter struggles! And what misery; how many workers died in prison, were transported to Australia, were shot or hanged, in order to win back the right to combine which—let it be remembered once more—every man free or serf practised freely so long as the State did not lay its heavy hand on societies.

But then, was it only the workman who was treated in this way?

Let us only recall the struggles that the bourgeoisie had to wage against the State to win the right to constitute itself into commercial societies—a right which the State only began to concede when it discovered a convenient way of creating monopolies for the benefit of its creatures and of filling its coffers. Think of the struggle for the right to speak, think or write other than the way the State decrees through the academy, the university and the church! Think of the struggles that have to be waged to this day in order to be able to teach children to read—a right which the State possesses but does not use! Even of the struggles to secure the right to enjoy oneself in public! Not to mention those which should be waged in order to dare to choose one's judge and one's laws—a thing that was in daily use in other times—nor the struggles that will be needed before one will be able to make a bonfire of that book of infamous punishments, invented by the spirit of the Inquisition and of the despotic empires of the Orient known under the name of the penal code!

Observe next taxation—an institution originating purely with the State—this formidable weapon used by the State, in Europe as in the young societies of the two Americas, to keep the masses under its heel, to favour its minions, to ruin the majority for the benefit of the rulers and to maintain the old divisions and castes.

Then take the wars without which States can neither constitute themselves nor maintain themselves; wars which become disastrous, and inevitable, the moment one admits that a particular region—simply because it is part of a State—has interests opposed to those of its neighbours who are part of another State. Think of past wars and of those that oppressed people will have to wage to conquer the right to breathe freely; of the wars for markets; of the wars to create colonial empires. And in France we unfortunately know only too well that every war, victorious or not, is followed by slavery.

And finally what is even worse than all that has just been enumerated, is the fact that the education we all receive from the State, at school and after, has so warped our minds that the very notion of freedom ends up by being lost and disguised in servitude.

It is a sad sight to see those who believe themselves to be revolutionaries unleashing their hatred on the anarchist—just because his views on freedom go beyond their petty and narrow concepts of freedom learned in the State school. And meanwhile, this spectacle is a reality. The fact is that the spirit of voluntary servitude was always cleverly cultivated in the minds of the young, and still is, on order to perpetuate the subjection of the individual to the State.

Libertarian philosophy is stifled by the Roman and Catholic pseudophilosophy of the State. History is vitiated from the very first page, where it lies when it speaks of the Merovingian and Carlovingian monarchies, up to the last page, where it glorifies Jacobinism and refuses to recognize the role of the people in creating its own institutions. Natural sciences are perverted in order to be put at the service of the double idol church-State. Individual psychology, and even more, that of societies, are falsified in each of their assertions in justifying the triple alliance of soldier, priest, and judge. Finally, morality, after having preached for centuries obedience to the church, or the book, only gains its emancipation today to preach servitude to the State: "No direct moral obligations towards your neighbour, nor even any feeling of solidarity; all your obligations are to the State" we are told, we are taught, in this new cult of the old Roman and Caesarian divinity. "The neighbour, the comrade, the companion—forget them. You will henceforth only know them through the intermediary of some organ or other of your State. And every one of you will make a virtue out of being equally subjected to it."

And the glorification of the State and of its discipline, for which the university and the church, the press and the political parties labour, is propagated so successfully that even revolutionaries dare not look this fetish straight in the eye.

The modern radical is a centralist, Statist, and rabid Jacobin. And the socialists fall in step. Just like the Florentines at the end of the fifteenth century who knew no better than to call on the dictatorship of the State to save themselves from the patricians, so the socialists only can call upon the same gods, the dictatorship of the State, to save themselves from the horrors of the economic regime, created by that very same State!

X

If one goes a little deeper into these different categories of phenomena which I have barely touched upon in this short outline, one will understand why—seeing the State as it has been in history, and as it is in essence today—and convinced that a social institution cannot lend itself to all the desired goals, since, like every organ, it developed according to the function it performed, in a definite direction and not in all possible directions—one will understand, I say, why the conclusion we arrive at is for the abolition of the State.

We see in it the institution, developed in the history of human societies, to prevent direct association among men, to shackle the development of local and individual initiative, to crush existing liberties, to prevent their new blossoming—all this in order to subject the masses to the will of the minorities.

And we know an institution which has a long past going back several thousand years cannot lend itself to a function opposed to the one for which and by which it was developed in the course of history.

To this unshakable argument for anybody who has reflected on history the reply we receive is almost infantile: "The State exists and it represents a powerful ready-made organization. Why not use it instead of wanting to destroy it? It operates for evil ends—agreed; but the reason is that it is in the hands of the exploiters. If it were taken over by the people, why would it not be used for better ends, for the good of the people?"

Always the same dream—that of the Marquis de Posa in Schiller's drama, seeking to make an instrument of emancipation out of absolutism; or again the dream of the gentle Abbé Pierre in Zola's *Rome* seeking to make of the church the lever for socialism.

Take a concrete example in France. All thinking people must have noticed the striking fact that the Third Republic, in spite of its republican form of government, has remained monarchist in essence. We all have reproached it for not having republicanized France—I do not only say that it has done nothing for the *social* revolution, but that it has not even introduced the morality or simply the *republican* outlook. For the little that has been done in the past twenty-five years to democratize social attitudes or to spread a little education has been done everywhere, in all the European monarchies, under pressure from the times through which we are passing. Then where does this strange anomaly of a republic which has remained a monarchy come from?

It arises from the fact that France has remained a State, and just where it was thirty years ago. The holders of power have changed the name but all that huge ministerial scaffolding, all that centralized organization of white-collar workers, all this aping of the Rome of the Caesars which has developed in France, all that huge organization to assure and extend the exploitation of the masses in favour of a few privileged groups, which is the essence of the State institution—all that has remained. And those cogs continue as in the past to exchange their fifty documents when the wind has blown down a tree onto the highway and to transfer the millions deducted from the nation to the coffers of the privileged. The official stamp on the documents has changed; but the State, its spirit, its organs, its territorial centralization, its centralization of functions, its favouritism, its role as creator of monopolies have remained. Like an octopus they go on spreading their tentacles over the country.

The republicans, and I am speaking of the sincere ones—had cherished the illusion that one could "utilize the organization of the State" to effect a change in the republican direction, and these are the results. Whereas it was necessary to break up the old organization, *shatter the State* and rebuild a new organization, by beginning from the very foundations of society—the liberated village commune, federalism, groupings from simple to compound, free workingmen's associations—they thought of using the "organization that already existed." And, not having understood that one does not make an historical institution follow in the direction which one seeks to indicate—in the opposite direction to the one it has taken over the centuries—they were swallowed up by the institution.

And this happened, though in this case it was not even a question yet of changing the whole of the economic relations in society! The aim was merely to reform only some aspects of political relations between men.

But after such complete failure, and in the light of such a pitiful experiment, there are those who still insist on telling us that the conquest of powers of the State by the people will suffice to accomplish the social revolution!—that the old machine, the old organism, slowly developed in the course of history to crush freedom, to crush the individual, to establish oppression on a legal basis, to create monopolists, to lead minds astray by accustoming them to servitude—will lend itself perfectly to its new functions: that it will become the instrument, the framework for the germination of a new life, to found freedom and equality on economic bases, for the destruction of monopolies, the awakening of society and the advance toward a future freedom and equality!

What a sad and tragic mistake! To give full scope to socialism entails rebuilding from top to bottom a society dominated by the narrow individualism of the shopkeeper. It is not as has sometimes been said by those indulging in metaphysical woolliness just a question of giving the worker "the total product of his labour"; it is a question of completely reshaping all relationships, from those which exist today between every individual and his churchwarden or his stationmaster to those which exist between neighbourhoods, hamlets, cities, and regions. In every street, in every hamlet, in every group of men gathered around a factory or along a section of the railway line, the creative, constructive, and organizational spirit must be awakened in order to rebuild life—in the factory, in the village, in the store, in production, and in distribution of supplies. All relations between individuals and great centres of population have to be made all over again, from the very day, from the very moment one alters the existing commercial or administrative organization.

And they expect this immense task, requiring the free expression of popular genius, to be carried out within the framework of the State and the pyramidal organization which is the essence of the State! They expect the State whose very *raison d'être* is the crushing of the individual, the hatred of initiative, the triumph of *one* idea which must be inevitably that of mediocrity—to become the lever for the accomplishment of this immense transformation!...They want to direct the revival of a society by means of decrees and electoral majorities...How ridiculous!

Throughout the history of our civilization, two traditions, two opposing tendencies have confronted each other: the Roman and the popular traditions; the imperial and the federalist; the authoritarian and the libertarian. And this is once more, on the eve of the social revolution.

Between these two currents, always manifesting themselves, always at grips with each other—the popular trend and that which thirsts for political and religious domination—we have made our choice.

We seek to recapture the spirit which drove people in the twelfth century to organize themselves on the basis of the free agreement and individual initiative as well as of the free federation of the interested parties. And we are quite prepared to leave the others to cling to the imperial, the Roman, and canonical tradition.

History is not an uninterrupted natural development. Again and again development has stopped in one particular territory only to emerge somewhere else. Egypt, the Near East, the Mediterranean coasts, central Europe have all in turn been centres of historical development. But every time the pattern has been the same, beginning with the phase of the primitive tribe, followed by the village commune, then by the free city, finally to die with the advent of the State.

In Egypt, civilization begins with the primitive tribe. It advances to the village commune and later to the period of the free cities, later still to the State which after a period in which it flourishes, leads to death.

Development starts afresh in Syria, in Persia, and in Palestine. It follows the same pattern: the tribe, the village commune, the free city, the all-powerful State and…death!

A new civilization then comes to life in Greece. Always through the tribe. Slowly it reaches the level of the village commune and then of the republican cities. In these cities civilization reaches its heights. But the East communicates its poisonous breath, its despotic traditions. War and conquests build up the empire of Alexander of Macedonia. The State asserts itself, grows, destroys all culture and again…it is death!

In its turn Rome starts civilization over again. Once more one finds at the beginning the primitive tribe, then the village commune followed by the city. At this phase Rome was at the height of its civilization. But then come the State and the empire and then…death!

On the ruins of the Roman Empire, Celtic, Germanic, Slavonic and Scandinavian tribes once more take up the threads of civilization. Slowly the primitive tribe develops it institutions and manages to build up the village commune. It lingers in this phase until the twelfth century when the republican city arises, and this brings with it the blossoming of the human spirit, proof of which are the masterpieces of architecture, the grandiose development of the arts, the discoveries which lay the foundations of natural sciences. But then the State emerges and then—death!

Yes: death—or renewal! *Either* the State for ever, crushing individual and local life, taking over in all fields of human activity, bringing with it its wars and its domestic struggles power, its palace revolutions which only replace one tyrant by another, and inevitably at the end of this development there is...death! *Or* the destruction of the State, and new life starting again in thousands of centres on the principle of the lively initiative of the individual and groups and that of free agreement.

The choice lies with you!

NOTES

1. The reasons which lead me to this hypothesis are put forward in a paper, "Desiccation of Eur-Asia," compiled for the Research Department of the Geographical Society of London, and published in its *Geographical Journal* for June 1904.

2. The reader interested in this subject, as well as in that of the communal phases and of the free cities, will find more detailed information and source references in my book, *Mutual Aid*.

3. It is already being done in Russia, the government having authorized pillaging of communal lands under the law of 1906 and favoured this pillage by its own functionaries.

4. See Dr. Gilbert Slater, "The Inclosure of Common Fields" in the *Geographic Journal of the Geographical Society of London*, with plans and maps, January 1907. Later published in volume form.

9 781895 431421